Fresh, original, engaging – this new contribution to the literature on trade governance is genuinely welcome and exciting. The chapters are of the highest quality, written by impressively experienced and knowledgeable authors who really know their stuff. This book will fully deserve the wide attention it will inevitably command.

Nicola Phillips, *Professor of Political Economy, University of Sheffield, UK*

Expert Knowledge in Global Trade brings together a first-rate group of scholars whose analysis provides valuable insights into the ways in which the ideas of 'experts' serve powerful interests and shape outcomes in the global trade regime.

Jennifer Clapp, *University of Waterloo, Canada*

These thought-provoking and diverse essays expose the explicit and subtle ways in which experts have shaped international trade policies to legitimize prevailing orthodoxies and, lately, to challenge them. This excellent volume is a significant contribution to scholarship on the role of ideas, from the commonsensical to the highly technical, in global political economy.

JP Singh, *George Mason University, USA*

Expert Knowledge in Global Trade

This book explores tensions in global trade by examining the role of experts in generating, disseminating, and legitimating knowledge about the possibilities of trade to work for global development. To this end, contributors assess authoritative claims on knowledge. They also consider structural features that uphold trade experts' monopoly over knowledge, such as expert language and legal and economic expertise. The chapters collectively explore the tensions between actors who seek to effect change and those who work to uphold the status quo, exacerbate asymmetries, and reinforce the dominant narrative of the global trade regime.

The book addresses the following key overarching research questions:

- Who is considered to be a trade expert and how does one become a knowledge producer in global trade?
- How do experts acquire, disseminate, and legitimate knowledge?
- What agendas are advanced by expert knowledge?
- How does the discourse generated within trade expertise serve to close off alternative institutional pathways and modes of thinking?
- What potential exists for the emergence of more emancipatory global trade policies from contemporary developments in the field of trade expertise?

This book will be of great interest to students and scholars of international political economy, trade politics, international relations, and international organizations.

Erin Hannah is Associate Professor at King's University College at the University of Western Ontario, Canada.

James Scott is Lecturer in International Politics in the Department of Political Economy at King's College London, UK.

Silke Trommer is University Lecturer in Global Sustainable Development and World Politics at the University of Helsinki, Finland.

Global Institutions

Edited by Thomas G. Weiss
The CUNY Graduate Center, New York, USA
and Rorden Wilkinson
University of Sussex, Brighton, UK

About the series

The "Global Institutions Series" provides cutting-edge books about many aspects of what we know as "global governance." It emerges from our shared frustrations with the state of available knowledge—electronic and print-wise, for research and teaching—in the area. The series is designed as a resource for those interested in exploring issues of international organization and global governance. And since the first volumes appeared in 2005, we have taken significant strides toward filling conceptual gaps.

The series consists of three related "streams" distinguished by their blue, red, and green covers. The blue volumes, comprising the majority of the books in the series, provide user-friendly and short (usually no more than 50,000 words) but authoritative guides to major global and regional organizations, as well as key issues in the global governance of security, the environment, human rights, poverty, and humanitarian action among others. The books with red covers are designed to present original research and serve as extended and more specialized treatments of issues pertinent for advancing understanding about global governance. And the volumes with green covers—the most recent departure in the series—are comprehensive and accessible accounts of the major theoretical approaches to global governance and international organization.

The books in each of the streams are written by experts in the field, ranging from the most senior and respected authors to first-rate scholars at the beginning of their careers. In combination, the three components of the series—blue, red, and green—serve as key resources for faculty, students, and practitioners alike. The works in the blue and green streams have value as core and complementary readings in courses on, among other things, international organization, global governance, international law, international relations, and international political economy; the red volumes allow further reflection and investigation in these and related areas.

The books in the series also provide a segue to the foundation volume that offers the most comprehensive textbook treatment available dealing with all the major issues, approaches, institutions, and actors in contemporary global governance—our edited work *International Organization and Global Governance* (2014)—a volume to which many of the authors in the series have contributed essays.

Understanding global governance—past, present, and future—is far from a finished journey. The books in this series nonetheless represent significant steps toward a better way of conceiving contemporary problems and issues as well as, hopefully, doing something to improve world order. We value the feedback from our readers and their role in helping shape the on-going development of the series.

A complete list of titles appears at the end of this book. The most recent titles in the series are:

World Trade Organization (2nd edition, 2016)
by Bernard M. Hoekman and Petros C. Mavroidis

Women and Girls Rising (2015)
by Ellen Chesler and Terry McGovern

The North Atlantic Treaty Organization (2nd edition, 2015)
by Julian Lindley-French

Governing Climate Change (2nd edition, 2015)
by Harriet Bulkeley and Peter Newell

The Organization of Islamic Cooperation (2015)
by Turan Kayaoglu

Contemporary Human Rights Ideas (2nd edition, 2015)
by Bertrand G. Ramcharan

The Politics of International Organizations (2015)
edited by Patrick Weller and Xu Yi-chong

Expert Knowledge in Global Trade

Edited by
Erin Hannah, James Scott and Silke Trommer

Routledge
Taylor & Francis Group
LONDON AND NEW YORK

First published 2016 by Routledge

4 Park Square, Milton Park, Abingdon, Oxon OX14 4RN
605 Third Avenue, New York, NY 10017

Routledge is an imprint of the Taylor & Francis Group, an informa business

First issuedinpaperback2017

British Library Cataloguing in Publication Data
A catalogue record for this book is available from the British Library

Library of Congress Cataloging in Publication Data
A catalog record for this book has been requested

ISBN: 978-1-138-78777-3 (hbk)
ISBN: 978-0-8153-7723-8 (pbk)

Typeset in Times New Roman
by Taylor & Francis Books

Contents

Table

Contributors

Joseph Conti is an Assistant Professor of Sociology and Law at the University of Wisconsin-Madison. He earned his PhD in Sociology in 2008 from the University of California, Santa Barbara. He is author of *Between Law and Diplomacy: The Social Contexts of Disputing at the World Trade Organization* (Stanford University Press, 2011). In 2011, he received the Best Article Award from the Law & Society Association for "Learning to Dispute: Repeat Participation, Expertise, and Reputation at the World Trade Organization," *Law & Social Inquiry* 35, no. 1 (2010): 625–62.

Matthew Eagleton-Pierce is a Lecturer in International Political Economy at the School of Oriental and African Studies, University of London. His primary research interests lie at the intersection between political economy and sociology, including the politics of world trade, the history of neoliberalism, and the conceptual analysis of power and legitimacy. He is the author of *Symbolic Power in the World Trade Organization* (Oxford University Press, 2013), a book which explores how the thought of Pierre Bourdieu can shed new light on trade diplomacy; and *Neoliberalism: The Key Concepts* (Routledge, 2015), a guide to the vocabulary of contemporary capitalism. He previously taught at the University of Oxford, the London School of Economics, and the University of Exeter.

Clive George is a retired Senior Research Fellow in the Institute for Development Policy and Management, University of Manchester, and Visiting Professor in the Department of International Relations at the College of Europe, Bruges. He is author of *The Truth About Trade* (London: Zed Books, 2010), and of numerous academic articles on the economic, social, and environmental impacts of international trade agreements.

Erin Hannah is Associate Professor of Political Science at King's University College at the University of Western Ontario. She is an international political economist specializing in global governance, trade, sustainable development, poverty and inequality, global civil society, and European Union trade politics. She examines the conditions under which knowledge and power asymmetries can be redressed through global governance and institutional reform, with a particular emphasis on social justice and equity issues. She has published articles in *Journal of International Economic Law, Journal of Civil Society, Journal of World Trade, Politics*, and *Third World Quarterly*. Her book, *NGOs and Global Trade*, is forthcoming with the Routledge Global Institutions Series.

Andrew Lang is an Associate Professor (Reader), teaching Public International Law, with a specialty in International Economic Law at the London School of Economics. His research explores a number of themes around global economic governance, including the relationship between law and expert knowledge, international law and economics, and sociological approaches to the study of international economic law. He is the author of *World Trade Law after Neoliberalism: Reimagining the Global Economic Order* (Oxford University Press, 2011).

James Scott is Lecturer in International Politics in the Department of Political Economy at King's College London. He works primarily on trade governance, particularly with regard to developing countries in the World Trade Organization, and also on rising powers in various areas of global governance. Dr. Scott has published extensively on these subjects and his latest book is the co-edited *Trade, Poverty, Development: Getting beyond the WTO's Doha Deadlock*, with Rorden Wilkinson (Routledge, 2013).

Gabriel Siles-Brügge is Lecturer in Politics at the University of Manchester. His research interests sit at the interface of European and International Political Economy, where he focuses on issues relating to trade and development, the role of economic ideas in politics, and responses to the financial and eurozone crises. He is the author of the book *Constructing European Union Trade Policy: A Global Idea of Europe* (Palgrave Macmillan, 2014); and of recent articles in the *Journal of Common Market Studies, New Political Economy*, the *Review of International Political Economy*, and *Contemporary Politics*. He tweets under @GabrielSilesB.

Silke Trommer is University Lecturer at the Department of Political and Economic Studies at the University of Helsinki. She is author of *Transformations in Trade Politics: Participatory Trade Politics in West Africa* (London: Routledge, 2014). Her doctoral dissertation on which the book is based won the 2013 Best Dissertation Award from the International Political Economy Section of the International Studies Association. Trommer has published peer-reviewed articles on trade politics in *New Political Economy*, *Globalizations* and *The Journal of Development Studies*, on trade law in *The Chinese Journal of International Law*, and on nongovernmental organizations in *West European Politics.* Her main research interests are global trade governance, trade and development, and trade and civil society.

Rorden Wilkinson is Professor and Chair of the Department of International Relations at the University of Sussex. He is also an Honorary Professorial Fellow at the Brooks World Poverty Institute at the University of Manchester. His most recent books include: *What's Wrong with the WTO and How to Fix it* (Polity, 2014); *International Organization and Global Governance* (Routledge, 2014); *Trade, Poverty, Development: Getting beyond the WTO's Doha Deadlock* (Routledge, 2013); and *The Millennium Development Goals and Beyond: Global Development after 2015* (Routledge, 2012). Rorden is a member of the editorial board of the international public policy journal *Global Governance*, co-editor of the Routledge *Global Institutions* series, a Fellow of the Royal Society of Arts, and the 2014 recipient of the International Studies Association Society for Women in International Political Economy (SWIPE) Mentoring Award.

Acknowledgement

We have assembled this edited collection with the intention of bringing together outstanding scholarship that can throw light on the role of experts and expert knowledge in the field of global trade governance, which we see as one key and under-researched node of authority constituting and reproducing the world as we know it. We are thrilled and very grateful that all of our contributors so marvelously stepped up to the task.

Since we first crossed paths in 2012 at the International Studies Association Annual Convention in San Diego and the World Trade Organization Public Forum in Geneva, we have shared concerns about a global trading system that we find asymmetrical in terms of distribution of benefits and access to decision making, inadaptable to urgent and well-founded demands for reform, and, consequentially, anachronistic and out of touch with social realities in the majority of countries across the world. We hope that our book can play a small part in motivating and driving forward scholarship that challenges received wisdom about world trade and crafts genuinely novel theoretical and analytical avenues for critically engaging with the way the world trades and who benefits from it.

We would like to thank Rorden Wilkinson and Thomas Weiss for the enthusiasm and support they have shown for our project from the start. We are deeply indebted to Amy Wood who provided tireless and invaluable editorial work, and to Nicola Parkin, Lydia de Cruz, and the team at Routledge for all their help and efforts. We would also like to thank the Social Sciences and Humanities Research Council of Canada for their generous support.

Erin Hannah, James Scott, and Silke Trommer
London, Canada, London, UK, and Helsinki, Finland
March 2015

Abbreviations

ACP	African, Caribbean and Pacific
ACWL	Advisory Centre on WTO Law
AfT	Aid for Trade
BRICS	Brazil, Russia, India, China, and South Africa
CAFTA	Central America Free Trade Agreement
CEPR	Centre for Economic Policy Research
CGE	computable general equilibrium
CPD	Centre for Policy Dialogue
CUTS	Consumer Unity and Trust Society
DDA	Doha Development Agenda
DFID	Department for International Development
DG	Director-General
DSM	dispute settlement mechanism
DSU	Dispute Settlement Understanding
EBA	Everything But Arms
EC	European Commission
ECDPM	European Centre for Development and Policy Management
ECOWAS	Economic Community of West African States
EFTA	European Free Trade Association
ENDA-CACID	Environment and Development of the Third World—African Centre for Commerce, Integration and Development
EPA	Economic Partnership Agreement
EU	European Union
FAO	Food and Agriculture Organization
FIT	Feed-in Tariffs
FTA	free trade agreement
GATS	General Agreement on Trade in Services
GATT	General Agreement on Tariffs and Trade

GDP	gross domestic product
GSP	Generalized System of Preferences
GTA	Global Trade Alert
ICTSD	International Centre for Trade and Sustainable Development
ILEAP	International Lawyers and Economists Against Poverty
IMF	International Monetary Fund
IO	international organization
IPE	international political economy
IR	International Relations
ISO	International Organization for Standardization
ITO	International Trade Organization
LDCs	least developed countries
LMG	Like-Minded Group
MDGs	Millennium Development Goals
MFN	most favored nation
NAFTA	North American Free Trade Agreement
NAMA	non-agricultural market access
NGO	nongovernmental organization
NTBs	non-tariff barriers
OECD	Organisation for Economic Co-operation and Development
PTA	preferential trade agreement
PV	photovoltaic
RoO	Rules of Origin
RTA	regional trade agreement
SACU	South African Customs Union
SADC	South African Development Community
SCM	Subsidies and Countervailing Measures
SDT	special and differential treatment
SP	sensitive products
SPS	Sanitary and Phytosanitary
SSM	special safeguard mechanism
TBT	Technical Barriers to Trade
TPP	Trans-Pacific Partnership
TPRTP	Trade Policy Research and Training Program
TRIMs	Trade-Related Investment Measures
TRIPs	Trade-Related Aspects of Intellectual Property Rights
TTIP	Transatlantic Trade and Investment Partnership
UN	United Nations

UNCTAD	United Nations Conference on Trade and Development
USTR	United States Trade Representative
WCA	West and Central African countries
WHO	World Health Organization
WTO	World Trade Organization

Introduction

Erin Hannah, James Scott and Silke Trommer

- **Experts and expert knowledge in global trade**
- **What our contributors say about expert knowledge**
- **Avenues for future research**

The role that expert knowledge plays in global trade governance has been crucial in practice, yet under-scrutinized in theory and analysis. The economic, legal and political complexities involved in global trade governance are such that every new student of its mysteries will sympathize with the famous words uttered by US Senator Eugene Millikin in 1951: "anyone who reads [the General Agreement on Tariffs and Trade] is likely to have his sanity impaired."[1] Consequentially, trade institutions and advocacy groups have long relied on staffing their ranks with highly trained experts, so-called "capacity building" in the field of global trade has become a cornerstone of the bulk part of the world's development programs, and universities provide courses and entire degrees geared exclusively at teaching the intricacies of the global trading system. Meanwhile, standard political economy approaches insist that trade policy outcomes are a function of states' economic interests, their power relations and aspirations, and the institutional frameworks in which trade decision making takes place.[2] As we explore below, numerous scholars have noted both the importance of expertise for reaching desired policy outcomes in trade governance and, indeed, in shaping the very policy preferences being pursued. Yet, few have pierced the veil of expert knowledge as a structural feature of trade governance in its own right, to ask essential questions such as: What knowledge is being disseminated through the global trading system, to whose benefit, and what is left un-conceptualized, unsaid, or omitted in trade-related political debates as a consequence of these patterns?

The central aim of this book is to shed light on expert knowledge and to begin to answer these core questions. From specialized language and terminology, to distinct techniques of economic analysis and legal reasoning, expert knowledge structures political debates the very moment any actor steps into the field of global trade to make their voice heard. From the coal face of trade negotiations and the texts that form trade agreements, through the bubble of actors involved in and around trade policy processes and the languages that they employ, up to the role of academia in analyzing and conceptualizing trade at its most abstract, bodies of expert knowledge channel and control what can be thought, who is able to act, and how the benefits of trade are created and distributed within and among countries and people.

It is widely acknowledged that the lack of expertise, resources, and technical capacity among developing countries are central factors underlying the negotiation of unfavorable rules that adversely impact on the poor.[3] As the World Trade Organization (WTO) approaches its fifteenth year of negotiations on the Doha Development Agenda with little sign of a forthcoming breakthrough, member states turn increasingly to preferential trade agreements (PTAs) to fill the gap. WTO-Plus rules in these PTAs not only fail to redress imbalances in global trade, but also serve to fragment the trading system further and, in some instances, undermine WTO flexibilities designed to address the challenges of poverty. The importance of expert knowledge to how the trade system functions is increasing with the continued extension of trade rules into new areas such as investment, services and intellectual property rights, while the emerging web of plurilateral agreements and PTAs have rendered negotiations more technical and multifarious.[4]

The resulting multiplicity of nodes of authority and increasing complexity of trade rules further empower experts relative to other trade political actors. Experts possess an authoritative claim on knowledge, and the ability to shape the terms of debate and construct narratives that define what is both conceivable and inconceivable in trade negotiations. In response, closed-door politics and ivory tower agendas are standard criticisms of global trade governance from economic and broader societal interest groups alike.

In order to explore these tensions and to put expert knowledge in global trade at the center of the analysis, we have invited contributors who collectively cover all of its core areas—including legal and economic aspects, discourse and ideational restraints, and the nongovernmental arena—to examine the structural features that uphold trade experts' monopoly over knowledge, to reflect on how existing forms of expert knowledge impact on trade policy formation and the application of trade rules, and to investigate the tensions between actors who work to uphold the status quo and those seeking to challenge dominant narratives about global trade. Given the wide range of academic disciplines and traditions required to tackle such an ambitious agenda, we have refrained from asking our contributors to adhere to a common analytical framework. Instead, we have directed them to engage one or several of the following overarching research questions:

- Who is considered to be a trade expert and how does one become a knowledge producer in global trade?
- How do experts acquire, disseminate and legitimate knowledge?
- What agendas are advanced by expert knowledge?
- How does the discourse generated within trade expertise serve to close off alternative institutional pathways and modes of thinking?
- What potential exists for the emergence of more emancipatory global trade policies from contemporary developments in the field of trade expertise?

In order to present the fruit of their efforts, we have arranged our book in three parts. In Part I, Rorden Wilkinson, Gabriel Siles-Brügge and Silke Trommer present accounts of the discourses and the ideas that structure the field of global trade and constrain political agency. In Part II, Joseph Conti, Clive George and Andrew Lang assess authoritative forms of legal and economic knowledge and provide avenues for studying their political implications. In Part III, Matthew Eagleton-Pierce, Erin Hannah, and James Scott examine the agency of experts and their role in producing knowledge that defines what is (in)conceivable in trade negotiations and opening up intellectual space for resistance and alternative policy options.

This pluralist approach harnesses the political nature of expert knowledge in the field of trade, unpacks received wisdom about the possibility of trade to work for global development, and problematizes both bodies of experts and the expertise they propagate. With the global economic and multilateralism crises raging, the inherently political nature of economic and legal expertise is today more obvious than ever. Speaking to ongoing debates in the trade literature, our book offers a detailed scrutiny of how ideas and interests interact in trade policymaking and highlights the role of expertise in shaping global trade governance.

We complete this introductory chapter by giving an overview of the existing literature on experts and expert knowledge in global trade, by summarizing chapter findings, and by suggesting avenues for future research on the basis of the analyses provided. Overall, we understand our book not as a complete treatment of the role of expert knowledge in global trade governance, but as a scholarly acknowledgement of its central importance in constructing and maintaining the global trading system as we know it, and as an invitation to the field to pay due analytical and theoretical attention.

Experts and expert knowledge in global trade

While we have argued above that there is a lacuna with respect to the analysis of the role of expert knowledge within global trade governance, there are certainly broader bodies of literature from which insights can be drawn. These can be usefully considered as forming two avenues of exploration—literature examining knowledge and power in global governance, and literature seeking to conceptualize the role of experts themselves in global governance.

Emanuel Adler and Steven Bernstein, for example, draw from constructivist thought to argue that knowledge plays a fundamental, rather than supplementary, role in both characterizing and facilitating global governance alongside the more traditional considerations of economic and political power.[5] They trace the limitations faced by developing countries in this regard and the difficulties that poor states have in exercising what Michael Barnett and Raymond Duvall characterize as "productive power." Productive power refers to the way in which systems of meaning and signification are socially produced and serve to determine what constitutes legitimate knowledge and whose knowledge matters.[6]

Building on this work, Erin Hannah examines the power of epistemes—shared, intersubjective or taken-for-granted causal and evaluative assumptions about how the world works—in global trade governance. She shows how epistemes are embedded in trade institutions and in common discourse through which people communicate about trade-related welfare gains, and how they work to enable and constrain nongovernmental organization (NGO) agency by defining the range of problems that can be addressed.[7]

Matthew Eagleton-Pierce makes another constructivist intervention into the study of power and knowledge. By drawing from the work of Bourdieu, he examines the role of "symbolic power" in global trade governance, and emphasizes how social and political orders are legitimated through particular discourses that draw from expertise as means of legitimation.[8] Similar in conceptualization but adopting a more rationalist methodological approach, liberal and institutionalist thinkers have also explored the way in which ideas intersect with material power to influence political outcomes, including influential work on the origins of US trade policy.[9] Farther afield, scholars such as Michael Strange have adopted post-structuralist methodologies to study the changing discursive and social contexts of global governance institutions, which are underpinned by evolving relations of material and ideational power.[10]

Knowledge is ultimately held by individuals and a related set of literature examines the way in which experts impact upon and shape global governance. In his work on epistemic communities, Peter Haas examines how networks of people with recognized claims of expertise are able to influence policy in areas of uncertainty.[11] Such experts "interpret the world for decision-makers and thus the governance arrangements which decision-makers negotiate."[12] In a similar vein, Ian Johnstone highlights the role that "interpretative communities" play in global governance, whose recognized expertise empowers them to determine which justifications of state action are to be considered legally acceptable and which are not.[13] Niilo Kauppi and Mikael Madsen identify transnational power elites as a distinct social group and conduct an empirical examination of these "operators of globalization" to help explain the authority and power structures produced by contemporary global governance.[14]

Susan Parks extends our theoretical understanding of policy change in global governance institutions by showcasing the central role that transnational environmental advocacy groups play in leveraging their scientific knowledge and socializing the World Bank Group to embrace sustainable development norms. Others favor the notion of a knowledge network, encompassing a range of individuals and institutions working on a given issue area.[15] Indeed, there are numerous examples of this line of constructivist work, where experts are considered important components in how we analyze global governance and understand how and why certain policies are chosen.[16]

A related set of thought highlights the importance of key, well-placed individual professionals and the influence they exercise over policy outcomes based on the privileged bodies of knowledge that they hold. Drawing from a variety of perspectives, Leonard Seabrooke identifies individuals who are able to engage in "epistemic arbitrage," defined as "exploit[ing] differences in professional knowledge pools for strategic advantage by positioning particular forms of knowledge as the most appropriate to deal with particular problems."[17] Such people are termed "epistemic arbiters" and are argued to be of increasing importance with the advancement of globalization and ever-greater transnational linkage. Craig Murphy and JoAnne Yates explore the role of engineers and other scientific experts in the process of standard setting in the International Organization for Standardization (ISO), to elucidate how technical standards lie at the heart of technological innovation and determine how trade is structured in industrial goods.[18]

While much of the work on epistemic communities concerns the role of scientific experts[19] and accords this body of knowledge a degree of objectivity, others have sought to problematize more deeply the nature of the knowledge that groups of experts propound,[20] perhaps reflecting the division in constructivist thought between conventional and critical strands that Katzenstein, Keohane and Krasner identify.[21] In a similar vein, scholars drawing from the work of Antonio Gramsci have argued that ideas are always linked to particular material interests.[22] For Gramsci, each social group brings with it a set of "organic intellectuals" who articulate the particular interests of that group in more abstract, theoretical terms.[23] These intellectuals define, promote, and sustain what Robert Cox terms "collective images of social order"—that is, "differing views as to both the nature and the legitimacy of prevailing power relations, the meaning of justice and public good, and so forth."[24] In this way, Gramscian-inspired analyses seek to connect ideas and the experts who produce and disseminate them back to material structures of power,[25] and highlight whose interests are being served by networks of intellectuals.[26] Though not overtly framed within a Gramscian approach, Diana Tussie's exploration of how research produced by, or at times commissioned from, expert bodies is used to support particular trade policies and mobilized to legitimize change, shares a concern with the political non-neutrality of such expert knowledge.[27]

Further critical work is to be found that draws from Foucault in particular. Jessica Lawrence, for instance, uses Foucault's concept of biopolitics to interrogate the privileging of expert participation within the WTO and whether this increases the legitimacy of the organization.[28] She highlights the problems of expert selection bias and how the claims regarding the objectivity and scientific nature of the expert knowledge embodied in the WTO may serve to silence critical voices.

The picture that emerges from this brief literature review is that there are multiple perspectives that can be drawn upon to explore the ways in which expert knowledge and the experts that produce and disseminate that knowledge contribute to bringing about particular policies, how they privilege certain interests and exclude others, and how bodies of knowledge get built into the structures of organizations. This book, rather than seeking to mediate between these or to favor one such approach over others, draws from all of them to give greater insight into the strengths and weaknesses of each. In particular, the chapters that follow allow us to interrogate the relationship between knowledge and power, and explore the political interests that different bodies of knowledge serve to advance. In addition, we seek to shed further light on the relationship between experts and expert knowledge, and show that there is value in analytically separating these two rather than treating them as almost synonymous, as is prevalent in much of the literature. The next section sets out the contribution that each chapter makes to the overall analysis.

What our contributors say about expert knowledge

The chapters in Part I present accounts of the discourses, metaphors, and ideas that structure the field of global trade and enable and constrain political agency. The authors are concerned with the epistemic foundations or "background knowledge" of global trade.[29] By asking what constitutes legitimate knowledge, the authors unpack the shared, intersubjective assumptions about how global trade does and should work. The way we talk about trade conveys, disciplines, and cements knowledge about trade. The chapters in this section examine the ways in which expert language serves as the key structural feature of global trade that upholds experts' monopoly over trade knowledge and determines which voices are heard and which are silenced and marginalized in global trade.

Rorden Wilkinson provides an account of common sense knowledge—comprising metaphors, stylized historical accounts, and crisis discourse—in global trade. He explores the ways in which these linguistic tools serve to normalize and depoliticize a deeply iniquitous global trade system. His central contention is that the way we talk about trade entrenches the illusion that the WTO and free trade are synonymous and that bargaining among unequals—the very basis of the multilateral trading system—can produce welfare gains for all.

Like Trommer in Chapter 3, Wilkinson shows how progressive debate and meaningful reform are stunted by the structural power of common sense knowledge and detractors and critics are delegitimized, villainized, and effectively silenced. Metaphors serve to convey common sense, oversimplify and obscure complex realities, and often infantilize opponents, particularly developing countries. When coupled with crisis discourse and stylized historical narratives, metaphors also tend to drive multilateral trade negotiations. Wilkinson argues that the language of crisis and collapse has been an intrinsic part of trade negotiations since the General Agreement on Tariffs and Trade (GATT) was first negotiated, and has played a key role in facilitating institutional development, pushing forward deeply asymmetrical bargains among members, and driving the trade agenda forward at moments when the institution appears deadlocked. In this chapter, he explores the content of common sense knowledge and examines the ways in which it has been generated and deployed by experts as a means of reframing trade negotiations in order to maintain forward momentum in the liberalization process. The way we talk about global trade is neither neutral nor objective, and Wilkinson calls on us to unpack and critically engage with the normative and ideological foundations of expert knowledge.

Chapter 2 in this section turns to the role of myth making and the power of ideas in global trade. Puzzled by the fact that there has been no significant move towards protectionism amongst most of the world's economics, despite the onset of the current economic crisis in 2008, Gabriel Siles-Brügge draws from constructivism to argue that particular ideas about the global trading system have become rooted in policymaking discourse, mediating the response of policy elites to protectionist pressures and temptations. Like Wilkinson, Siles-Brügge shows how stylized historical accounts of global trade reflect and advance particular national interests. In this case, leading economists and policymakers enjoying reified positions as experts in trade matters have constructed an ideational imperative for continued openness by drawing on a questionable reading of economic history (the Smoot-Hawley myth) and by continually stressing the role of protectionism as a cause of the Great Depression.

Like the other chapters in this section, Siles-Brügge unpacks the role of ideas in silencing alternative policy narratives; non-liberal responses to the current crisis have been all but ruled out by the ideational strength of the Smoot-Hawley myth. Nonetheless, Siles-Brügge finds reason for hope in Argentina where decision makers have responded differently by explicitly rejecting this narrative and implementing wide-ranging protectionist measures to deal with the crisis. The non-conformity of Argentina shows that the dominant myths and ideas underpinning trade expertise have not completely closed off alternative modes of thinking.

Silke Trommer deepens our understanding of the discursive foundations of global trade by exploring the role expert language plays in constituting the trade policy elite and in shaping its perceptions of politically feasible lines of action. She applies tools from anthropological and feminist scholarship to trace the gate-keeping function that global trade expert language plays in shaping who can talk and what they can say in trade politics. Trommer builds upon Wilkinson's chapter by investigating how one becomes a trade expert by acquiring and legitimating the "talk." The technocratic nature of global trade language not only serves to marginalize and exclude non-experts from trade policymaking processes but also obscures the deeply political nature of learning and using expert language, acts that reproduce a particular worldview and understanding of reality. Trommer argues that this language as currently constituted results in a dehumanization of the global trading order, in which human, social, and environmental conditions become second-order issues and the role of human agency in producing social and political outcomes is obscured.

The three chapters in this section provide compelling accounts of the role and structural power of expert language in global trade. By identifying the ideas, myths, metaphors, and common sense that constitute expert language, the authors identify what agendas are advanced by trade experts and the ways in which the discourse generated within trade expertise serves to close off alternative institutional pathways and modes of thinking. Wilkinson, Siles-Brügge, and Trommer concur that trade experts have constructed an ideational imperative for further liberalization that uncritically accepts the notion that free trade is an end in itself which promotes welfare for all, however unevenly. The central contention of this section is that global trade will never work for development so long as political agents remain shackled to this received wisdom.

The three chapters of Part II explore the two most central areas of expertise at play in trade governance, namely economics and law. While economics has always been a natural source of expertise at work within the global trade system, the increasing legalization of trade relations, most notably with the strengthening of the dispute settlement mechanism in the Uruguay Round, has propelled legal expertise to a more prominent role. The chapters by Joseph Conti and Andrew Lang each concern the legalization of trade but explore different stages of that process. Lang examines the dynamics at play when a legal agreement is created and how that process encodes a body of (often economic or scientific) knowledge into the text, while Conti's chapter, by contrast, concerns the subsequent period and how that legal agreement structures relations between states.

Lang's chapter gives a highly nuanced account of how the process of encoding a body of expertise into a legal text enables subsequent recourse to that expert knowledge as a means of achieving objectivity in dispute rulings, while simultaneously opening the possibility of doing the very opposite of this, namely allowing legal rulings to make judgments explicitly contrary to that encoded expertise. Lang terms this twin process a "double movement" and goes on to explore how it plays out in the agreements on Subsidies and on Sanitary and Phytosanitary Standards (SPS). In each, the Appellate Body has opted at times to utilize bodies of expert knowledge as an "objective" basis on which to make rulings, while at other times it has deliberately departed from that basis to exert an opposing legal basis for rulings. In this way, the Appellate Body chooses different paths in different circumstances that serve to produce legal objectivity. How this takes place and how one option in the "double movement" is chosen over another is discovered through the process of legal interpretation that takes place within the dispute settlement system, where the boundaries between law and other forms of expert knowledge are constructed and reconstructed.

This ongoing process of learning through the dispute settlement mechanism (DSM) highlights the importance of deep knowledge and experience of the DSM if it is to be utilized effectively, which is a key finding of Conti's chapter. The juridification (that is, the expansion of legal regulation) that took place with the creation of the WTO has not only created a greater role for legal experts within the trade system, but has generated new forms of expert knowledge and new paths to acquiring necessary legal expertise. As Joseph Conti argues in Chapter 4, the expanded dispute settlement system of the WTO compared with that of the GATT has made it necessary for states to develop legal expertise in order to allow them to make use of the DSM. Failure to do so risks being unable to secure benefits from the trade system. In this, Conti finds, from detailed empirical work, that actual experience of using the DSM is crucial for building the expertise that is peculiar to the WTO as a legal entity. For this reason large, rich trading nations are at an advantage in that they are more prolific users of the DSM and have larger bodies of in-house expertise. Developing countries, by contrast, are sometimes caught in a vicious cycle: lack of in-house legal expertise precludes their use of the DSM, which in turn hampers their ability to create in-house legal experts. Conti highlights how outside organizations have played a role in mitigating this problem, particularly the Advisory Centre on WTO Law, through offering outside assistance in accessing the DSM. This operates as a stepping stone to developing in-house experts, but Conti concludes that such measures will have to be supplemented with institutional reform if developing countries are to be enabled to have equal practical use of the DSM.

Such institutionalization of inequalities and the need for institutional reform is also a key insight of Clive George's chapter. George examines a particular form of economic expertise, namely that produced by computable general equilibrium (CGE) modeling. This, he argues, is used to bolster support for further liberalization despite the dubious basis for the claims made by such analyses and the tiny economic gains that they predict. He highlights how it is the numerical output of CGE models specifically that gives them an unwarranted "scientific" veneer, serving to mask the politics that underlies trade agreements. Despite this, or perhaps because of it, CGE models have become the tool of choice for trade analysis.

George's chapter also highlights how the rise of CGE models serves to sideline alternative economic perspectives, particularly those that question the benefits of ever greater liberalization. The orthodox trade agenda is thereby reinforced at the expense of alternative traditions such as those advocating the use of infant industry protection as a tool of the developmental state.[30] One form of expertise thereby serves to exclude others.

All three chapters of this section touch in varying degrees upon how expert knowledge is used instrumentally in the pursuit of other aims, and on the role played by notions of objectivity within expertise. The three chapters here form a powerful examination of the (at times problematic) interconnection between the trade system and bodies of expert knowledge and how these forms of expertise serve to reify certain actors, traditions and interests over others.

Filling structures with names and faces, contributors to our closing section on the agency of expert knowledge focus on individuals and organizations that can be considered to be experts of trade policy today. In line with our overall goal of searching for alternative pathways to make trade policy work for global development, all three chapters in Part III examine what may be called new or atypical actors in the global trade regime by focusing on representatives of civil society and the global South. In this sense, they deviate from the standard, outdated, and exclusive focus in trade policy analysis on state agents and private sector representatives of the global North.

Matthew Eagleton-Pierce builds on Bourdieusian insights to examine changes in knowledge production and policy practice that have occurred in trade governance since the Washington Consensus' falling into disrepute and the WTO's legitimacy crisis of the late 1990s and early 2000s. His chapter provides an in-depth analysis of how the global North NGO Oxfam International successfully built alternative trade policy strategies that were informed by their social critique of contemporary capitalism centered around notions of global social justice. Using the West and Central African cotton issue as a focal point in his case study, Eagleton-Pierce traces the NGO's gradual emergence as a knowledge producer and credible voice in trade policy debates through a process of learning and adapting to global trade orthodoxy, which opened inroads into the global trade policy elite and culminated in Oxfam's ability to utter a critique from within. Similar to Scott's chapter in the same section, Eagleton-Pierce reveals the decisive role of individuals in making strategic policy decisions that determine which types of knowledge are being produced. At the same time, his analysis provides clear evidence showing how the discursive and epistemic structures analyzed in the first two sections of our book constrain the policy field by exerting influence over the types of expert knowledge that any normative goal must be pressed into if its agents hope to attain policy influence.

Erin Hannah examines what she calls embedded NGOs and the emergence of demand-driven advocacy in the global trade regime. She defines embedded NGOs as non-profit knowledge producers from the global North and global South who work to address injustices in the trading system by institutionally empowering low-income countries, and push an embedded liberalist agenda of inserting sustainable development priorities into the global market economy. As Hannah notes, these types of actors have multiplied since the WTO's legitimacy crisis—a crucial turning point in the actor landscape of global trade also identified by Eagleton-Pierce. While Hannah finds that embedded NGOs work to improve accountability criteria and negotiating capacity among poor-country WTO members, she questions to what extent their work can be seen to undermine power asymmetries within both global trade itself and in the dominant discourses and forms of knowledge about global trade. Instead, the Western-centric make-up of these groups, their selectiveness in the issues they pick up, their own transparency record, and their liberal economic bias all appear to limit embedded NGOs' transformative potential.

James Scott's account of Southern intellectuals in contemporary trade governance suggests that we are witnessing an empowerment of global South trade political actors to a position of providing intellectual leadership to developing countries. He engages in an indicative mapping exercise of the epistemic communities that these individuals form and assesses the alternative narratives around global trade that arise from their agency. Scott finds that Southern intellectuals provide a coherent narrative that challenges the traditional powers' reading of the trajectory and purpose of the global trade system and that this narrative, along with the growing leadership Southern intellectuals provide, has played an important role in bolstering developing countries' negotiating positions in the Doha Development Round. Like Hannah, Scott, however, ultimately emphasizes the role of the dominant episteme in shaping trade experts' perceptions of politically feasible positions to take on questions of global trade. Given that this group is closely linked to the leading emerging economies, and thus presumably their trade political outlooks and interests, Scott issues a warning that the concerns of the most marginalized will remain just that, even with new expert knowledge emanating from individuals associated with the global South.

The various actors under scrutiny in this section are of course not new to trade governance as such. As the authors acknowledge in their chapters, some of the trade political agents they examine predate the dawn of trade multilateralism and certainly the WTO era. What is new, and what all contributors to this section analyze, are the increased levels of influence that these actors have gained over recent years. This suggests that there is room for novel types of agency in trade governance. At the same time, taken together, the authors in this section also find agency to remain constrained by the various structural features of expert knowledge analyzed in the previous two sections of our book. Eagleton-Pierce's observations about the gate-keeping functions of language as well as economic and legal technical knowledge in particular, brings our book back to its starting point of emphasizing the relevance of these structural features.

Curiously, the three contributions expose a tension in their assessments of how successful the new trade experts are in forging alternative pathways for the global trade regime. Despite acknowledging important shortcomings and epistemic constraints, the chapters of Scott and Eagleton-Pierce highlight the ability to create counter-narratives and successful articulations of heterodox voices. Hannah, on the other hand, questions the transformative reach of the organizations she examines when suggesting that embedded NGOs crowd out alternative voices from the debate. The tension between these views seems exacerbated by the fact that taken together, the chapters indicate that there are overlaps and revolving doors among the analyzed individuals and groups in the real world. Overall, the section thus leaves us with both a need for and some pointers towards refined research agendas on the role of experts and expertise in global trade, to which we turn in the closing section of our introduction.

Avenues for future research

This book focuses on the origins, legitimacy, and structural power of expert knowledge in global trade. Contributors highlight the various ways in which expert knowledge constrains political agency, disciplines policymaking, and limits the potential for global trade to work for sustainable development. They show that in order to gain and maintain expert status, individuals are compelled to assimilate and reproduce dominant forms of expert knowledge in policy and academia, thus shielding the field from transformative influences. Given these conditions, we conclude that the prospects for global trade to generate welfare gains for the world's poorest people and redress injustices in global trade seem bleak. Our hope is that scholars will challenge this conclusion by exploring the conditions under which the shackles of received wisdom might be loosened.

Future research should address how experts' monopoly over trade knowledge can be politicized, whether meaningful reform of global trade is possible in light of the structural power of expert knowledge, and whether and how global trade expert knowledge can be reconstituted to correct the shortcomings of the global trading system. Building upon the insights in the first section of this volume, scholars could examine circumstances under which dominant discourses, myths, historical narratives, and metaphors can be successfully challenged and resisted. Perhaps by looking beyond the field of trade to other, overlapping areas such as finance, environment, and development, scholars could generate insight into how global trade governance could be made fit for purpose. Another potential avenue is to study the impact of evolving expert knowledge in other contexts (institutional and policy-wise) for global trade governance. For instance, do changing policy narratives around sustainable development within the United Nations system impact the generation and legitimation of expert knowledge in global trade governance? Scholars might also examine whether deliberations in different political arenas that include a broader range of voices can impact discourses and ideas about global trade.

Certain types of knowledge are particularly prominent within trade governance—none more so than economics and law. Further work might be done to flesh out how individual experts are chosen within these areas, particularly as they feed into processes within the dispute settlement, and the potential biases that may result. As the trading system becomes more heterogeneous in terms of influential actors, research might elaborate on the implications that encounters of different legal traditions—those originating in "the West" and those originating in "the Rest"—have for rule application and dispute settlement. Similarly, the fusion between legal, economistic, and science-based reasonings and how legally reformulated understandings of key economic and scientific concepts feed back into policymaking deserve further scholarly scrutiny. With regard to economics, there is potential for further study to explore how certain economic theories are privileged over others in the processes of expert knowledge provision and the developmental and distributional consequences this has. What heterodox approaches in economics and law compete with the orthodoxy and how they do or do not succeed in acquiring policy influence might also provide a future research agenda worth delving into.

One central argument of our book is that experts as political actors in their own right constitute an understudied category of trade political agents. This is an insight from which we hope subsequent research may depart, as the analytical work of identifying, mapping, and making sense of the actions of those in the global trade policy community who participate in policy processes on the basis of their expert status has only just begun. One pertinent question is, if the traditional club model of trade policymaking has given way to a much more complex reality, in which experts play a prominent role, how can we theoretically capture all aspects of trade governance in order to be able to analyze it in meaningful ways? Furthermore, do changing assessments of what constitutes valid knowledge in global trade accompany the ongoing power shifts in the global economy that many observers currently report?

Such research may benefit from addressing some blank spots in the analyses provided here. Potential areas to examine include such questions as the agency of experts in other forums of global trade governance outside the institutional boundaries of the WTO; the agency of experts vis-à-vis more frequently studied non-state actors, notably business, labor and consumers; and, as one glance at Scott's indicative list of trade intellectuals suggests, the gendered nature of global trade expertise. Scholars might also conduct comparative research on the transformative potential of state and non-state agents of global trade governance. Politicizing dominant forms of expertise undermines claims to authoritative knowledge. Given the often-invoked need for trade political "thinking outside the box," such research may be exactly what is required in order to identify the social forces that can help unleash the potential of global trade to work for sustainable development.

Notes

1 Cited in Roderick Abbott, "The World Trade Organization," in *The New Economic Diplomacy: Decision-Making and Negotiation in International Economic Relations*, ed. Nicholas Bayne and Stephen Woolcock (Aldershot: Ashgate Publishing, 2007), 316.

2 Bernard Hoekman and Michel Kostecki, *The Political Economy of the World Trading System*, 3rd edition (Oxford: Oxford University Press, 2010).

3 Rorden Wilkinson, *What's Wrong with the WTO and How to Fix It* (Cambridge: Polity Press, 2014); and Fatoumata Jawara and Aileen Kwa, *Behind the Scenes at the WTO: The Real World of International Trade Negotiations*, 2nd edition (London: Zed Books, 2004).
4 Tony Heron, *Pathways from Preferential Trade: The Politics of Trade Adjustment in Africa, the Caribbean and Pacific* (Basingstoke: Palgrave Macmillan, 2013); Alisa DiCaprio and Silke Trommer, "Bilateral Graduation: The Impact of EPAs on LDC Trade Space,"*Journal of Development Studies* 46, no. 9 (2010): 1607–27.
5 Emanuel Adler and Steven Bernstein, "Knowledge in Power: The Epistemic Construction of Global Governance," in *Power in Global Governance*, ed. Michael Barnett and Raymond Duvall (Cambridge and New York: Cambridge University Press, 2005), 294–318.
6 Michael Barnett and Raymond Duvall, *Power in Global Governance* (Cambridge and New York: Cambridge University Press, 2005), 3–4.
7 Erin Hannah, *NGOs and Global Trade: Non-State Voices in EU Trade Policymaking* (Abingdon: Routledge, forthcoming).
8 Matthew Eagleton-Pierce, *Symbolic Power in the World Trade Organization* (Oxford: Oxford University Press, 2012).
9 Judith Goldstein, "The Impact of Ideas on Trade Policy: The Origins of US Agricultural and Manufacturing Policies," *International Organization* 43, no. 1 (1989): 31–71; Judith Goldstein and Robert O. Keohane, ed., *Ideas and Foreign Policy: Beliefs, Institutions, and Political Change* (Ithaca, NY and London: Cornell University Press, 1993).
10 Michael Strange, *Writing Global Trade Governance: Discourse and the WTO* (Abingdon: Routledge, 2013).
11 Peter Haas, "Introduction: Epistemic Communities and International Policy Coordination," *International Organization* 46, no. 1 (1992): 1–35.
12 Peter Haas, "Ideas, Experts and Governance," in *The Role of "Experts" in International Decision-Making: Advisors, Decision-Makers or Irrelevant?* ed. Mónika Ambrus, Karin Arts, Ellen Hey and Helena Raulus (Cambridge: Cambridge University Press, 2014), 19–43.
13 Ian Johnstone, "The Power of Interpretive Communities," in *Power in Global Governance*, ed. Michael Barnett and Raymond Duvall (Cambridge and New York: Cambridge University Press, 2005), 185–204.
14 Niilo Kauppi and Mikael R. Madsen, "Fields of Global Governance: How Transnational Power Elites Can Make Global Governance Intelligible," *International Political Sociology* 3, no. 8 (2014): 324–42, 324.
15 Susan Park, *World Bank Group Interactions with Environmentalists: Changing International Organization Identities* (Manchester: Manchester University Press, 2010); Diane Stone, "'Shades of Grey': The World Bank, Knowledge Networks and Linked Ecologies of Academic Engagement," *Global Networks* 13, no. 2 (2013): 241–60; Janice Stein, *Networks of Knowledge: Collaborative Innovation in International Learning* (University of Toronto Press, 2001).
16 For an example of the impact of nationally based epistemic communities on global governance, see Emanuel Adler, "The Emergence of Cooperation: National Epistemic Communities and the International Evolution of the Idea of Nuclear Arms Control," *International Organization* 46, no. 1 (1992): 101–45.

17 Leonard Seabrooke, "Epistemic Arbitrage: Transnational Professional Knowledge in Action," *Journal of Professions and Organization* 1, no. 1 (2014): 50.
18 Craig N. Murphy and JoAnne Yates, *The International Organization for Standardization: Global Governance through Voluntary Consensus* (Abingdon and New York: Routledge, 2009).
19 Mai'a K. Davis Cross, "Rethinking Epistemic Communities Twenty Years Later," *Review of International Studies* 39, no. 1 (2012): 137–60.
20 Gabriel Siles-Brügge, *Constructing European Union Trade Policy: A Global Idea of Europe* (Basingstoke: Palgrave Macmillan, 2014); Niilo Kauppi and Mikael Rask Madsen, ed., *Transnational Power Elites: The Professionals of Law, Governance and Security* (Abingdon and New York: Routledge, 2013).
21 Peter J. Katzenstein, Robert O. Keohane and Stephen D. Krasner, "International Organization and the Study of World Politics," *International Organization* 52, no. 4 (1998): 676–77.
22 Stephen Gill, "Epistemology, Ontology and the 'Italian School'," in *Gramsci, Historical Materialism and International Relations*, ed. Stephen Gill (Cambridge: Cambridge University Press, 1993), 24.
23 Antonio Gramsci, *Selections from the Prison Notebooks* (London: Lawrence and Wilshart, 1971), 5–7.
24 Robert W. Cox, *Approaches to World Order* (Cambridge, New York and Melbourne: Cambridge University Press, 1996), 99.
25 Andreas Bieler, "Questioning Cognitivism and Constructivism in IR Theory: Reflections on the Material Structure of Ideas," *Politics* 2, no. 2 (2001): 93–100.
26 Timothy J. Sinclair, "Reinventing Authority: Embedded Knowledge Networks and the New Global Finance," *Environment and Planning C: Government and Policy* 18, no. 4 (2000): 487–502; Inderjeet Parmar, "American Foundations and the Development of International Knowledge Networks," *Global Networks* 2, no. 1 (2002): 13–30.
27 Diana Tussie, ed., *The Politics of Trade: The Role of Research in Trade Policy and Negotiation* (Ottawa: International Development Research Centre, 2009). See also Paul Mably, "Centralized Production: The Group of G33," in *The Politics of Trade: The Role of Research in Trade Policy and Negotiations*, ed. Diana Tussie (Ottawa: International Development Research Centre, 2009), 239–70; and James Scott, "The Use and Misuse of Trade Negotiation Simulations," *The Journal of World Trade* 42, no. 1 (2008): 87–103.
28 Jessica Lawrence, "Structural Logic of Expert Participation in the WTO," in *The Role of "Experts" in International Decision-Making: Advisors, Decision-Makers or Irrelevant?* ed. Mónika Ambrus, Karin Arts, Ellen Hey and Helena Raulus (Cambridge: Cambridge University Press, 2014), 173–93.
29 Michel Foucault, *The Order of Things: An Archeology of the Human Sciences* (New York: Pantheon, 1970); and Adler and Bernstein, "Knowledge in Power," 294–318.
30 For more in this line of thought, see UNCTAD, *Trade and Development Report 2014* (Geneva: UNCTAD, 2014).

Part I

The language of expert knowledge

The power of discourse, metaphors, and myth making

1 Talking trade

Common sense knowledge in the multilateral trade regime[1]

Rorden Wilkinson

- **It's all common sense, right?**
- **Pestilence, history, villains, and who to blame**
- **All for nothing**
- **Infants and insults**
- **Of boats, bicycles, and other dramatic catastrophes**
- **Targeting recalcitrants**
- **The WTO the unfortunate**
- **Conclusion**

The way we talk about trade is unique. It is unique because, unlike any other area of economic and political debate, conversations often distill complex arguments into easily consumable ways of deliberating. These ways of talking—often in the form of metaphorical sound bites and, less frequently, more involved but nonetheless stylized historical accounts—present those reading or listening with snippets of logic that convey a subjective position about how the trade (and wider) world works. They also frequently portray opponents of free trade in highly unflattering ways designed to undermine the credibility of contrary views using what we imagine is a "common sense" logic.

Yet, we have become so consumed with stylized ways of talking about trade that we are apparently unable to see that these forms of communicating help blind us to a form of trade governance that has, in the post-World War II era, produced a series of trade deals that have offered developed countries disproportionately greater economic advantages than their developing counterparts. Moreover, we seem unable to see that these stylized ways of talking distract our attention sufficiently to maintain the illusion that equitable trade outcomes can be negotiated by bargaining among member states varying dramatically in economic size and capability in an institutional setting that clearly favors the advanced industrial countries over their smaller, less able developing counterparts. Equally, we have failed to realize that these subjective positions are presented as if they were true "facts" and their biases—ideological, interest-wise or other—are hidden behind the logic of a metaphor, an historical account, a constructed identity and/or common sense reasoning (that we might just be able to "level the playing field" or harvest "low-hanging fruit") with which the reader or listener is presented.

The problems here are twofold. The presentation of metaphor, historical logic or constructed identity as fact and common sense simultaneously encourages (i) particular forms of behavior consistent with maintaining the status quo, while at the same time (ii) safeguarding that logic from critical scrutiny. Our acceptance of these ways of talking about trade constrains us not only from asking questions about where we are going but also from having debates about the future of trade and its governance that are genuinely "outside the box."

If we are to reform the existing system—even install a new one—we need to recognize that the problems that exist are more than the way the General Agreement on Tariffs and Trade (GATT) and World Trade Organization (WTO) has functioned and was designed. We need to change fundamentally the way we think and talk about trade. We need to move beyond simply regurgitating received wisdom about trade—as George Orwell advised, we need to resist using language without thinking and repeating words and phrases simply because their use has become habit.[2] We need to subject to critical interrogation the meanings underpinning (and often obscured by) the way we speak and the language we use, and we need to filter out the forms of behavior that preclude others from engaging in genuine conversations about trade.

The aim of this chapter is to show how the way that we talk about trade affects the way we think and act, which in turn has an effect on how we conceive the form of trade governance that we *actually* (rather than imagine we) have. Its purpose is to get us to think about the way we talk and listen to arguments about trade so that we no longer take common sense wisdom at face value and are not persuaded by simple assertions that trade is like a "bicycle" which needs to be kept in perpetual motion, that the world economy will collapse if liberalization is halted, that "rising tides will lift all boats," or that "free-riders" (a label more often than not attached to developing countries) are necessarily "free-riding." Put simply, the chapter is intended to get us to think twice about the value of what we take to be common sense trade logic.

The chapter begins by setting out some conceptual markers that help us understand how the metaphorical and historical devices and the constructed identities we deploy when thinking and talking about trade bind us into unhelpful intellectual circuits from which we struggle to extract ourselves. Thereafter, the chapter examines how the way we talk about trade can have an impact on encouraging forward momentum at moments of intransigence in trade rounds, making the production of asymmetrical trade bargains more—rather than less—likely; it explores the tensions between on the one hand the pursuit of freer trade as an inalienable good in itself, and on the other hand claims that the WTO is not a development organization; and it points to those new frontiers that have opened up in the way we talk about trade but which do little to move us beyond existing common sense wisdom. The chapter concludes by showing how the way that we currently talk about trade forces us to think inside the box at a moment when we need to do just the opposite.

It's all common sense, right?

One way language contributes to the maintenance of particular relations of power is through the dissemination of "common sense"—what we think of as those words and phrases that convey everyday wisdom, what we all ought to know, what is obvious, what is in front of one's nose (as Orwell remarked).[3] As Antonio Gramsci put it, common sense is the "traditional popular conception of the world,"[4] that which is instinctive, rarely questioned, seldom subjected to scrutiny.[5] Yet, it is not just "wisdom" and "knowledge" that common sense conveys; it also suggests particular courses of action and forms of behavior that we assume are, or must be, appropriate.[6]

Common sense is particularly important in understanding how language contributes to the perpetuation of particular ideas that are held to be "right." Precisely because common sense is held to be "true" or "fact," it is seldom challenged. It suggests, nevertheless, modes of behavior that are consistent with the ideas and ideologies that underpin a social order. In so doing, common sense helps shape what it is that we deem politically possible. Other forms of wisdom and attendant modes of behavior—ones that may or may not be equally or more appropriate—are either obscured from view, dismissed as nonsense, or else they are rendered plain false; and the penalties can be sufficiently high to militate against challenging common sense (as the story of Socrates and his demise poignantly illustrates).[7] Yet, it is precisely because common sense embodies assumptions that treat authority and hierarchy as natural—because they reflect the wisdom of dominant ideologies—and which presuppose that particular courses of action or modes of behavior are the most appropriate, that it needs to be challenged.[8]

Metaphors play an important role in conveying common sense. They help create social realities, construct ideas of what is "true" and "false," and specify particular kinds of action.[9] Metaphors can also change the way events are perceived and understood, thereby altering conceptions of what is understood to be true, prescribing particular courses of action while crowding out or delegitimizing others. This is done by replacing an act, event, instance, or attribute with a word or phrase that conveys a particular meaning intended to underline or alter perceptions such that they serve a set of interests. Medical metaphors, for instance, are often used in political discourse to underline the dangers of particular ideologies or courses of action as well as to celebrate others.[10] For instance, in the West during the Cold War, the use of the word "cancer" in association with the spread of communism served not only to reinforce negative perceptions of an alternative form of socio-economic and political organization, but also prescribed (and legitimized) practices consistent with halting its spread.[11]

The words, metaphors, phrases, and linguistic constructions that convey common sense form part of a wider discourse. Discourses are organic aspects of any social order. They emerge out of particular historical moments and change with, are reproduced by, and influence the shape of the orders from which they emerge. They create exclusionary arenas (locking in some kinds of wisdom while crowding out others) empowering particular individuals to speak. Those who have been assimilated into, learnt or have been socialized by a dominant discourse and use it in communicating (verbally, in writing or otherwise) are "heard," while those who do not, or are excluded by it, are silenced.[12] Moreover, discourses are seldom static. They are reproduced and mutate through usage as well as change in response to challenges both to their credibility as well as to underlying ideas and interests. They also intensify at some moments and fall into relative abeyance at others. In so doing, they assist in perpetuating their underlying interests and relations of power.

What we know, then, is that language can shape behavior and that it develops and is deployed in a wider social context. As such, it reflects those hierarchies and power relationships that are prevalent at any given moment in time. We know that behavior is shaped not just through direct instructions, but also by the received wisdom embodied in common sense (whether it is through stock phrases, metaphors, or other linguistic constructions). We know that the use of a particular language creates some possibilities for action (consistent with the ideas and interests that underpin a discourse) while crowding out others. We know that it matters who speaks; and that by speaking, which voices are heard. We know that at moments wherein threats to the interests and power relationships underpinning a discourse emerge, an intensification and/or subtle (and sometimes dramatic) change in the substance of a discourse can result. It is with these conceptual markers in mind that we now turn to the way we think and speak about trade.

Pestilence, history, villains, and who to blame

The relationship between trade and war is one area wherein metaphors and pithy accounts purporting to be accurate historical renditions are presented in ways that overly simplify the complex relationship between commerce and conflict.[13] The key to this form of argumentation is the use of metaphorical and/or distilled examples wherein the logic of the story illustrates clearly the necessity of taking one course of action over another. In the early twentieth century, for instance, in accounts seeking to associate freer trade with the pursuit of world peace, stylized and abstracted stories were common. Demonstrating clearly the utility of metaphorical argument in presenting his case for freer trade in 1919, J. Russell Smith used the fixing of a broken sewage pipe to stem a typhoid outbreak as a proxy for the necessity of treating the root causes of conflict (of which the lack of trade was one) and the primary care given to patients by hospital nurses as a synonym for the hopelessness of treating the symptoms of war once it had broken out.[14] This form of argumentation was also prevalent in the immediate post-World War II era. Here commentators such as Clair Wilcox crafted their case for freer trade using metaphorical and stylized historical argument to support common sense messages by using disease both as a metaphor and a selective reading of the passage of world events in the preceding 150 years.[15]

Yet it is not just what commentators like Smith (who was professor of economic geography at Columbia) or Wilcox said that was important, it was also who they were. For instance, it is precisely because of Wilcox's role in the American polity and academy that his version of events gained credibility. He was professor and chair in the Economics Department at Swarthmore (1927–68). He co-authored (with Paul H. Douglas—a University of Chicago economist and later Democratic senator for Illinois) a petition against the 1930 Smoot-Hawley tariff (signed by 1,028 economists). He led the Office of International Trade Policy at the State Department between 1945 and 1948 (the competencies of which were later transferred over to form part of what is now the Office of the United States Trade Representative—USTR). He was head of the US delegation to London in 1946 charged with the task of negotiating the International Trade Organization (ITO), and he was vice-chairman of the US delegation to the 1948 Havana Conference on Trade and Employment that concluded the ITO Charter.

Others, too, were instrumental in putting forward these common sense messages like Wilcox's: University of Chicago and Princeton economics professor and sometime advisor to the US Treasury Jacob Viner; William Adams Brown, a contemporary of Wilcox's during the ITO negotiations and at Swarthmore; Wilcox's student and Council on Foreign Relations stalwart William Diebold Jr.; and Cambridge professor, a director of the Bank of England and co-author of the Bretton Woods system John Maynard Keynes.[16]

In arguing their case, what Wilcox, Viner, Brown, Diebold, Keynes, and others did was help put in place a core story that warned against the follies of not liberalizing trade married to a strong vision of what would transpire should this logic not be followed. This story was then disseminated domestically (particularly within the United States) and internationally which, in turn, helped secure the necessary support for liberalization to begin under the GATT. It also served to frame a particular kind of liberalization that simultaneously opened up trade in particular areas of importance to the United States, while protecting others.

These liberalization-cum-war arguments have not been confined to the annals of history, however. They resurface in more contemporary (and rather hyperbolic) accounts worrying about the future of the multilateral trading system. What is common to all is a form of historical reductionism that grooms the "lessons" of history in ways that are permissive to the arguments being pursued. As Gabriel Siles-Brügge puts it in Chapter 2, they create "an ideational imperative ... by drawing on a questionable reading of economic history."[17]

Three points about the way these arguments are manifest contemporarily are worth dwelling on momentarily, as the chapter returns to them throughout. The first is the use of catastrophe as a mechanism for driving a point home and encouraging the recipient of that wisdom to act with expediency. The second is the unique way that—more than any other challenger before—China is constructed as a threat, a state that for many has such potential that it will inevitably challenge the existing system.[18] The third is the manner in which all of these accounts rely on the capacity to easily identify a foe. In the early literature, the foes were identifiable as reactionary, mercantilist, anti-free trade forces. These forms of identification persist but more often than not they have moved from unidentifiable faces and shady political movements to nameable foes. This most commonly takes the form of laying blame in a highly predictable game of upstaging that unfolds after each hiccup in a trade round. The pattern is familiar to all. An agreement cannot be reached—often because it was impossible from the outset—and the countries deemed to have been the blockers to any deal are widely harangued. This haranguing goes largely uncommented upon, however.

What is worrying is that we come to acknowledge, even accept it when those being blamed are our favorite villains—favorites because we deplore their continued protection of agricultural markets, their strong-arm tactics, their neo-imperialist ways, or their domestic political structures—irrespective of whether domestic or other considerations meant a deal was never likely. We sometimes turn a blind eye when situations are engineered to collapse so that a foe can be identified for political purchase (as China was after the July 2008 mini-ministerial collapse over the Special Safeguard Mechanism).[19] Yet we almost never comment when the individuals identified are labeled "free-riders." This is the ultimate *faux pas.*

All for nothing

The accusation that a member is accruing benefits without contribution (that is, free-riding) renders us unable to see that this label has often been used for political purposes—particularly with regard to developing countries. Sometimes it is leveled at developing countries in what is imagined is a benign fashion—they matter little in terms of their overall contribution to world trade so their lack of reciprocity also does not matter. Or else, it is deployed with more intent—to highlight a lack of contribution. Joseph Stiglitz and Andrew Charlton's claim that "[a]fter effectively sitting out the first four decades of multilateral trade negotiations, developing countries' participation in the Uruguay Round led them to accept substantial liberalization of their trade regimes,"[20] is an example of the former. Reducing GATT/WTO participation to activity in trade negotiations alone and developing theoretical models designed to show that the application of the most-favored-nation clause generates a "free-rider problem"[21] is an example of the latter.

Whether stated passively or more intentionally, both forms of expression reinforce the common sense logic that the largest trading countries—that is, the "principal suppliers"—distribute benefits that are then accrued by smaller, less able states without reciprocation. What matters here is less the fact that—contrary to existing wisdom[22]—the historical record shows that developing countries have actually always been actively engaged in the multilateral trading system[23] and are structurally disadvantaged from participating fully in negotiations (both by institutional factors as well as their own economic complexion),[24] and more that the brandishing of the term "free-rider" conjures up notions of states not pulling their weight while at the same time celebrating the contribution of non-free-riders (who just happen to be, and have been, the principal beneficiaries of the trade regime).

Irrespective of its intent, and like all aspects of the "blame game," these accusations are unhelpful. In any social environment the leveling of blame, particularly if it is done so repeatedly, generates resentment. This, in turn, can lead to a hardening of positions, disaffection, or worse, all of which are entirely unhelpful in moving negotiations forward. Moreover, because of the uncritical way we treat accusations of foe and free-rider, we often gloss over the very real reasons why heightened moments of contestation have come about. As with the rest of the way we talk about trade, we need to look beneath the words and phrases that are commonly deployed—what Orwell likened to "*phrases* tacked together like the sections of a prefabricated henhouse"[25]—to understand the consequences of talking in the way that we do.

Infants and insults

A more worrying trend in the way we talk about trade concerns the tendency of some commentators to infantilize opponents to undermine their arguments (thus presenting them as naïve and immature), to construct developing countries as if they were at some early stage of childhood development requiring the instruction of a well-meaning parent, and to dismiss the arguments of critics in ungenerous ways—a tendency that becomes more pronounced at pressure points in negotiations. As with many other metaphorical expressions, these ways of talking are unhelpful and belie ideologically subjective positions, but are nevertheless presented as common sense. Developing countries are no more like children, or their citizens infantile, than advanced industrial countries are mature adults and appropriately qualified parents. Certainly there is a dramatic gulf in knowledge between industrial and developing countries and a pressing need for its transfer, but to belittle countries and populations in this way is at best inappropriate.

Bhagwati has used some of these techniques in advancing his case for free trade. He writes:

> The protection of infant industries against imports much too often tends to be indiscriminate and creates strong incentives for the

> infant producers to remain inefficient and to continue demanding protection which then becomes politically difficult to remove. The result is that the infant does not learn and grows up wearing protectionist diapers into premature senility.[26]

While Bhagwati is trying to use the language of infant industries in a witty fashion to develop his argument, it is an unfortunate choice of metaphors. The message is nonetheless clear. Those states and commentators that advocate the protection of infant industries are resigning developing countries to a fate of perpetual infancy (whether they physically age—as the image of a diaper-wearing senile adult invokes—or not). This is designed both to ridicule opponents and to present a subjective and contested understanding of development as a linear process. The point here is that these are not helpful ways of talking. Development is a complex process and not one that is akin to the human lifecycle; and ridiculing opponents—as Bhagwati, Friedman and others on occasion do—is not an act that helps create an arena in which genuine debate can take place. What Bhagwati and others are doing is smuggling in ideological positions via metaphorical argument without being open and honest about those positions or their essentially contested nature.

Of boats, bicycles, and other dramatic catastrophes

The metaphorical repertoire of trade politics is uniquely and peculiarly replete. Precisely because liberalization requires action and freer trade is constructed as progress forward (from more restricted trade and unenlightened times), WTO politics is laden with metaphors of motion occasionally mixed in with ideas of natural forces and physical phenomena. The idea that liberalization will be a tide that "lifts all boats" is one such instance that is both natural and rather gentile in the vision it evokes;[27] the use of "sunshine" as a metaphor for the effect transparency in the WTO's dispute settlement system creates is another.[28] The use of a train, and in particular the necessity of keeping it firmly on its rails lest it crash (with catastrophic consequences), is a more dramatic but nonetheless comparable construction.[29]

The highly political nature of trade politics, the manner in which trade governance has evolved, and the way unequals are pitched together in adversarial negotiations has ensured that trade negotiations were, from the very outset, contested affairs. The drama that has ensued during every round of trade negotiations has imbued them with a propensity to crisis, and on occasion, collapse. These moments of drama are taken seriously, particularly as they threatened to undermine the institution and the purpose for which it had been designed. They also threaten to undermine the case for further liberalization. The result is that worries about what might result if liberalization should be allowed to stall continually frames negotiations, and the case for its forward march has been made repeatedly, particularly at moments when the institution has been in crisis. What has emerged is a "crisis discourse," one that encourages a particular kind of political behavior by framing trade negotiations in a manner consistent with their conclusion by warning against what might transpire should the liberalization process be interrupted.[30]

What is interesting about this crisis discourse is that not only has it become a key part of the common sense history of global trade governance, but it has come to be expressed in one unique and tenacious metaphor: the bicycle. At its simplest, the bicycle suggests that trade liberalization, like the forward motion required to keep a bicycle moving, needs to be in a state of perpetual motion. If that motion were to cease, the process (like the bicycle) would collapse and cause injury to the global economy/the bicycle's rider. The use of this metaphor serves, at one and the same time, to simplify, clarify, and intensify the mental image constructed by the crisis discourse of what would happen if the multilateral process was allowed to stall despite the self-evident fact that the trading system is very unlike a bicycle or its movement linear in the way the metaphor would encourage us to believe. Moreover, it creates an imperative around the perpetuation of a particular kind of liberalization—one that primarily benefits core interests while at the same time offering only limited prospects to those on the periphery—which has resulted in the conclusion of successive trade bargains that have been deeply asymmetrical.[31]

It is no mistake that the bicycle metaphor emerged as serious impediments to further liberalization began to emerge in the late 1960s and early 1970s. By this point, GATT negotiations had become progressively harder to conclude because of increases in the number of contracting parties (which posed logistical as well as political problems, especially because of the growing militancy of newly independent states), the growing depth and extent of the trade agenda, mounting tensions between the then European Economic Community and the United States and growing protectionist sentiment in both, a worsening international economic environment, and mounting concern among developing countries that their interests were not being served.[32]

Attributed to C. Fred Bergsten,[33] the bicycle metaphor conveyed the message of the lengthier and more involved core story put forward by

Wilcox and others to a domestic US and international public and polity that was nearly 30 years removed from the end of World War II, nearly 40 years from the inter-war depression, and had enjoyed (at least in the United States) two decades of unrivalled prosperity. It did not require recipients of this received wisdom to understand the intricacies of what had caused the depression, but the necessity of maintaining forward motion sought to encourage support for further liberalization. In so doing, it made common sense of the notion that unless the trade bicycle continually moved forward it would topple over. As Bergsten put it, the "[s]teady movement toward trade liberalization is necessary to halt the acceleration of the trend toward increasing trade restrictions."[34]

Since they were first articulated, a consensus has emerged around the logic of the crisis discourse and the bicycle metaphor. Both have become staples of trade politics and are widely known and frequently used. Moreover, in that process wherein subjective views are assimilated as social truths, the metaphor has itself been elevated to the status of both "theory" and "fact." As James Bacchus, former chair of the WTO's appellate body, puts it, "[a]ccording to the 'bicycle theory,' the history of trade, and of trade policymaking, teaches us that a failure to move steadily forward toward freer trade condemns the world trading system to topple over."[35]

As the Doha Round negotiations have progressed and the talks have ground to a seemingly intractable halt, subtle changes in the content of the crisis discourse have occurred. These changes are neither unheard of, nor unprecedented. Rather, they are consistent with other intensifications that have occurred across the life of the trade regime. On occasion this intensification appears passive—such as WTO Director-General (DG) Roberto Azevêdo's pre-Bali ministerial conference appeal to members, echoing similar calls made by each of the three previous DGs, to bear in mind that what is "at stake is the credibility of the multilateral trading system itself."[36] It can also be much more active and aggressive, as in the use of a dramatic and high-stakes language to comment on the state of the round and the plight of the organization[37]—a mutation in the crisis discourse to which we now turn.

What is notable about the more active and aggressive turn in language is that all too often the state of the Doha Round is presented in life and death terms, with commentators competing to be the first to proclaim it "dead" (and to write *the* obituary);[38] or else they suggest that with enough energy the round's impending demise can be averted. In many cases, this life and death struggle is sharpened with the use of pointed metaphors. These metaphors are often medical, such as likening the state of the round to a "coma" or else encouraging us to imagine that it is on "life support," though other metaphors are also used. The point here is that, once deployed, arguments are developed that take these metaphors to their logical conclusion to reinforce the need to pursue a particular course of action. For example, we are encouraged to accept the round's failure and let the patient "die," drum up support for dramatic intervention to salvage the negotiations (such as "surgery," "amputation," "chemical correction"), engage in a spot of "euthanasia," or sanction a distasteful, but nonetheless necessary, "assassination."[39]

The problem with talking in such dramatic ways is that they presuppose and necessitate that quite dramatic action *is* necessary. In so doing, they hook readers into forms of argumentation that suggest that only a particular course of action consistent with the commentator's predisposition is worth pursuing. This, in turn, limits debate to those options associated with a diagnosis that sees the situation as chronic and the solution as dramatic. The issue here is that the use of such high-stakes language crowds out discussion of solutions that are *not* dramatic and which *do not* speak to the solutions proposed by the original commentator. Hence, the momentum of the "bicycle" must be maintained; the "train" must be prevented from coming off the rails; and the "patient" must be treated immediately and robustly or else put out of his or her misery.

The point here is that the entailments that accompany a metaphor, or for that matter the manner about which a subject is spoken, set the boundaries of what is understood to be politically possible. The message is clear: bridge the divides and conclude the round, or else the breakdown of the multilateral trading system and something akin to the nightmare of the 1930s will be upon us. Yet, the perceived urgency of the situation ensures that we continue to think inside the box, to carry on doing things just the way we always have *without* allowing space and time for thinking about how we might solve the ills of the multilateral trading system. As Alan Winters put it during that moment when scholars and pundits alike presumed the Uruguay Round was on the edge of a precipice,

> [for] many commentators the era of liberal and multilateral international trade is in the melting pot, if not actually doomed. To them the Uruguay Round … represents the last chance to re-assert the virtues of multilateralism which, if unsuccessful, will herald a descent into restricted and bilateral or plurilateral trading arrangements.[40]

What is important here is that the rationale for the GATT was consciously constructed for a particular purpose. That rationale brought with it a constructed history that has since become a core part of common sense wisdom about the GATT. As such, it represents only a partial, subjective, and problematic account of both the GATT and the logic upon which it is based. The language deployed, particularly relating to the dangers of not pursuing multilateral trade, is nevertheless sufficiently compelling and reasonably close to the historical reality to have become *the* story. This, in turn, has assisted in generating and maintaining a consensus around both the GATT/WTO as an institution and the kind of liberalization pursued therein. In the absence of a credible alternative, it has focused attention on fettling, but nevertheless persisting with the existing system, rather than fundamentally overhauling its core practices and attendant principles.

These metaphors and their related ways of talking do not, of course, constitute the sum of the ways commentators have chosen to express their subjective and politically instrumental view about trade. Susan Schwab, for instance, has asked us to imagine that the act of trying to conclude a multilateral trade round is one akin to "pole-vaulting."[41] Elsewhere, Bhagwati has suggested that constructing the Doha Round as a "hanging" might just be enough to focus minds and get the negotiations going again. He also accused the *Financial Times* of "cluster-bombing" the negotiations, likened proclamations of the "death" of the Doha Round to Mark Twain's premature obituary, and suggested that the outcome of the WTO's Bali ministerial conference resembled "decaf … coffee."[42] Duncan Green has encouraged us to see the WTO as sliding into a "zombie" state of irrelevance.[43]

What talking in these ways does is limit discussion. In so doing, it precludes from the realm of debate other solutions, an acceptance that periods of reflection may indeed be useful and essential components of trade rounds, and an acknowledgement that at particular times it might not be possible—politically or otherwise—to close a deal. Moreover, talking about trade in this way encourages respondents to engage with the chosen metaphor, twisting it to fit their point of view. The consequence, however, is that in so doing they become bound up in a language and a realm of political possibility from which they cannot escape. Hence, counter-claims of the need for "intensive treatment," "incisive surgery," "palliative care," and the like to save the round fail to get us beyond Doha as life and death struggle. In short, they force us to think about solving the ills of Doha in too high-pressured a fashion, crowding out time for measured contemplation of the problem, goal, and solution.

The use of terminal medical metaphors, as with those requests for us to think of trade rounds as akin to material things that need to be kept in motion, are unhelpful. They create a pressure to act with speed that is not always helpful. They are also discursive tools that belie ideological dispositions and claims about how trade ought to be organized. They encourage us to take a leap of faith, and they often encourage us to deny empirical evidence to the contrary.

Targeting recalcitrants

It is also worth noting that much of the leverage that the crisis discourse is designed to realize is often directed at developing countries. The run-up to the 2005 Hong Kong Ministerial Conference provides a good example of this, though similar examples can be found in the run-up to many of the WTO's other ministerial gatherings. Precisely because developing countries were seen to be the principal spoilers of any deal that might be struck, the crisis discourse began to be tailored towards what the consequences might be for them were the round to fail.

Former World Bank President Paul Wolfowitz, for instance, argued that:

> The stakes are too high—not just for the poor, but also for the global economy—to let the trade talks conclude without real progress. The Doha Round presents an opportunity to rewrite the rules of an unfair trading system that holds back the potential of the poorest people … [I]f Doha fails it's the world's poor … who will suffer most.[44]

Likewise, in a speech to the United Nations Conference on Trade and Development (UNCTAD), former WTO DG Pascal Lamy warned that:

> Hong Kong is not just another checkpoint in the negotiations. It is our best chance to move this Round to a successful conclusion … If we fail, we would all have lost a unique opportunity to rebalance the world trading system to the interests of developing countries.[45]

As one developing country delegate put it at the time,

> we [developing countries] feel continually on the back foot. Because we were seen to get our way in Cancún, we were being steadily forced to agree to positions [in the run-up to Hong Kong] we didn't feel comfortable with and sometimes didn't even

> understand, yet we were being warned of what might happen [to the multilateral trading system] if we didn't [agree to move forward].[46]

These sentiments were echoed by Dipak Patel, former Zambian minister of commerce, trade and industry and then chair of the Least Developed Countries (LDC) Group, when he put it that "the LDC group feels the most pressure to conform. We do not want to be blamed for another collapse or for any harm that might be done to the multilateral trading system."[47] Barbadian Minister of Foreign Affairs and Foreign Trade and Vice-Chair of the Hong Kong Ministerial Conference Antoinette Miller noted that the pressure to reach an agreement, even though the expectations had been rolled back, had been motivated as much by the necessity of maintaining forward momentum and avoiding a repeat of Cancún as it had been about the substance of the agreement itself.[48] Likewise, a senior figure in the South African delegation to the WTO stated that despite the rolling back of expectations in the run-up to the meeting, "the pressure was … incredible. Many of the developing countries felt that if a deal wasn't reached they'd be primarily to blame."[49]

The point here is that the intensification of the crisis discourse in the run-up to the Hong Kong Ministerial Conference played a role in ensuring that despite continuing tensions over the shape and direction of the negotiations, an agreement was reached. Significantly, this intensification involved key core trade public intellectuals as well as those only peripherally connected with trade. This, in turn, helped shape the way delegations approached the negotiations and influenced the reframing of the negotiations in such a manner that preventing their potential collapse was perceived to be the overriding objective.

This strategy remains a key part of the ratcheting-up of the discourse that occurs in the run-up to ministerial conferences. As USTR Michael Froman put it in his keynote address to the October 2013 WTO Public Forum, "if Bali shows that the WTO is not a viable forum for negotiations, bilateral and plurilaterals will likely be the only avenue for trade negotiations … [and] small countries and poor countries would feel the loss the most."[50]

The WTO the unfortunate

One final construction warrants our attention in the twists and turns of contemporary trade discourse: the presentation of the WTO as an unfortunate institution. What is important about this construction is that it behooves us to accept that the organization is far from perfect, that it was the product of compromise, and in some ways we should pity it and get on with what passes for liberalization under its auspices nonetheless. Here we are asked to accept that the organization was born out of opportunism and happenstance, it was imbued with certain "birth defects"[51] that have rendered it slightly less than fit for purpose, and it is rather unfortunately caught in the crosshairs of trade politics.

Yet, closer examination of the historical record suggests that rather than a slightly hapless body, we find an institution reasonably well suited to the task at hand, whose performance has actually been quite strong in terms of the objectives it was set up to achieve and whose development has been consistently focused on the task ahead.[52] Moreover, far from being the slightly unfortunate institution caught in the crossfire of great power trade politics, the WTO is a more instrumental body which has been more effective and dynamic than is commonly understood, and whose basic form and function has changed little since its was created. Yet, we continue to paint a picture of an organization that struggles to function, thereby obscuring the asymmetric gains that this mechanism of liberalizing trade has produced. There is, in short, little to pity.

Conclusion

We should bear in mind that even the best of the earliest accounts of the genesis of multilateral trade offers a partisan narrative. This is perhaps inevitable as the telling of history is inherently subjective.[53] It is nevertheless worth noting that like most histories, the lenses that are deployed tend to be tinted in ways that reflect dominant ideas and interests. The standard history of the GATT is no different. Most accounts focus on the GATT as seen from the viewpoint of Washington, London, and Brussels. Few explore the role developing countries have played, leaving aside much of the industry and energy many exerted in the GATT's negotiation and evolution. Instead, as we have seen, developing countries tend to be portrayed as either determinedly negotiating relief from various commitments, focused on the pursuit of industrialization through import substitution and/or free-riding on the commitments made by their industrial counterparts, or else as "quiet bystanders" lacking the expertise or political representation to participate fully, or attempting to redress biases in the institution's design. Either way, the presentation of their participation in this way is used to encourage developing countries to reciprocate for (often inappropriate) concessions received and to become "paid-up" members of the trading system.

It is also worth reiterating that the received history of the multilateral trading system—and the metaphors and ways of talking that have come to perpetuate its common sense logic—has come to dominate, in part, because alternative ideas either do not exist or else they have been discredited, and in part because of the path-dependent way of thinking that this history and its underlying set of assumptions encourage. The consensus that has emerged around the current global economic model has, in turn, solidified further the logic presented by the narrative of the GATT and WTO and has, inevitably, focused attention on the pursuit of minor adjustments for the sake of efficacy rather than fundamental reform. While it may well be widely acknowledged that the WTO is not working well—particularly for its least developed members—the dominance of this model continues to underpin perceptions of the WTO as the only—or perhaps better still, least ineffective—game in town.

Nonetheless, it is important to remind ourselves that the stories we commonly encounter about the GATT/WTO are not neutral or objective; rather, they are subjective accounts that encase a core political purpose—the advancement of a set of national trade interests—in a common sense story about the value of free trade. One of the many problems, of course, is that these accounts tend to be incongruous with one another. The GATT was established as a mercantilist instrument in which some areas of commercial activity were to be liberalized while restrictions were to remain in others. This continues to be the case with the WTO. Equally, the necessity of keeping liberalization in perpetual motion is at odds with the record of trade politics wherein some areas have been opened up, others have remained protected, while still others have seen more protection emerge as other barriers to trade (particularly non-tariff barriers) have been imposed. All of this has occurred in the absence of a slide into war. This, of course, does not mean that we should discard these stories as wholly meaningless. It means that we should acknowledge them for what they are: particularist views of how the world ought to be governed.

The task ahead is thus to reconstruct an alternative trade narrative which better captures the history of the multilateral trading system, which uses the past as a motivation for change, which has at its core a concern for the interests of all, and which enables broader debate to occur in a less ideologically constrained fashion. Yet, it is precisely because the narratives that inform the multilateral trading system have proven so malleable, and accommodated challenges and accounted for changes through time, that they have continued to exude an appearance of relevance.

Notes

1 This chapter is a revised version of cChapter 3 of Rorden Wilkinson, *What's Wrong with the WTO and How to Fix It* (Cambridge: Polity Press, 2014).
2 George Orwell [1946], "Politics and the English Language," reprinted in *Inside the Whale and Other Essays* (London: Penguin 1962).
3 George Orwell, "In Front of Your Nose," *Tribune*, 22 March 1946. This section draws on Rorden Wilkinson, "Language, Power and Multilateral Trade Negotiations," *Review of International Political Economy* 16, no. 4 (2009): 597–619.
4 Antonio Gramsci, *Selections from the Prison Notebooks*, ed. and trans. by Quintin Hoare and Geoffrey Nowell Smith (London: Lawrence and Wishart, 1998), 198–9.
5 Norman Fairclough, *Language and Power* (Harlow: Pearson, 2001), 64.
6 Fairclough, *Language and Power*, 64.
7 See Alain de Botton, *The Consolations of Philosophy* (London: Penguin, 2000), 14–42.
8 Fairclough, *Language and Power*, 2; Gramsci, *Selections from the Prison Notebooks*, 348–350.
9 George Lakoff and Mark Johnson, "The Metaphorical Structure of the Human Conceptual System," *Cognitive Science* 4, no. 2 (1980): 195–208.
10 Susan Sontag, *Illness as Metaphor and AIDS and its Metaphors* (London: Penguin Books, 2002).
11 Glenn D. Hook, "The Nuclearization of Language: Nuclear Allergy as Political Metaphor," *Journal of Peace Research* 21, no. 3 (1984): 262.
12 See Carol Cohn, "Sex and Death in the Rational World of Defense Intellectuals," *Signs* 12, no. 4 (1987): 687–718.
13 See David H. Bearce and Eric O'N. Fisher, "Economic Geography, Trade, and War," *Journal of Conflict Resolution* 46, no. 3 (2002): 365–393.
14 J. Russell Smith, "Trade and a League of Nations or Economic Internationalism," *Annals of the American Academy of Political and Social Science* 83 (1919): 287.
15 Clair Wilcox, *A Charter for World Trade* (New York: Macmillan, 1949), 3–10, 12–13.
16 Jacob Viner, "Conflicts of Principle in Drafting a Trade Charter," *Foreign Affairs* 25, no. 4 (1947): 612–628; William Adams Brown Jr., *The United States and the Restoration of World Trade* (Washington, DC: Brookings Institution, 1950); William Diebold Jr., "The End of the ITO," *Essays in International Finance* 16 (International Finance Section, Department of Economics, Princeton University, 1952); John Maynard Keynes, "The Balance of Payments of the United States," *Economic Journal* 56, no. 222 (1946): 172–187.
17 See Chapter 2 of this volume.
18 For an extended discussion see Shaun Breslin, "China and the Global Order: Signalling Threat of Friendship?" *International Affairs* 89, no. 3 (2013): 615–634.
19 See Daniel Drezner, "The Contradictions of Post-Crisis Global Economic Governance," in *Handbook of Global Economic Governance*, ed. Manuela Moschella and Catherine Weaver (London: Routledge, 2014), 345–360. For an alternative view see James Scott and Rorden Wilkinson, "China Threat? Evidence from the WTO," *Journal of World Trade* 47, no. 4 (2013): 775–7.
20 Joseph Stiglitz and Andrew Charlton, *The Right to Trade: Rethinking the Aid for Trade Agenda* (London: Commonwealth Secretariat, 2013), 3.

21 See, for instance, Rodney D. Ludema and Anna Maria Mayda, "Do Countries Free Ride on MFN?" *Journal of International Economics* 77, no. 2 (2009): 137–150.
22 Javed Maswood and Larry Crump, "Introduction," in *Developing Countries and Global Trade Negotiations*, ed. Larry Crump and Syed Javed Maswood (London: Routledge, 2007), 1.
23 Rorden Wilkinson and James Scott, "Developing Country Participation in the GATT: A Reassessment," *World Trade Review* 7, no. 3 (2008): 473–510.
24 See Emily Jones, *Negotiating Against the Odds: A Guide for Trade Negotiators from Developing Countries* (London: Commonwealth Secretariat/Palgrave Macmillan, 2013); Fatoumata Jawara and Aileen Kwa, *Behind the Scenes at the WTO: The Real World of International Trade Negotiations* (London: Zed Books, 2003).
25 Orwell, "Politics and the English Language," 145.
26 Jagdish Bhagwati, "Reshaping the WTO," *Far Eastern Economic Review* 168, no. 2 (2005): 26–7.
27 James R. Hines Jr., Hilary W. Hoynes and Alan B. Krueger, *Another Look at Whether a Rising Tide Lifts All Boats*, Working Paper No. 8412 (Cambridge, Mass.: National Bureau of Economic Research, 2001), 1–68; Andrew Berg and Anne Krueger, "Lifting all Boats: A Critical Survey of Recent Studies in Trade Liberalization," in *Financial Globalization: A Compilation of Articles from Finance & Development*, ed. Jeremy Clift and Elisa Diehl (Washington, DC: IMF, 2007).
28 Robert Wolfe, "Does Sunshine Make a Difference: How Transparency Brings the Trading System to Life," in *Handbook of Global Economic Governance*, ed. Manuela Moschella and Catherine Weaver (London: Routledge, 2014), 40–56.
29 Daniel Drache, *Trade, Development and the Doha Round: A Sure Bet or a Train Wreck?* Working Paper No. 5 (Waterloo, Canada: Centre for International Governance Innovation, 2006); Ken Haydon, *After the WTO Hong Kong Ministerial Meeting: What is at Stake?* Trade Policy Working Paper No. 27 (Paris: OECD, 2006).
30 Wilkinson, "Language, Power and Multilateral Trade Negotiations."
31 Rorden Wilkinson, *The WTO: Crisis and the Governance of Global Trade* (London: Routledge, 2006).
32 Tigani E. Ibrahim, "Developing Countries and the Tokyo Round," *Journal of World Trade Law* 12, no. 1 (1978): 1–26.
33 Bergsten did not actually use the term "bicycle" at first, though Jagdish Bhagwati credits him with putting forward the idea. See Jagdish Bhagwati, *Protectionism* (Cambridge, Mass.: MIT Press, 1988), 41.
34 C. Fred Bergsten, "Trade Liberalization in Agricultural Products," *American Journal of Agricultural Economics* 55, no. 2 (1973): 280.
35 James Bacchus, "The Bicycle Club: Affirming the American Interest in the Future of the WTO," *Journal of World Trade* 37, no. 3 (2003): 429.
36 WTO, "Azevêdo Sends Letter Asking Ministers for 'Personal, Active Engagement' Ahead of Bali," *WTO News Item*, 30 September 2013, www.wto.org/english/news_e/news13_e/tnc_infstat_30sep13_e.htm.
37 See, for example, Jagdish Bhagwati's comments in the run-up to the WTO's December 2013 Bali Ministerial Conference: CUTS, "The Multilateral Trading System is Dead: Professor Jagdish Bhagwati," press release, 27

September 2013, www.cuts-international.org/30thAnniversaryLectures/Press_release-Multilateral_Trading_System_is_Dead-Bhagwati.html.

38 D. Kleimann and J. Guinan, "The Doha Round: An Obituary," Global Governance Programme Policy Brief No. 2011/1 (Fiesole, Italy: Robert Schuman Centre for Advanced Studies, European University Institute, 2011), www.eui.eu/Projects/GGP/Documents/Publications/PolicyBriefs/PolicyBrief20111final.pdf.

39 Stuart Harbinson, "Calls to Pull the Doha Plug Show Naivety Not Realism," *Financial Times*, 5 May 2011.

40 L. Alan Winters, "The Road to Uruguay," *The Economic Journal* 100, no. 403 (1990): 1288.

41 Susan Schwab, "After Doha," *Foreign Affairs* 90, no. 3 (2011): 104.

42 Jagdish Bhagwati, "The Doha Round's Premature Obituary," *Project Syndicate*, 28 April 2013, www.project-syndicate.org/commentary/bhagwati12/English; CUTS, "The Multilateral Trading System is Dead."

43 Duncan Green, "The Doha Round has Run its Course but New Trade Realities Demand Solutions" (2011), www.guardian.co.uk/global-development/poverty-matters/2011/may/04/doha-trade-realities-demand-solutions. For a commentary on the uses and abuses of zombie metaphors, see Erin Hannah and Rorden Wilkinson, "Zombies and IR: A Critical Reading," *Politics early view* (2015).

44 Paul Wolfowitz, *Message from the World Bank President, Paul Wolfowitz, on the Doha Development Round*, 6 December 2005, http://tinyurl.com/onk3zq4.

45 Pascal Lamy, *Speech to UNCTAD*, Palais des Nations, Geneva, 6 October 2005, www.wto.org/english/news_e/sppl_e/sppl05_e.htm.

46 Interview with a member of the Nigerian delegation (anonymous), Hong Kong, 13 December 2005.

47 Comments during press briefing at the WTO Hong Kong Ministerial Conference, 15 December 2005.

48 Conversation with the author during the Joint Initiative for Policy Dialogue/Brooks World Poverty Institute task force on trade meeting, University of Manchester, UK, 2–3 February 2006.

49 Conversation (anonymous) with the author during the Joint Initiative for Policy Dialogue/Brooks World Poverty Institute task force on trade meeting, University of Manchester, 2–3 February 2006. Similar views were also expressed in interviews with delegates from Nigeria, Togo, Malawi, Indonesia, Costa Rica, India, Pakistan, Uruguay and Malaysia during the Hong Kong Ministerial Conference, 13–18 December 2005, and in follow-up telephone interviews in January/February 2006.

50 WTO, "USTR Froman Warns Poor Countries would be the Biggest Losers if Bali Fails," *WTO News Items*, 1 October 2013, www.wto.org/english/news_e/news13_e/pfor_01oct13_e.htm.

51 John H. Jackson, *The Jurisprudence of GATT and WTO: Insights on Treaty Law and Economic Relations* (Cambridge: Cambridge University Press, 2000), 455.

52 See Rorden Wilkinson, "Measuring the WTO's Performance: An Alternative Account," *Global Policy* 2, no. 1 (2011): 43–52; also Faizel Ismail, "Is the Doha Round Dead? What is the Way Forward?" *World Economics* 13, no. 3 (2012): 143–169.

53 E.H. Carr, *What is History?* (Basingstoke: Palgrave, 2001), 2.

2 The specter of Smoot-Hawley and the global trading system

Sustaining free trade through the crisis[1]

Gabriel Siles-Brügge

- **Deconstructing trade discourse: the bicycle metaphor and the Smoot-Hawley myth**
- **The Smoot-Hawley myth in action (2008–14)**
- **Challenging Smoot-Hawley: explaining (non-)conformity**
- **Conclusion**

The global financial crisis of 2008 and the ensuing economic recession had a hugely negative effect on world trade volumes.[2] What is more significant from a political economy perspective is that the crisis slump in output was not accompanied by a significant increase in trade barriers, despite much talk of the rise of "creeping" "behind-the-border" protectionism.[3] Tariff levels have remained fairly stable, while the impact of a seemingly increasing number of non-tariff barriers (NTBs) such as quotas, import licensing, or subsidies has also been limited.[4] Such developments surprised many of those who study trade policy from the perspective of standard public choice models, where given collective action problems protectionists are often seen to be more likely to mobilize and shape policy than the "winners" from liberalization.[5] Echoing the views of others,[6] one World Bank research paper noted that "[s]trikingly, despite the trade collapse, the 2008 crisis and its recessionary aftermath did not fuel protectionism."[7]

One possible explanation for this state of affairs is offered by what could be termed a "rational institutionalist" literature in the field of International Political Economy (IPE). The argument is that international trading institutions—especially the World Trade Organization (WTO) and its system of judicialized dispute-settlement—have legally "locked-in" trade liberalization, incentivizing compliance with global trading rules.[8] This explanation has also been commonly invoked in recent years to justify the conclusion of the current Doha Round of multilateral trade talks, as this would allow for additional policy binding to supposedly guard against the threat of protectionism.[9] Such explanations, however, overlook the fact that most countries have remained open in areas where they have not bound their liberalization. In other words, they have either continued applying lower tariffs than they are legally obliged to and/or not made significant use of NTBs that are not subject to WTO disciplines.[10]

For their part, even when endogenous trade policy models have accorded a greater role to pro-liberalization interest groups, this only partially accounts for the resilience of free trade. The argument here is that where trade liberalization is undertaken on the basis of reciprocity, as in the WTO,[11] the pressure exerted by those interested in liberalization can offset the influence of protectionists. Applied to the recent crisis, the point is that given increasingly interconnected global supply chains, the domestic demand for protection is outweighed by the interests of importers and exporters in avoiding retaliatory measures.[12] While there is considerable merit to such an argument in terms of explaining why demand for protection was not as significant as may have been expected (as suggested by the relatively low incidence of trade defense measures),[13] it does not tell the full story. The maintenance of free trade was more widespread than the variable of global market integration might have implied, with the poorest regions of the globe accounting for a very small proportion of the (otherwise also few) barriers that have been implemented.[14] Moreover, Argentina—a country strongly dependent on its export earnings and thus sensitive to retaliation from its trading partners—has bucked the general trend and introduced very visible and wide-ranging import restrictions since the start of the crisis.

As a result, I argue that we need to complement such explanations with a perspective that focuses on the role of ideas in mediating elite responses to the crisis. More specifically, I develop a constructivist argument, which emphasizes how particular ideas about the global trading system have become rooted in policymaking discourse, with those bucking the trend choosing to reject the dominant view. Echoing the findings of other contributors to this volume, I argue that trade experts (more specifically, trade policymakers and a group of leading economists) have contributed to constructing an ideational imperative for continued openness (and for concluding the Doha Round) by drawing on a questionable reading of economic history (what I refer to as the Smoot-Hawley myth). By continually stressing protectionism's role as one of the causes of the Great Depression, non-liberal responses to the recent crisis have been all but ruled out by all except those willing to question the received wisdom. My aim in developing this argument is twofold. For one, I challenge the dominant discourse about the WTO found in scholarly circles, which uncritically accepts the institution's role in providing the supposed "public good" of free trade. Second, I show how ideas, long neglected in the study of trade decision making, are crucial determinants of policy outcomes. In particular, I suggest that we need to challenge the power inherent in a *contestable* reading of economic history deployed by experts. This serves to limit policy debates on international trade and entrench a limited range of responses, with my research pointing to the additional policy space that Argentina crafted for itself by explicitly rejecting the dominant discourse.

The remainder of this chapter is structured as follows. In the next section, I outline a constructivist account of trade policy, which emphasizes the importance of discourses of external constraint, in particular the so-called Smoot-Hawley myth. In the third section, I trace how this idea—that the Great Depression was in large part caused and/or exacerbated by protectionism in the 1930s—has been invoked since the collapse of Lehman Brothers in September 2008 by experts and other elite actors within the international trading system. Combined with a consistent exaggeration of the extent of protectionism in public discourse, this has significantly contributed to rendering a protectionist response to the crisis unthinkable while strengthening the discursive armory of those pushing for a conclusion to the Doha Round (especially in the aftermath of the alleged "success" of the Bali Ministerial). In the fourth section I then underscore the importance of this myth by considering the case of Argentina, which chose to implement meaningful barriers to trade following the start of the crisis while articulating an alternative vision of trade-led development. I conclude in the final section, offering some thoughts on the importance of challenging the Smoot-Hawley myth.

Deconstructing trade discourse: the bicycle metaphor and the Smoot-Hawley myth

My aim in this section is to map out a constructivist approach to explaining the resilience of free trade during the crisis, pointing to the important role of agents in constructing social reality. Drawing on Colin Hay,[15] my ontological position is that social and political reality is *constructed* by agents through ideas rather than being *fixed* by particular material constraints, as in rationalist accounts. This is not to say that material factors do not exist or matter, but rather, in a social context, what is decisive is *how* they are interpreted by relevant actors.

Thus, although there may be material constraints to action, what is ultimately the determining factor is how an actor responds to these. This is what, according to Emanuel Adler, could be called the "middle ground" between rationalism—where ideas are best adjunct to material forces—and "interpretivist" approaches (such as post-structuralism or the Frankfurt School)—where it is only ideas that matter.[16] Making the case for such a constructivism, Adler argues that "collective understandings, such as norms, endow physical objects with purpose and therefore help constitute reality."[17] This shows how constructivism can complement the insights of endogenous trade theory, with ideas mediating and defusing the way policy elites respond to domestic (interest group) pressure.

This suggests that it may be fruitful to consider a literature that has concerned itself with the discursive construction of globalization as an economic constraint. This takes as its point of departure the debate between advocates of the "hyperglobalization thesis" and its skeptics. Rather than accepting the parameters of this rationalist argument—that is to say, entering into a debate over whether globalization is an empirically verifiable *material* process that restricts the choices facing political actors—such writers adopt the constructivist view that it is the ideas that agents hold (and invoke) about "globalization" that are key.[18] The perceived material rationality of the hyperglobalization thesis becomes meaningful in shaping outcomes only because they treat it as though it were a *real*, material constraint rather than just a (contestable) economic framework.[19] The power of such ideas thus resides in that they present a (politically) contingent phenomenon as immutable (economic) fact, often being deployed by policy elites to justify unpalatable socioeconomic reforms. In this vein, the literature also underscores the often "coercive" nature of ideas that some have claimed has often been absent from political analysis. The argument is that regardless of whether a particular set of ideas has been internalized by one's political opponents, these "can prove critical to success in political contests" by "leav[ing] their opponents without access to the rhetorical materials needed to craft a socially sustainable rebuttal."[20]

Whereas much work on discourses of economic constraint has focused on the invocation of *current* processes allegedly constraining policy choices—e.g. globalization and the necessity to meet competitiveness objectives[21]—what is interesting in the case of trade policy is that similar discourses have often had an *historical* dimension. In other words, rather than just stressing the inevitability of contemporaneous process, such discourses have drawn on a contestable historical interpretation to draw an analogy to the present. One such discourse is highlighted by Susan Strange, who seeks to expose it as a "myth."[22] This is the idea, commonly articulated by liberal economists and scholars of international political economy (IPE), that the global Great Depression of the 1930s was, if not caused by trade protection, certainly exacerbated by it, as countries shortsightedly pursued "beggar-thy-neighbor" policies. These, so the conventional argument goes, led to a significant decline in world trade in manufactures with dire consequences for the global economy. It could be termed the "Smoot-Hawley myth," in "honor" of the two US legislators who attached their names to the infamous protectionist bill passed by the Congress in 1930, and which is often depicted as the catalyst for subsequent protectionism. Strange challenges this myth by invoking the evidence collected by several economic historians, arguing that the collapse of world trade and the rise of protectionism was a *symptom*, rather than a *cause*, of worldwide economic collapse. To this effect she cites not only the perhaps more heterodox development economist Arthur Lewis, but also one of the doyens of the realist school of IPE, Charles Kindleberger, both of whom argued that tariffs had a "minimal" impact on "the volume of world trade or to its direction."[23]

Another influential "myth" tackled by Strange is what she refers to as the "bicycle theory"—the idea that "if you do not keep up the momentum of trade liberalization [of multilateral trade rounds], disaster will follow."[24] This particular discourse has also been critiqued by Rorden Wilkinson in Chapter 1, although he uses the term "metaphor" to convey the manner in which such ideas are used to inculcate a discursive "common sense." Wilkinson's aim, not unlike Strange's, is to expose this metaphor as false. More importantly, however, he also seeks to explore (in a similar vein to this chapter) "the way in which the discourse has been deployed as a means of reframing trade negotiations in such a way that the likelihood of their continuation and ultimate conclusion increases."[25] These ideas are thus powerful instruments used by trade policymaking elites—in particular those with close ties to the United States—in order to further their interest in concluding the Doha Round of multilateral trade talks.

To a large extent both discourses are, of course, entwined. The argument expounded in the conventional economics/IPE literature on the value of concluding the Doha Round in terms of its ability to *bind* current levels of trade openness in the context of an economic recession clearly resonates on both counts.[26] Moreover, the Smoot-Hawley myth also had its origins in US policymaking circles; as prominent IPE trade scholar Judith Goldstein notes of this myth, which she herself accepts as fact, in the aftermath of the Great Depression in US trade policymaking circles, "[t]he failure of the Smoot-Hawley tariff of 1929–30 to deal with economic decline set up a policymaking crisis. The delegitimization of protectionism forced the political community to search for an alternative theoretical approach to explain past errors and provide guidelines for future behavior."[27] In this chapter, however, I choose not only to differentiate between both but also to focus primarily on the Smoot-Hawley myth. The fact that protectionism has not been brought about despite the advent of the crisis *and* despite the stagnation of the Doha Round—bicycle metaphor *notwithstanding*—suggest why this latter discourse may have become more prevalent in recent years.[28] That being said, and as we shall see later, the alleged "success" of the Bali Ministerial has shown how both still remain deeply entwined.

Whereas there is insufficient space here to completely deconstruct the Smoot-Hawley myth, there are clear grounds to challenge the accuracy of its historical interpretation. While some economists have sought to argue that the macroeconomic effect of tariffs during the Great Depression was significant (leading, among other things, to escalating tariff wars),[29] the consensus among economic historians has been to challenge this interpretation, despite its prevalence in public and expert discourse on global trade. As perhaps one of the foremost exponents of this view, Douglas Irwin has calculated that Smoot-Hawley only increased tariffs by an average of around 20 percent. His conclusion is that while deflationary price shocks may have been significant, "Smoot-Hawley itself appears to have been a very small direct shock to trade and therefore, it is likely, to the economy at large."[30] Moreover, it only "played a modest role in the spread of protectionism and the collapse of world trade in the early 1930s,"[31] while the incidence of other measures such as quotas and exchange controls during this period was driven by instability in the financial system rather than protectionist pressures.[32] Similar conclusions are mirrored in a number of other econometric studies.[33] Using the term *myth* thus serves to highlight the power that this *contestable* idea, wielded by trade policy experts, ultimately holds in the international trading system.

The Smoot-Hawley myth in action (2008–14)

The Smooth-Hawley myth has played a key role in legitimating free trade policies following the financial crisis, with near universal acceptance among leading world economic decision makers in the G20 leading economies (with the notable exception of Argentina, see below) and in the WTO. This can be seen especially following the collapse of the

Lehman Brothers investment bank—widely understood to be the point at which the brewing subprime mortgage crisis in the United States escalated to become a worldwide financial meltdown.[34] Among the G20, metaphorical alarm bells were rung as early as November 2008 (only two months after Lehman) when the leaders of the world's leading economies met for their first summit in Washington, DC. Among the issues on the agenda was the subject of "committing to an open global economy." The final summit communiqué was very explicit in this regard, with G20 members,

> underscor[ing] the critical importance of rejecting protectionism and not turning inward in times of financial uncertainty. In this regard, within the next 12 months, we will refrain from raising new barriers to investment or to trade in goods and services, imposing new export restrictions, or implementing World Trade Organization (WTO) inconsistent measures to stimulate exports.[35]

This statement is quite significant for two reasons. First of all, rejecting protectionism was argued to be of "critical importance … in times of financial uncertainty," clearly echoing the experience of the Great Depression of the 1930s, which itself had roots in the financial turmoil experienced at the time. The Smoot-Hawley discourse, moreover, has become a common feature of G20 summit declarations.[36] There has been at least an implicit reference to protectionism in the context of the Depression in most of the leaders' communiqués, with a clear correlation (as implied by the Smoot-Hawley myth and its interpretation of economic history) being drawn between trade protection and economic stagnation or collapse. Some of the references have been quite explicit. At the London summit, leaders agreed that they would "not repeat the historic mistakes of protectionism."[37]

Second, the excerpt from the Washington summit communiqué cited above contained a formal commitment from policymakers—from practically the beginning of the worldwide economic recession we should not forget—not to implement new trade barriers. This "standstill pledge" would be extended until the end of 2010 at the London G20 summit in April 2009. It was then reaffirmed at Pittsburgh (September 2009) and subsequently extended until the end of 2013 at Toronto (June 2010), with this extension of the pledge being reaffirmed at Seoul (November 2010) and Cannes (November 2011), and again extended at Los Cabos (June 2012) until 2014, and at St Petersburg (September 2013) until 2016. Moreover, at London the standstill pledge was expanded to include a commitment to "rollback," which

G20 members undertook to "rectify promptly any such measures" that they imposed.[38]

This would appear, at first sight, to substantiate an institutionalist argument about the resilience of free trade. Not only were these a form of international cooperation, but they also entailed *quasi-legal* pre-commitments to liberal trade policies that were to be monitored by the WTO, Organisation for Economic Co-operation and Development (OECD) and United Nations Conference on Trade and Development (UNCTAD) (as agreed at the London G20 summit). However, although Terry Collins-Williams and Robert Wolfe credit this "[e]nhanced monitoring and surveillance of emergency measures [as] … central to the international effort to mitigate the effects of the financial crisis,"[39] their own paper reports that the WTO's overall monitoring record is patchy at best. This is, in large part, due to the reliance on self-reporting, with only those bodies within the WTO having clearly defined reporting arrangements yielding promising outcomes.[40] This problem also besets the specific reporting arrangements for the G20 pledge, as they are governed by nothing more than an undertaking to "notify promptly the WTO of any such measures."[41] Indeed, Collins-Williams and Wolfe note that these reports "are hampered by the failure of governments to notify more."[42] In this chapter I therefore suggest that what matters is not so much the quasi-legal pledge itself and its role in shaping the rational expectations of actors, but rather the discursive context of which it is symptomatic, where free trade is seen as the only possible response to the crisis.

The G20 summits and 2011 WTO ministerial conference have been perhaps the most high-profile instance of the prevalence of this discourse among trade policymaking circles. However, it is also commonplace in the statements of key WTO figures, such as its previous director-general (DG), Pascal Lamy. Following the collapse of Lehman Brothers in September 2008, Lamy was to make a series of four speeches in quick succession (24 September, 27 October, 29 October and 3 November), in which he explicitly invoked the "Smoot-Hawley" myth.[43] Thus, on 24 September Lamy, addressing the WTO Public Forum, was to stress that "one of the important lessons of the Great Depression, which we must not forget, is that 'protectionism' and economic isolationism do not work."[44] On 27 October, the reference to the Smoot-Hawley myth was even more explicit in a speech Lamy was to give at Stanford University:

> The notorious Smoot-Hawley Act sharply raised already high US tariffs, triggered retaliatory measures by trading partners and led

> to a two-thirds contraction in the value of global trade. This trade contraction deepened the Great Depression which pushed the US jobless rate to 25 percent. It also shaped the thinking of the visionaries who created the post-World War II system of multilateralism. Never again would the world lurch toward blinkered beggar-thy-neighbor trade policies that did so much to destabilize the world in the 1930s.[45]

The same can be said of a speech he subsequently gave on 29 October, in which Lamy stressed how "Smoot-Hawley touched off a domino effect of retaliation and counter-retaliation among trading partners which provoked a severe contraction of international trade, depressed growth and rising unemployment around the industrial world."[46] More generally, the Great Depression—and by extension the Smoot-Hawley myth—has become a consistent feature of the discourse of the DG since a peak in 2008 (there was a total of eight references that year to the "Depression" in his public speeches, all occurring after the collapse of Lehman Brothers in September), after not featuring whatsoever in his pronouncements in either 2006 or 2007.[47] Highlighting the continued prevalence of such ideas, Roberto Azevêdo (the WTO's DG since September 2013) has also drawn explicitly on the Smoot-Hawley myth in more recent public interventions.[48]

Exaggerating the threat of protectionism and the need to conclude Doha

One aspect of the Smoot-Hawley crisis discourse has been the fact that the extent of (and by extension, the threat posed by) global protectionism has been consistently exaggerated by a group of influential economists. Foremost among these have been Richard Baldwin and Simon Evenett (both of the Centre for Economic Policy Research—CEPR—and then also, respectively, of the Graduate Institute, Geneva and of the University of St Gallen), who in December 2008 edited a book on *What World Leaders Must Do to Halt the Spread of Protectionism*. This included contributions from the likes of Jagdish Bhagwati, Arvind Panagariya, Gary Hufbauer, and Jeffrey Schott—all well-known advocates of the multilateral trading system and, more broadly, of free trade. The following excerpt from Baldwin's contribution is particularly significant, as it highlights not only the centrality of the Smoot-Hawley myth to these economists' discourse, but also the explicit purpose of their intervention—to restate the logical *necessity* of continued trade openness (an abridged version of this passage was also replicated on the back cover as a form of synopsis):

> The futility of protectionism in a global recession is not a new lesson—every world leader knows the morality tale of protectionism in the Great Depression. But leaders find themselves in ageless "two brain" situation. Their intuitive "right brain" hears the cries of workers losing jobs and firm-owners losing money; protectionism feels like a natural reaction. Their logical "left brain," however, knows that protectionism in a global slowdown is a self-defeating tactic. The challenge facing world leaders is to find mechanisms that help them mutually commit to doing the right thing.[49]

Baldwin and Evenett subsequently launched the "Global Trade Alert" (GTA) website in June 2009.[50] Its "mission" is to "provide information in real time on state measures taken during the current global economic downturn that are likely to discriminate against foreign countries."[51] GTA also publishes analysis of protectionist trends as so-called "GTA Reports." These are ultimately a "naming and shaming" exercise aimed at holding the G20 to their standstill (and future rollback) pledges, supplementing existing monitoring initiatives by the WTO, OECD, and UNCTAD by rendering "murky protectionism" transparent. However, despite the fact that the GTA data seem to suggest that the number of trade restrictions imposed each quarter has been declining since an early 2009 peak,[52] the GTA reports have consistently stressed the failure of G20 countries to live up to their promises.[53] In sum, it is clear that both the extent and the threat of protectionism have been exaggerated by leading academics (an opinion shared by a number of other economists),[54] with the Smoot-Hawley myth underpinning the crisis discourse of the GTA and of other leading economists.

To highlight the impact of such pronouncements among policy-makers, one need only consider how the WTO, OECD, and UNCTAD G20 monitoring reports (carried out since the London summit to hold G20 countries to their "standstill" and "rollback" commitments) have painted a similarly grim picture. Some of the first such reports, from March 2010 and May 2011, called for vigilance in safeguarding an open trading system.[55] Since then, however, several reports have struck a more alarmist tone. In May 2012 it was claimed that "the past seven months have not witnessed any slowdown in the imposition of new trade restrictions,"[56] while the June 2013 report stressed that "[s]ome G20 economies have continued to implement trade restrictive measures."[57] Moreover, both reports concurred that the "accumulation" of trade barriers was of "concern,"[58] even as the June 2012 report conceded in a footnote that "[t]his may well be an underestimation of the real rate of elimination, as very few G20 delegations provided information on the termination of old measures."[59] Unsurprisingly, the then WTO DG Pascal Lamy did not pick up on the degree of uncertainty in the 2012 report's data in a speech (on 7 June 2012) ahead of the Los Cabos G20 summit. Instead, he was to underscore how "[f]or the first time since the beginning of the crisis in 2008, [the monitoring] report is alarming."[60]

By exaggerating the threat of protectionism and invoking the ghost of Smoot-Hawley, such policymakers have also sought to underscore the necessity of concluding the Doha Round. This has dovetailed with a particular scholarly narrative that has stressed the value of the Doha Round as a means of binding tariff levels and otherwise restricting the scope for protectionism.[61] Thus, while so far I have sought to treat them as distinct discourses for analytical purposes, it makes sense at this juncture to acknowledge that there is an important degree of overlap between the functions (and content) of the Smoot-Hawley myth and the bicycle metaphor; stressing the need to avoid the "past mistakes" of the Great Depression has reinforced the argument that the multilateral "juggernaut" has to proceed apace.

This is particularly relevant in the light of the Bali Ministerial of December 2013, which resulted in the first significant multilateral agreement since the WTO's inception, albeit only on a "fraction of the outstanding issues in the Doha Round" (such as trade facilitation, a few agricultural issues and specific developmental provisions), while "skirt[ing] the most difficult ones."[62] Both discourses were not only invoked in the run-up to the summit, but have also formed part of the discursive armory of those pushing (with renewed urgency) for a conclusion of the Doha Round on the back of the Bali Package. Thus, a few months before Bali, the June 2013 G20 "trade and investment" monitoring report by the WTO and others was to underscore how "[t]o overcome protectionist threats and to prevent a self-destructive lapse into economic nationalism, G20 economies need to refocus their attention on reinforcing the multilateral trading system," emphasizing the importance of working towards "a successful outcome" in Bali.[63] In a similar vein, the following monitoring report, issued only a few weeks after the conclusion of the ministerial, was to note both the need "to move forward on the positive momentum generated by the adoption of the Bali package," and that "[t]he multilateral trading system remains the best defense against protectionism."[64]

Roberto Azevêdo's subsequent calls to complete the Doha Round by the end of 2014 were even more explicit in their invocation of both the

Smoot-Hawley and bicycle discourses. In a March 2014 speech, he referred not only to the "mistake" of the Smoot-Hawley Tariff Act, but also the multilateral trading system's role in constraining protectionism. Bali, meanwhile, "has created an opportunity which we now have to seize."[65] Similar themes emerged from an interview with *The Guardian* newspaper, where the WTO's DG spoke of the consequences of not reaching a deal in the Doha Round in the same breath as he spoke of the protectionism of the 1930s (although he did note a difference in response during the two periods).[66] While it is beyond the scope of this chapter to examine the extent to which the "success" of the Bali Ministerial is owed to the entwined bicycle metaphor and Smoot-Hawley myth, or indeed to assess whether they will facilitate the conclusion of the still ongoing Doha Round talks, the fact remains that they are still at the heart of how the experts and elites talk about global trade.

Challenging Smoot-Hawley: explaining (non-)conformity

Few countries have been willing to challenge openly the "Smoot-Hawley" myth. Argentina is one notable exception. Since 2008 it has made increasing use of non-automatic import licensing and in January 2012 also introduced a policy of requiring companies to file affidavits for prior import authorization by the government, with the issuing of such permits being delayed. Moreover, it has put in place policies requiring importers to balance imports with exports, invest in Argentine production facilities and increase local content. Such visible (and indeed onerous) measures soon attracted the attention of Argentina's peers at the WTO. In March 2012, the policies were roundly condemned in a statement issued by 14 delegations (including the United States, European Union (EU), Japan, Mexico, Thailand, Turkey, and a number of other G20 members).[67] Criticism was again leveled against Argentina in June 2012 by the United States (with concerns also raised by 11 other WTO delegations, including a number of G20 members), but Argentina has largely resisted pressure so far from its peers. Although it did announce in January 2013 that it was scrapping the policy of import pre-approval, it has maintained many of the other measures, even as formal disputes in the WTO challenging these—lodged by the United States, EU and Japan—have reached the panel stage.[68] In criticizing Argentina, its peers have drawn on the Smoot-Hawley myth's implied link between import protection and global economic collapse/stagnation; in the March 2012 statement condemning its policies, WTO delegations noted that "[i]n light of the shared goal of making every effort to sustain global economic growth, Argentina's measures, which clearly limit the growth-enhancing prospects of trade, are particularly troubling."[69]

There are those who have argued that in recent years, "Argentina has gone in the opposite direction of most successful emerging countries, by refusing to integrate into international markets."[70] The reality is more nuanced, even if the neoliberal policies of the Menem era (1989–99)—including deregulation of economic activity, privatization and trade liberalization under the auspices of the fixed exchange rate Convertibility Plan—were thoroughly discredited in the wake of the Argentine financial crisis (2000–02).[71] However, rather than closing it off from the world, the alternative set of economic policies that emerged under the leadership of President Néstor Kirchner (2003–07)—which have largely remained in place under his successor Cristina Fernández de Kirchner[72]—seek to carve out a role for the state in managing Argentina's integration into the global economy. Crucially, this model implies a strategy of state-led export promotion in the agricultural sector through an undervalued exchange rate.[73] In the light of the continuing vulnerability of Argentina to commodity price fluctuations,[74] the government has also pursued industrial policy as a means of diversifying its export earnings into the area of manufacturing. This has involved selective tariffs on manufactures, as well as subsidies and credit facilities, with the undervaluation of the Argentine peso also contributing to boosting manufacturing exports.[75]

A growing consensus among scholars studying Argentina appears to be that this set of policies is underpinned by a new policy paradigm, even if such authors have identified elements in this of Peronist import-substitution industrialization (1940s–50s) and Menemist neoliberal policies. It is variously called neodevelopmentalism (or its Spanish-language equivalent, *neodesarrollismo*) and post-neoliberalism (in the light of a pronounced trend amongst left-wing governments in Latin America to reject the prescriptions of the Washington Consensus).[76] As argued by Jean Grugel and Pía Riggirozzi, this "has involved a more dynamic role for the state in the pursuit of growth and social stability."[77] Indeed, the policy of export promotion of agricultural commodities has played a key role in subsidizing (through export taxes) social welfare programs and promoting national economic development more broadly—with moves towards carving out a similar role for manufacturing exports.[78] Of course, the policy itself has also been assisted by a favorable interest group coalition bringing together agricultural exporters, the manufacturing sector and trade unions, and has been underpinned by an international commodity boom.[79] However, it also represents a policy paradigm for re-interpreting the role of the

Argentine state in economic development,[80] and a set of ideas through which interest group politics and global market events have been mediated.

My aim in this chapter, of course, is not to enter into debates about how best to characterize this emerging policy paradigm, but rather to underscore that it is a departure from pure neoliberal precepts in trade (i.e. through selective protectionism in manufacturing). More specifically, I contend that Argentine policymakers' post-neoliberal paradigm of *neodesarrollismo* led them to reject the Smoot-Hawley myth's policy prescriptions. Import protection was seen as a legitimate policy instrument to protect their "infant" manufacturing industries in the wake of the crisis' export demand shock in developed economies and the erosion of competitiveness brought on by continued inflation.[81] This was particularly so given the perceived injustices of the global trading system, which was seen to privilege the interests of developed economies. In this vein, President Cristina Fernández de Kirchner not only defended Argentina's policy measures as legitimate, but also accused developed countries of hypocrisy (thus implicitly underscoring the inequality of the global trading regime): "It's as if there was a legal form of protectionism, the one that developed countries engage in, and a populist one when it involves emerging economies … [Protectionism] is also being confused with the concept of patriotism and defense of our own interests."[82] In another speech to the Common Market of the South (MERCOSUR) summit in Brasilia in December 2012, the link between the rejection of the Smoot-Hawley myth's prescription of unchallenged trade liberalization and the logic of Argentine *neodesarrollismo* was rendered even more apparent by the Argentine President. Fernández de Kirchner also highlighted the imbalances in the global trading system that Argentine policy was seeking to remedy:

> For decades the terms of trade between our region and developed countries were stacked against us. Now the terms of trade have been favorable for the past decade. But this has not been the work of the Holy Spirit … [W]e have achieved this thanks to public policies and to projects which have prioritized growth with inclusion … and which have abandoned the neoliberal policies that the Washington Consensus had imposed on the region.[83]

One naturally should not overstate the extent to which Fernández de Kirchner is rejecting "neoliberalism," the Washington Consensus, and its ("imposed") policy prescription of trade liberalization. After all, Argentina's proclaimed successes stem from a state-led policy of integration into the global economy. In this respect, Argentina appears to have adopted a very similar developmental paradigm to other emerging powers, which have also sought to re-articulate a role for the state while adopting some neoliberal policy prescriptions.[84] This underscores my argument here (borrowed from a broader literature on Argentine political economy) that Argentine trade policy has to be understood through the lens of particular policy ideas. This allows me to highlight how Argentina's nonconformity in the WTO should be understood in terms of its discursive rejection of the (otherwise coercive) logic of *no alternative* associated with current debates on global free trade. In other words, Argentina has been able and willing to articulate an alternative in the face of exercises of publicly "naming and shaming" WTO members for their import policies during the crisis—exercises, one should not forget, that appear to carry considerable legitimacy by appealing to a shared narrative about the ultimate necessity of free trade (with the Smoot-Hawley myth lurking in the background).

Conclusion

In this chapter, I began with a puzzle: how to explain the resilience of free trade despite the onset of the 2008 financial crisis and subsequent economic recession. I challenged the dominant, rational-institutionalist account of mainstream IPE scholars and economists, who (in large part) argued that the resilience of free trade is a product of the constraining role of the global trading regime embodied by the WTO. My argument was that it made little sense to point to policy "lock-in" when most countries have had considerable legal leeway to raise tariffs and/or NTBs and appear not to have done so to a significant degree. Endogenous trade policy models pointing to the effects of increasingly interconnected supply chains only tell part of the story. While they may explain the reduced demand for protection following the start of the crisis, integration into the global marketplace did not always correlate with support for free trade, as the significant non-conformity of Argentina showed. As a result, I made a constructivist argument that pointed to the important role played by ideas, as articulated by trade experts such as policymakers and economists, in structuring social reality and mediating the response of elites to protectionist pressures and temptations—in particular so-called discourses of external constraint. I focused on the role of the so-called Smoot-Hawley myth—the idea that the Great Depression was caused and/or exacerbated by global protectionism in the 1930s that had been initiated in the United

States—in ruling out any non-liberal response to the global financial crisis among most of the world's trade policymaking elites (especially among the G20 and in the WTO). Moreover, the willingness of Argentine decision makers to respond differently to the crisis by implementing very visible and wide-ranging import barriers was strongly shaped by their explicit rejection of this logic of no alternative.

The conclusions I have reached in this chapter are, of course, still tentative. However, I have been able to challenge the idea that it is largely the legal or other rational-institutional mechanisms of the WTO that guarded against protectionism. In this vein, I have been able to advance the cause of those who critically argue that we need to take ideas more seriously in the study of the international trading system. Much as Wilkinson bemoans that the crisis discourse "obscures the search for solutions to the problems that generate tensions in trade negotiations,"[85] so too the Smoot-Hawley myth—a highly contested historical narrative—can be seen to constrain the debate on policy responses to the economic crisis. My aim in this chapter has been to expose this discursive straightjacket for what it is: a *contestable* social construction with considerable political impact. Combined with, as we have seen, the questionable idea that it is the WTO's rules-based system of rational incentives that has prevented the descent into protectionism, the Smoot-Hawley myth and its associated crisis discourse have resulted in a powerful ideational imperative for continued openness. They have also helped to exaggerate the threat of protectionism and underscored the need to conclude the Doha Round, especially in the wake of the Bali Ministerial.

Bali notwithstanding, the fact that the current round of trade talks has not yet been completed (at least at the time of writing) is, of course, evidence of the limitations of my constructivist explanation emphasizing rhetorical coercion through the Smoot-Hawley myth; these ideas have not (yet?) been sufficient to secure a comprehensive agreement in the Doha Round even if they have played a key role in inhibiting non-liberal responses to the crisis (and may have played a role in achieving the more limited Bali Package). What is particularly noteworthy here, is that Argentina's discursive rejection of the logic of Smoot-Hawley—highlighting the "hypocrisy" of developed economies and imbalances in the global trading system—mirrors statements it (and other emerging economies) has consistently made in the Doha Round.[86] In this sense, it reflects the malaise of emerging powers with the current WTO system, as well as the potential for challenging the discourses of external constraint deployed in its defense. However, it is fair to say that the Smoot-Hawley discourse of the trade policy experts—while not entirely unquestioned—still carries considerable legitimacy.

This serves to obscure the need for a wider debate on how to respond to the crisis and how to shape the present round of multilateral trade talks. In so doing, it entrenches the political economic interests of those who benefit from the current trading system's oft-remarked asymmetry: delivering trade liberalization and openness in those areas of interest to a number of developed economies while doing little in the way of serving the interests of many developing countries.[87]

Notes

1 This is an abridged and revised version of an article first published as "Explaining the Resilience of Free Trade: The Smoot-Hawley Myth and the Crisis," *Review of International Political Economy* 21, no. 3 (2014): 535–74. I kindly thank the publisher Taylor & Francis for allowing me to reproduce this material here.

2 WTO, *WTO Statistics Database*, 2007, http://stat.wto.org.

3 See, for example, Anne Capling and Richard Higgott, "Introduction: The Future of the Multilateral Trade System—What Role for the World Trade Organization," *Global Governance* 15, no. 3 (2009): 313–25.

4 Kishore Gawande, Bernard Hoekman and Yue Cui, *Determinants of Trade Policy Responses to the 2008 Financial Crisis*, World Bank Policy Research Paper No. 5862 (Washington, DC: World Bank, 2011): 15–18.

5 See, for example, Gene M. Grossman and Elhanan Helpman, "Protection for Sale," *American Economic Review* 84, no. 4 (1994): 833–50.

6 See, for example, Hiau Looi Kee, Cristina Neagu and Alessandro Nicita, *Is Protectionism on the Rise? Assessing National Trade Policies during the Crisis of 2008*, World Bank Policy Research Working Paper No. 5274 (Washington, DC: World Bank, 2011), 1.

7 Gawande et al., *Determinants of Trade Policy Responses to the 2008 Financial Crisis*, 2.

8 For example, Judith Goldstein, Douglas Rivers and Michael Tomz, "Institutions in International Relations: Understanding the Effects of the GATT and the WTO on World Trade," *International Organization* 61, no. 1 (2007): 37–67; and Terry Collins-Williams and Robert Wolfe, "Transparency as a Trade Policy Tool: The WTO's Cloudy Windows," *World Trade Review* 9, no. 4 (2010): 551–81.

9 Capling and Higgott, "Introduction: The Future of the Multilateral Trade System—What Role for the World Trade Organization," 313–25; and Bernard Hoekman, Will Martin and Aaditya Mattoo, "Conclude Doha: It Matters!" *World Trade Review* 9, no. 3 (2010): 505–30.

10 On tariffs, see WTO, *World Tariff Profiles 2006–2012* (Geneva: WTO, 2006–12). On NTBs, see Simon Evenett, *Trade Tensions Mount: The 10th GTA Report* (London: GTA/CEPR, 2011), 28; Gawande et al., *Determinants of Trade Policy Responses to the 2008 Financial Crisis*, 17.

11 Michael J. Gilligan, *Empowering Exporters: Reciprocity, Delegation and Collective Action in American Trade Policy* (Ann Arbor, MI: University of Michigan Press, 1997).

12 Olivier Cattaneo, Gary Gereffi and Cornelia Staritz, "Global Value Chains in a Postcrisis World: Resilience, Consolidation, and Shifting End Markets," in *Global Value Chains in a Postcrisis World: A Development Perspective*, ed. Olivier Cattaneo, Gary Gereffi and Cornelia Staritz (Washington, DC: The World Bank, 2010), 3–20; and Gawande et al., *Determinants of Trade Policy Responses to the 2008 Financial Crisis.*

13 See Chad P. Bown, *Emerging Economies and the Emergence of South-South Protectionism*, World Bank Policy Research Working Paper No. 6162 (Washington, DC: World Bank, 2012).

14 Simon Evenett, ed., *Africa Resists the Protectionist Temptation: The 5th GTA Report* (London: Global Trade Alert (GTA)/Centre for Economic Policy Research (CEPR), 2010); Simon Evenett, *The Debacle: The 11th GTA Report on Protectionism* (London: GTA/CEPR, 2012).

15 Colin Hay, *Political Analysis: A Critical Introduction* (Basingstoke: Palgrave Macmillan, 2002), 201.

16 Emmanuel Adler, "Seizing the Middle Ground: Constructivism in World Politics," *European Journal of International Relations* 3, no. 3 (1997): 319–63.

17 Adler, "Seizing the Middle Ground," 324.

18 See, among others, Ben Rosamond, "Discourses of Globalization and the Social Construction of European Identities," *Journal of European Public Policy* 6, no. 4 (1999): 652–68; Colin Hay and Ben Rosamond, "Globalization, European Integration and the Discursive Construction of Economic Imperatives," *Journal of European Public Policy* 9, no. 2 (2002): 147–67; and Matthew Watson and Colin Hay, "The Discourse of Globalization and the Logic of No Alternative: Rendering the Contingent Necessary in the Political Economy of New Labour," *Policy & Politics* 31, no. 3 (2003): 289–305.

19 Hay and Rosamond, "Globalization, European Integration and the Discursive Construction of Economic Imperatives," 148.

20 Ronald R. Krebs and Patrick Thaddeus Jackson, "Twisting Tongues and Twisting Arms: The Power of Political Rhetoric," *European Journal of International Relations* 13, no. 1 (2007): 36.

21 Gabriel Siles-Brügge, *Constructing European Union Trade Policy: A Global Idea of Europe* (Basingstoke: Palgrave Macmillan, 2014).

22 Susan Strange, "Protectionism and World Politics," *International Organization* 39, no. 2 (1985): 239–42.

23 Strange, "Protectionism and World Politics," 239–40.

24 Strange, "Protectionism and World Politics," 241–2.

25 Strange, "Protectionism and World Politics," 597.

26 Hoekman et al., "Conclude Doha: It Matters!" 505–30.

27 Judith Goldstein, "Ideas, Institutions and American Trade Policy," *International Organization* 42, no. 1 (1988): 187.

28 See also Rorden Wilkinson, "Of Butchery and Bicycles: The WTO and the 'Death' of the Doha Development Agenda," *The Political Quarterly* 83, no. 2 (2012): 395–401.

29 Mario J. Crucini and James A. Kahn, "Tariffs and Aggregate Economic Activity: Lessons from the Great Depression," *Journal of Monetary Economics* 38, no. 3 (1996): 427–67.

30 Douglas Irwin, "The Smoot-Hawley Tariff: A Quantitative Assessment," *The Review of Economics and Statistics* 80, no. 2 (1998): 333.

31 Douglas Irwin, *Trade Policy Disaster: Lessons from the 1930s* (Cambridge, Mass.: MIT Press, 2012), 18.
32 Irwin, *Trade Policy Disaster*, 32.
33 See, for example, Barry Eichengreen, *The Political Economy of the Smoot-Hawley Tariff*, National Bureau of Economic Research (NBER) Working Paper No. 2001 (Cambridge, Mass.: NBER, 1986).
34 Randall Germain, *Global Politics and Financial Governance* (Basingstoke: Palgrave Macmillan, 2010), 70–2.
35 G20, *Declaration of the Summit on Financial Markets and the World Economy*, Washington, DC, 15 November 2008, www.g20.utoronto.ca/2008/2008declaration1115.html.
36 See G20, *Declaration of the Summit on Financial Markets and the World Economy*; G20, *Global Plan for Recovery and Reform: Statement Issued by the G20 Leaders*, London, 2 April 2009, www.g20.utoronto.ca/2009/2009communique0402.html; G20, *G20 Leaders Statement: Pittsburgh Summit*, 24–25 September 2009, www.g20.utoronto.ca/2009/2009communique0925.html; G20, *The G20 Toronto Summit Declaration*, 27 June 2010, www.g20.utoronto.ca/2010/to-communique.html; G20, *The G20 Seoul Summit Leaders' Declaration*, 12 November 2010, www.g20.utoronto.ca/2010/g20seoul.html; G20, *Cannes Summit Final Declaration—Building Our Common Future: Renewed Collective Action for the Benefit of All*, 4 November 2011, www.g20.utoronto.ca/2011/2011-cannes-declaration-111104-en.html; G20, *G20 Leaders Declaration at Los Cabos*, 19 June 2012, www.g20.utoronto.ca/2012/2012-0619-loscabos.html; and G20, *G20 Leaders' Declaration*, St Petersburg, 6 September 2013, www.g20.utoronto.ca/2013/2013-0906-declaration.html.
37 G20, *Global Plan for Recovery and Reform.*
38 G20, *Global Plan for Recovery and Reform.*
39 Collins-Williams and Wolfe, "Transparency as a Trade Policy Tool," 551.
40 Collins-Williams and Wolfe, "Transparency as a Trade Policy Tool," 572–4.
41 G20, *Global Plan for Recovery and Reform.*
42 Collins-Williams and Wolfe, "Transparency as a Trade Policy Tool," 577.
43 Pascal Lamy, *Keynote Address to the WTO Public Forum*, Geneva, 24 September 2008, www.wto.org/english/news_e/sppl_e/sppl101_e.htm; Pascal Lamy, *The Stabilizing Influence of a Rules-based Trading System*, Speech at Stanford University, 27 October 2008, www.wto.org/english/news_e/sppl_e/sppl104_e.htm; Pascal Lamy, *Restoring Citizens' Confidence in Trade Requires Sound Domestic Policies*, Speech at the University of California, Berkeley, 29 October 2009, www.wto.org/english/news_e/sppl_e/sppl105_e.htm; Pascal Lamy, *Opening Address to the Geneva Shipping and Trading Association's Commodities Week*, 3 November 2008, www.wto.org/english/news_e/sppl_e/sppl106_e.htm.
44 Lamy, *Keynote Address to the WTO Public Forum.*
45 Lamy, *The Stabilizing Influence of a Rules-based Trading System.*
46 Lamy, *Restoring Citizens' Confidence in Trade Requires Sound Domestic Policies.*
47 See WTO, *Director-General Pascal Lamy—Speeches and Statements*, 2013, www.wto.org/english/news_e/sppl_e/sppl_e.htm.
48 Roberto Azevêdo, *The WTO Needs America, and America Needs the WTO*, Speech at the US Chamber of Commerce, Washington, DC, 10

March 2014, www.wto.org/english/news_e/spra_e/spra9_e.htm; and Larry Elliott, "Time Running Out for International Trade Deal, Says WTO Boss," *The Guardian*, 8 April 2014, www.theguardian.com/world/2014/apr/08/time-international-trade-deal-wto-boss.

49 Richard Baldwin, "The Crisis and Protectionism: History Doesn't Repeat Itself, but Sometimes it Rhymes," in *What World Leaders Must Do to Halt the Spread of Protectionism*, ed. Richard Baldwin and Simon Evenett (London: VoxEU.org/CEPR, 2008), 32.

50 See Global Trade Alert, www.globaltradealert.org.

51 GTA, *About Global Trade Alert*, 2012, www.globaltradealert.org/about.

52 See figure 2 in Evenett, *Trade Tensions Mount: The 10th GTA Report*, 28.

53 Simon Evenett, *Broken Promises: A G-20 Summit Report by Global Trade Alert* (London: GTA/CEPR, 2009); Simon Evenett, *The Unrelenting Pressure of Protectionism: The 3rd GTA Report, A Focus on the Asia-Pacific Region* (London: GTA/CEPR, 2009); and Evenett, *The Debacle: The 11th GTA Report on Protectionism*.

54 See, for example, Kati Suominen, *A New Age of Protectionism? The Economic Crisis and Transatlantic Trade Policy*, Brussels Forum Paper Series (Washington, DC: The German Marshall Fund of the United States, 2009).

55 WTO, OECD and UNCTAD, *Report on G20 Trade and Investment Measures (September 2009 to February 2010)* (Geneva and Paris: WTO, OECD and UNCTAD, 8 March 2010); and WTO, OECD and UNCTAD, *Report on G20 Trade and Investment Measures (Mid October 2010 to April 2011)* (Geneva and Paris: WTO, OECD and UNCTAD, 24 May 2011).

56 WTO, OECD and UNCTAD, *Report on G20 Trade and Investment Measures (Mid October 2011 to Mid May 2012)* (Geneva and Paris: WTO, OECD and UNCTAD, 31 May 2012), 4.

57 WTO, OECD and UNCTAD, *Report on G20 Trade and Investment Measures (Mid October 2012 to Mid May 2013)* (Geneva and Paris: WTO, OECD and UNCTAD, 17 June 2013), 4.

58 WTO et al., *Report on G20 Trade and Investment Measures (Mid October 2011 to Mid May 2012)* (Geneva: WTO, 2012), 6; and WTO, OECD and UNCTAD, *Report on G20 Trade and Investment Measures (Mid October 2012 to Mid May 2013)*, 4.

59 WTO et al., *Report on G20 Trade and Investment Measures (Mid October 2011 to Mid May 2012)* (Geneva: WTO, 2012), 10.

60 Pascal Lamy, *Rise in Trade Restrictions Now Alarming*, Speech to Heads of WTO Delegations, Geneva, 7 June 2012, www.wto.org/english/news_e/sppl_e/sppl234_e.htm.

61 For example, Hoekman et al., "Conclude Doha: It Matters!" 505–30.

62 International Centre for Trade and Sustainable Development (ICTSD), "Success in Bali Sparks Questions Over Doha, WTO Future," *Bridges Weekly Trade News Digest*, no. 17 (Geneva: ICTSD, 2013), http://ictsd.org/i/news/bridgesweekly/181294/.

63 WTO et al., *Report on G20 Trade and Investment Measures (Mid October 2012 to Mid May 2013)*, 6.

64 WTO, OECD and UNCTAD, *Report on G20 Trade and Investment Measures (Mid May 2013 to Mid November 2013)* (Geneva and Paris: WTO, OECD and UNCTAD, 18 December 2013), 2.

65 Azevêdo, *The WTO Needs America, and America Needs the WTO.*
66 Elliott, "Time Running Out for International Trade Deal, Says WTO Boss."
67 ICTSD, "Argentina Import Controls Come Under Fire at WTO," *Bridges Weekly Trade News Digest*, no. 3 (Geneva: ICTSD, 2012), http://ictsd.org/i/news/bridgesweekly/130486/.
68 ICTSD, "Four Argentina WTO Disputes Reach Panel Stage," *Bridges Weekly Trade News Digest*, no. 3 (Geneva: ICTSD, 2013), http://ictsd.org/i/news/bridgesweekly/153150/.
69 Cited in ICTSD, "Argentina Import Controls Come Under Fire at WTO."
70 Andres Gallo, "Trade Policy and Protectionism in Argentina," *Economic Affairs* 32, no. 1 (2012): 59.
71 Jean Grugel and Pía Riggirozzi, "The Return of the State in Argentina," *International Affairs* 83, no. 1 (2007): 92–4.
72 Jean Grugel and Pía Riggirozzi, "Post-neoliberalism in Latin America: Rebuilding and Reclaiming the State after Crisis," *Development and Change* 43, no. 1 (2012): 12.
73 Grugel and Riggirozzi, "The Return of the State in Argentina," 97–106.
74 Grugel and Riggirozzi, "Post-neoliberalism in Latin America," 15.
75 Christopher Wylde, "The Developmental State is Dead, Long Live the Developmental Regime! Interpreting Néstor Kirchner's Argentina 2003–2007," *Journal of International Relations and Development* 17, no. 2 (2014): 194–5.
76 Wylde, "The Developmental State is Dead, Long Live the Developmental Regime!" 191–219; and Grugel and Rigirozzi, "Post-neoliberalism in Latin America," 1–12.
77 Grugel and Rigirozzi, "The Return of the State in Argentina," 87.
78 Wylde, "The Developmental State is Dead, Long Live the Developmental Regime!" 191–219.
79 Neal P. Richardson, "Export-oriented Populism: Commodities and Coalitions in Argentina,"*Studies in Comparative International Development* 44, no. 3 (2009): 228–55; and Sebastián Etchemendy and Ruth B. Collier, "Down But Not Out: Union Resurgence and Segmented Neocorporatism in Argentina (2003–2007)," *Politics & Society* 35, no. 3 (2007): 363–401.
80 Wylde, "The Developmental State is Dead, Long Live the Developmental Regime!" 215.
81 Mario E. Carranza, *Mercosur, the Global Economic Crisis, and the New Architecture of Regionalism in the Americas*, Latin American Trade Network Working Paper No. 125 (San José, Costa Rica: Facultad Latinoamericana de Ciencias Sociales, 2010), 5; Gallo, "Trade Policy and Protectionism in Argentina," 59.
82 Cited in ICTSD, "Argentina Trade Tensions Escalate with Six New WTO Cases," *Bridges Weekly Trade News Digest*, no. 30 (Geneva: ICTSD, 2012), http://ictsd.org/i/news/bridgesweekly/144563/.
83 Author's translation from Cristina Fernández de Kirchner, "Palabras de la Presidenta de la Nación en la Cumbre del Mercosur," *Casa Rosada, Presidencia de la Nación Argentina*, 7 December, 2012, www.presidencia.gov.ar/discursos/26229-cumbre-del-mercosur-en-brasilia-palabras-de-la-presidenta-de-la-nacion.

84 See Cornel Ban and Mark Blyth, "The BRICs and the Washington Consensus: An Introduction," *Review of International Political Economy* 20, no. 2 (2013): 241–55.

85 Rorden Wilkinson, "Language, Power and Multilateral Trade Negotiations," *Review of International Political Economy* 16, no. 4 (2009): 614.

86 See, for example, Amrita Narlikar, "Fairness in International Trade Negotiations: Developing Countries in the GATT and WTO," *The World Economy* 29, no. 8 (2006): 1005–29.

87 Anthony J. Payne, *The Global Politics of Unequal Development* (Basingstoke: Palgrave Macmillan, 2005); and Rorden Wilkinson, *What's Wrong with the WTO and How to Fix It* (Cambridge: Polity Press, 2014).

3 Trade policy communities, expert language, and the dehumanization of world trade

Silke Trommer

As part of the evolution and moving center stage of critical political economy approaches to trade, the literature pays growing attention to the discursive foundations of trade politics. While scholars have examined episodes of language formation, discursive practices and struggles over terminology, this literature has tended to retain state-centric lenses and focuses on how specific terms and phrases affect the setting or application of international trade rules at distinct historical moments. At the same time, the World Trade Organization (WTO) published a glossary of 227 terms on its website that the organization refers to as "WTO speak."[1] More wide-ranging, meticulously assembled reference works such as the *Dictionary of Trade Policy Terms* (hereafter, the *Dictionary*) contain around 2,500 entries,[2] running from "actionable subsidies," "built-in agenda" and "cross-retaliation," to "unforeseen developments," "variable geometry," and "water in the tariff," of which the ordinary speaker will be hard-pressed to make sense. These compilations capture (parts of) the expert language of global trade, through which state and non-state trade policy actors communicate daily, and in which struggles over specific expressions are embedded.

A number of studies in the trade literature have produced insights into how linguistic practices within global trade governance affect its course.[3] Rorden Wilkinson analyzes what he calls, "the way we talk about trade" and critiques its impact on trade political processes, notably at the WTO. He exposes commonplace rhetorical devices like the "bicycle metaphor," or the notion that the multilateral trading system is in a state of crisis, as providing political pressure for reproducing existing patterns of trade liberalization. He sees the way we talk about trade as complicit in perpetuating a governance mechanism that repeatedly results in poor benefits for marginalized countries.[4]

Matthew Eagleton-Pierce has introduced a Bourdieu-inspired notion of symbolic power that draws attention to the interactions between the exercise and the legitimization of power in WTO politics. Analyzing episodes of political struggles during the Doha Round that developing countries championed, Eagleton-Pierce shows how countries that lack standard vehicles of negotiating power, such as economic and military strength, can utilize political language as a tool for pursuing their goals.[5] Insightful as they are, these studies examine discursive interactions among people who are insiders to the field. In other words, they focus on discursive practices among the global elite of trade policy-makers and experts. The question remains: What role does broader expert language, as compiled in the above-mentioned reference works, play in constituting this elite, and in shaping its perceptions of politically feasible lines of action?

Scholarship across the social sciences has observed that speaking expert language is an important element of how people become and are recognized as experts on a given issue area. This identification function of expert language can work independently from an individual's mastery of the body of expert knowledge associated with the language. In his 1997 article "The UN Security Council, Indifference, and Genocide in Rwanda," Michael Barnett explains that although having little prior knowledge on the country, "my standing as an expert [on Rwanda in the US Mission to the United Nations in 1994] derived from my ability to formulate questions and responses, to pose talking points, to use language and to carry on conversations in ways that were consistent with the understandings and discourses of my superiors and colleagues."[6] In her 1987 piece, "Sex and Death in the Rational World of Defense Intellectuals," Carol Cohn recalls from her engagement with US defense specialists, "that no matter how well-informed my questions were, if I spoke English rather than expert jargon, the men responded as though I were ignorant, simple-minded, or both," while "using the right phrases opened my way into long, elaborate discussions." Cohn further finds that "at the same time as the language gave me access to things I had been unable to speak about before, it radically excluded others." She concludes, "this language does not allow certain questions to be asked or certain values to be expressed."[7]

Relying on existing trade scholarship, my previous professional engagement with trade policy,[8] and the *Dictionary* as one authoritative source of global trade expert language, I apply tools in the anthropological and feminist traditions of Barnett's and Cohn's pieces, respectively, to provide scrutiny of how expert language shapes the trade policy field. Based on this methodology, I argue that global trade expert language performs distinct and traceable gate-keeping functions of who can talk and what they can say in trade politics. Overall, my chapter speaks to the literature that is engaged in unpacking the political foundations of technocratic language in economic policy. As Doreen Massey argues, "the whole vocabulary we use to talk about the economy, while presented as a description of the natural and the eternal, is in fact a political construction that needs contesting."[9] Andreas Bieler and Adam Morton further remind us that also in relation to discourse, one question that political economy has to ask systematically is "who benefits?"[10] Developing a complete theoretical framework that satisfies this criterion requires an empirical and conceptual exercise that is beyond the scope of this short piece. Examining how expert language seals off trade policy processes from non-experts and identifying which concerns it marginalizes, nonetheless presents a step towards making visible the inherently political nature of global trade expert language, on which future scholarship may subsequently build.

In section two, I categorize the linguistic elements that turn trade expert language into incomprehensible jargon for the ordinary speaker. On the basis of Celina Del Felice's, Erin Hannah's and my own previous works,[11] I contend that joining the global trade policy community requires learning the expert language, while speaking it requires discursively reproducing its underlying perspectives and normative commitments, irrespective of the speaker's own worldviews and understandings of reality. The point is thus not that the speaker of global trade expert language has to internalize the understandings of reality and normative commitments on which the language is built and adopt them as his or her own; the speaker may well hold values and causal understandings that differ from those that the language validates. The point is, as Cohn notes, that the individual cannot express those without risking being considered as speaking from a non-professional, non-expert position. In other words, the social function of the language, that is to say signaling who is a member of the trade policy elite, also upholds a hierarchy of worldviews—those normative underpinnings, values and causal understandings that echo the language's perspective on reality are considered part of expert discourse, while alternative perspectives appear ill-informed, naïve, or inappropriate.

In order to discern what realities are captured and validated through global trade expert language, in section three I ask—in line with the feminist tradition—from which perspective the language speaks. I find that global trade expert language creates an image of reality that is built on abstract and socially constructed entities, such as commodities, states, and corporations, as the basic units constituting this reality and existing in it. At the same time, humans are not an important reference point in the expert terminology per se. That is, the language privileges the vantage point of goods and services traveling through the global economy, to the detriment of the people who are doing the trading. I argue that this bias in perspective results in a dehumanization of the current global trading order, in which human, social and environmental conditions become second-order issues, and the role of human agency in producing social and political outcomes is obscured. As long as these biases persist, trade experts can reasonably be expected to continue reproducing existing material and political patterns in global trade relations. It is in this context that we can make better sense of Director-General Roberto Azevêdo's address to the opening session of the 2014 WTO Public Forum in which he asserted the urgent need to "put the human dimension in the heart of our work and change the terms of the debate."[12]

Expert language and the constitution of the trade policy communities

Bringing together insights from the works of Barnett, Cohn, Del Felice, Hannah, and my previous research, I argue in this section that the ability to handle expert terminology signals who is a member of the community of global trade experts and who is not. Expert language performs this function because, due to a large number of technical terms that I categorize, it cannot be understood nor spoken by the uninitiated. At the same time, those who do not speak expert language, either voluntarily or involuntarily, typically find themselves disqualified from meaningful participation in trade policy processes. In order to acquire effective trade political agency, expert language thus needs to be learned, which requires discursively reproducing the worldview on which the expert terminology implicitly or explicitly rests.

Recent scholarship finds that in trade politics, adopting expert language is one element that affects perceptions of who is a legitimate actor. International trade negotiations between the European Union (EU) and the Economic Community of West African States (ECOWAS), in which a network of West African global social justice movements took a critical stance towards the global trade agenda and over time gained access and influence in the negotiating process, provide one example. I have argued elsewhere that adopting technical language was a strategic advocacy decision that bestowed trade political legitimacy on these atypical participants to trade talks.[13] Trade officials reported in my interviews that once civil society organizations had engaged in producing technical expertise, their contributions to trade political debates were useful, "as opposed to earlier stages, where it was just rhetoric and lack of substance."[14] Civil society organizations, on the other hand, asserted that rather than changing their positions, they had simply learned over time to translate their concerns into technical language.

In her study of the same set of negotiations, Del Felice finds that activists deliberately tried to break "the barriers between legal-technical and popular texts."[15] She observes that: (i) activists consciously and purposely reproduced the established ways of communicating inside the technocratic sphere of trade negotiations, while aiming to politicize the issues through more provocative language in the broader public debate; and (ii) although a broader range of positions entered trade politics in this way, the overall result was to limit discourse to those established iterations that rely on liberal assumptions. Taken together, our studies suggest that while activists attempted to break down the barriers between expert language and popular language, the necessity to speak expert language in order to be part of the trade political process ultimately posed challenges to the range of positions that they found politically feasible to take. By contrast, Hannah shows in her broader study of nongovernmental organizations (NGOs) on global trade that some NGOs reject speaking expert language in a conscious effort to avoid assimilation and instead engage in protest and resistance from outside the formal trade political process. In response, policy-makers actively attempt to delegitimize, silence, and marginalize actors who refuse to speak expert language.[16]

Expert language can fulfill this gate-keeping function because it is laden with acronyms and shorthand terminology for complex economic, legal, and political constellations that are incomprehensible to the outsider. This is a typical feature of expert languages across governance fields. Recalling his early days as Rwanda expert in the US Mission to the UN, Barnett reports, "my colleagues could speak full sentences in acronyms that I had never heard of [and] use slang that referred to events and processes of which I had no knowledge."[17] As Cohn writes, these codes "restrict communications to the initiated, leaving all others both uncomprehending and voiceless in the debate."[18] In global trade expert language, three broad categories of expert terminology exist: acronyms, legal-administrative codes, and concepts derived from economic theory.

The vast majority of elements in the WTO's treaty structure are typically expressed in acronyms. Next to the better-known General Agreement on Tariffs and Trade (GATT), GATS,[19] the Agreement on the Trade-Related Aspects of Intellectual Property Rights (TRIPS) and the Agreement on Trade-Related Investment Measures (TRIMs),[20] feature the texts on RoOs,[21] the SCM,[22] SPS,[23] and TBT[24] Agreements, and the DSU.[25] In the steadily growing network of bilateral agreements, often interchangeably referred to as FTAs,[26] RTAs,[27] or PTAs,[28] individual deals are captured in ciphers that are at times distinguishable by one or two letters only. Such is the case for the TPP[29] and TTIP,[30] SACU[31] and SADC,[32] or NAFTA,[33] CAFTA,[34] and EFTA.[35] Several key principles, rules and negotiating areas are equally coded, such as MFN,[36] SDT,[37] GSP,[38] NTBs[39] or NAMA.[40] Entire WTO negotiating groups hide behind certain acronyms that are WTO specific and do not necessarily correspond to abbreviations used in other fields of global governance. Examples include the G20,[41] the G33,[42] and the G90,[43] but also the NAMA 11[44] or the Cotton 4.[45] Others are captured under slang-type expressions, like the Cairns Group[46] or the Quad.[47] Elaborate use of these terms and flawless incorporation into statements is an essential condition for trade experts. Within the global trade policy elite, acronym use is generalized to the point of providing the basis of insider jokes. Thus, it has been noted that the EU's EBA scheme should really have been called "Everything But Farms."[48] Today less popular in WTO circles is the pun that UNCTAD stands for "Under No Circumstances Take a Decision."[49] The fact that both witticisms play on the politically and morally charged trade and development debate is testimony to the way in which trade expert language distances the speaker from the human realities behind traded products, on which I elaborate in the next section.

In addition to acronyms, terms relevant to the practices of customs administrations, the body of international trade law and concepts drawn from economic theory further pose barriers to non-expert participation in trade policy debates. It might be possible to second-guess the meaning of "customs valuation,"[50] "import licensing,"[51] or "transit trade,"[52] for instance. The list of expressions that have acquired specialized and technically complex content as a result of state practice and judicial interpretation is, however, long. It includes examples such as "amber box,"[53] "causality,"[54] "commercial presence,"[55] "parallel import,"[56] "retaliation,"[57] or "risk assessment,"[58] to name but a few. The administrative and legal terminology is supplemented with concepts and theorems of economic theory, such as "comparative advantage,"[59] "factor endowment,"[60] or "trade diversion."[61] Trade economists regularly deplore that trade policymakers and experts do not necessarily grasp the concepts behind these terms fully or correctly.[62] The point underscores that speaking expert language has a social and political function that is in principle related to, but can effectively be distinct from, mastering the body of expert knowledge associated with the language.

The above suggests that in trade, as in other policy fields, expert language is "something that ha[s] to be learned."[63] Both Cohn and Barnett find that the process of learning expert language has transformational effects on the individual's sense of identity, rationality, and appropriate political action. According to Cohn, learning the acronyms and the language more generally comes with the "thrill of being able to manipulate an arcane language, the power of entering the secret kingdom, being someone in the know."[64] She sees learning expert language as a rewarding experience because it instills the individual with a sense of belonging to a global elite. As Cohn writes, "few know and those who do are powerful."[65] Similarly, Barnett notes that once he had learned the expert language,

> not only had I entered the bureaucratic world, but the bureaucratic world had entered me. My long days of intense interaction with my colleagues were slowly transforming how I understood, identified, and presented myself. Whereas once I had effected certain practices and discourses because of their instrumentality and strategic value, now I did so because they felt comfortable and consistent with who I was and how I understood myself.[66]

How learning global trade expert language affects the individual's sense of identity, rationality, and appropriate political action is an empirical question that requires further research. The next section examines global trade expert language as assembled in the *Dictionary* through the lens of its dominant perspectives in order to discern which aspects of global trade the language allows experts to talk about, and which aspects it excludes from the realm of trade expertise. The exercise ultimately suggests that despite fashionable calls for "thinking outside the box," global trade expert language, as currently constituted, hinders rather than promotes the finding of innovative, holistic solutions to contemporary global problems.

Expert language and the dehumanization of global trade

In this section I contend that from the perspective of global trade expert language, the two most significant entities in world trade are states and commodities. To the extent that other policy fields have an impact on trade flows, they are classified as "trade related," indicating their subordinate character. One notable perspective missing in the language is that of the people behind the traded goods and services, as well as their general social and environmental conditions. Given the above-mentioned gate-keeping function of global trade expert language, this absence of a human focus has identifiable socio-political implications for debates among global trade policy elites, namely: (i) lifting social and environmental concerns above concerns for the circulation of goods and services becomes by default unprofessional; and (ii) human agency as an impact factor on trade policy outcomes appears constrained by seemingly invariable political economy forces.

In her paper, Cohn finds expert language to be both enabling, by providing access to political debates from which one would otherwise be excluded, and constraining, by privileging certain worldviews and perspectives at the expense of others, thus excluding the latter from the realm of expertise. One key political question lurking behind the use of expert language more generally is thus whether existing patterns of inclusion and exclusion are appropriate. To tease out the constraints that the existing expert language imposes, Cohn analyzes expert language in defense policy by "ask[ing] myself the question that feminists have been asking about theories in every discipline: What is the reference point? Who (or what) is the *subject* here?"[67] Applying this technique to global trade expert language, it becomes clear that all entries in the *Dictionary* relate either to state actions under public international law or domestic customs law, or their references are internationally traded goods and services, with the occasional mention of corporations associated with either category.

It may seem uncontroversial that global trade expert language relies on states and commodities as the two basic units with which it crafts its image of reality, since exchanging goods and services across national borders is what trade is traditionally understood to be about. It is, however, equally clear that commodity circuits and the way they are regulated and organized internationally and globally interact with other fields of governance and policy areas, which may or may not contain a primary focus on economic activity. As mentioned above, global trade expert language acknowledges this fact and groups concerns that are recognized as overlapping under the label of "trade-related." Nonetheless, when trade policy experts begin talking about these broader issues, they are constrained by expert language to mediate human, social and environmental concerns through the basic units of states and commodities. Thus, the exclusive state/commodity perspective removes experts from the concrete human realities that they are talking about. It is not that the human realities behind the traded goods and services do not matter. It is that privileging human realities in deliberations about the global trading order is inexpert.

The field of trade and public health provides one example to illustrate these points. Excluding treaties and state practice in international law and specific country groups, the *Dictionary* contains 12 entries that relate to policy overlap between trade and public health, although a number of them are broader in reach and apply to other regulatory fields, such as environmental protection. They are: "acceptable level of risk," "access to medicines," "appropriate level of protection," "necessity test," "non-trade objectives," "precautionary principle," "risk assessment," "sanitary and phytosanitary measures," "specified risk material," "technical barriers to trade," "trade and human rights," and "zero risk."

Since the entry into force of the TRIPS Agreement, the interface between public health measures and trade rules has been an important field of political contestation.[68] In broader global governance, a right to health was first internationally proclaimed in the 1946 Constitution of the World Health Organization, and reiterated in the 1948 Universal Declaration of Human Rights, the 1966 International Covenant on Economic, Social and Cultural Rights, and a number of subsequent international legal instruments.[69] On its website, the World Health Organization (WHO) declares "the highest attainable standard of health as a fundamental right of every human being" and notes that "the right to health includes access to timely, acceptable, and affordable health care of appropriate quality."[70]

In 2001, the African Group of the TRIPS Council brought an initiative to address perceived problems in pursuing effective domestic public health policies as a result of their patenting obligations under TRIPS. Following tough negotiations, the initiative culminated in the adoption of the Doha Declaration on TRIPS and Public Health at the Doha Ministerial Conference in December 2001. In Article 4 of the Doha Declaration, WTO members:

> agree that the TRIPS Agreement does not and should not prevent members from taking measures to protect public health. Accordingly, while reiterating our commitment to the TRIPS Agreement, we affirm that the Agreement can and should be interpreted and implemented in a manner supportive of WTO members' right to protect public health and, in particular, to promote access to medicines for all.[71]

The *Dictionary* evokes the political struggles leading up to the Doha Declaration when it defines access to medicines as "deal[ing] with the balance between obligations under the TRIPS Agreement and the expectations of developing countries for affordable medicines," and adds that:

> developing countries claim that compulsory licenses and parallel imports are essential for their governments to carry out effective health policies through affordable medicines. In their view, the TRIPS agreement is biased in favor of pharmaceutical companies residing in developed countries.[72]

The underlying perspectives within the two bodies of expert language expose radical differences. While the WHO and related international institutions focus on the human being as the bearer of a right to health, the global trade expert language excludes this human perspective to the benefit of states, commodities and in the instance of the *Dictionary* definition, companies associated with certain states. While for the WHO a right to health includes a right to care, global trade language debates a right to acquire a commodity, namely medicines. Different types of expert language contain different reference points that lead to different mechanisms of inclusion and exclusion. The question remains whether existing inclusion/exclusion mechanisms are appropriate to resolve the political problem at hand.

Analyzing defense policy, which takes the vantage point of arms rather than people, Cohn summarizes the concrete effects in the following words:

> if human lives are not the reference point, then it is not only impossible to talk about humans in this language, it also becomes in some sense illegitimate to ask the paradigm to reflect human concerns … No one will claim that the questions are unimportant, but they are inexpert, unprofessional, irrelevant to the business at hand to ask … It is not that the men I spoke with would say that these are invalid questions. They would, however, simply say that they are separate questions, questions that are outside what they do, outside their realm of expertise.[73]

Similarly, by decoupling the things that are being traded from the people who are doing the trading, as well as the broader social realities in which the trading activity is embedded, global trade expert language disconnects these contexts from the realm of trade policy. Anyone who has ever taught an international trade law class has witnessed this mechanism in operation. Once the global trade expert language is learned, students can become so immersed in sophisticated deliberations on how the principle of freedom of transit in Article V of the GATT relates to the general obligations of enforcement of intellectual property rights in Article 41 of the TRIPS Agreement, for example, that they are often genuinely surprised to discover that what is at stake in the case at hand is the ability of a government to run a public health program intended to save the very real lives of its very real citizens. We may excuse the students for failing to remember this, because the subjects of global trade expert language are not people, but products and services.

Nonetheless, focusing on commodities at the expense of human realities sets important limits on our ability to think innovatively about trade policy reform. Although we know that interconnections between trade and labor rights, environmental protection, public health and so forth exist, the expert language does not allow adopting a holistic perspective. The political implication is that policymakers and experts can call for new approaches to tackle these interfaces, but in order to appeal to the global trade policy community, pathways for trading into sustainable futures necessarily need to focus around commodities at their core. Whether policy solutions driven by this preoccupation are genuinely sustainable is a question that the expert language cannot ask.

If the people behind the traded goods and services are not visible in the expert language of global trade, this further leaves conceptualizations of the trading activity with a curious agency gap. In similar fashion to Stuart Hall's observation that public discourse regularly depicts globalization as a force of nature,[74] global trade expert language leaves open the question of where the often-cited "forces of global trade" exactly originate. This agency gap elevates said forces to a category of constraints on human behavior that resides outside the realm of agency. Global trade expert language thus not only naturalizes the view that a number of allegedly inevitable trade political phenomena are limiting the possibilities for political agency to that of reaction. If we cannot (exactly) pinpoint the acting subject(s) that drive a particular trade political phenomenon, this also diffuses responsibility for trade political outcomes to forces that reside outside the reach of human actions.

One example to illustrate these points is provided in the terminology relating to the trade and development debate, and notably the term "preference erosion." Excluding specific treaties and country groups, the *Dictionary* contains 21 entries pertaining to the trade and development debate. They are: "Doha Development Agenda," "enabling clause," "flying geese paradigm," "graduation," "graduation box," "GST," "GSTP," "Haberler report," "poverty reduction," "preference erosion," "reverse preferences," "reverse special and differential treatment," "reverse transfer of technology," "right to development," "special and differential treatment," "special agricultural safeguards," "sustainable development," "sustainable trade policy," "trade and poverty," "trade related aspects of sustainable development," and "variable geometry." According to the *Dictionary*, preference erosion denominates "the gradual disappearance of or reductions in margins of preference as countries proceed with non-discriminatory trade liberalization."[75]

Preference erosion can, in principle, affect all WTO members. It is, however, more regularly discussed as a problem for developing country members, since their special, non-reciprocal preferences diminish during the course of other members' multilateral, unilateral or bilateral liberalizations with third parties. While the term "preferences," according to the *Dictionary*, refers to "favors extended to some trading partners,"[76] the term "erosion" is commonly associated with the field of geology. In geology, erosion is the transportation of sediment, whereby the application of a force, notably water or wind, over time breaks down a block of material and moves it to a different location. Other than through natural forces, erosion occurs when one block of material is moved across another.[77] It is therefore a natural phenomenon that lies outside the immediate realm of agency, in the sense that human attempts to eliminate erosion from the spectrum of natural phenomena would be laughable. Instead, our actions need to take the invariable process of erosion into account in the way in which we plan, organize and live our lives. The analogy of preference erosion projects this attitude into global trade expert language. It cements the view that trade policymakers and experts can lament or regret that preference erosion is occurring. They can mitigate its effects or, at best, use them to their benefit. However, erosion as such is an inevitable phenomenon that is naturally tied to the passage of time.

As a result of the lack of agency, the analogy portrays an image whereby it is not the fault of anybody in particular that the special preferences for poor countries diminish as trade negotiations proceed. Since erosion is simply a natural phenomenon, attempts to hold anybody responsible for stopping preference erosion would be absurd; expectations that anyone would be responsible for repairing the damage would be ludicrous. The analogy implies that it is the responsibility of affected countries to remove themselves from the situation where they are vulnerable to preference erosion. Although in cases of preference erosion someone is demanding a deal, someone is negotiating concessions, and someone is applying trade rules, these events are obscured through a metaphor that purports the view that the underlying forces of global trade, including their inherent power relations, reside outside the reach of human agency.

The agency gap inherent in global trade expert language depoliticizes trade policy debates in three distinct and interrelated ways. First, it downgrades the relevance of the distinct historical path through which the global trading system has evolved for contemporary trade politics. Scholars may well write volumes on how the global trading system became deeply asymmetrical and biased towards certain members and their economic interests. Against this perspective, global trade expert language posits a view of the forces of trade as quasi-natural phenomena that all human societies are ultimately exposed to and grapple with. Second, it has ethical implications, because identifying an acting subject is one precondition for according responsibility for the outcomes of our actions in human relations. Instead, global trade expert language promotes the idea that some trade political outcomes are unavoidable, because they are quite simply beyond human control. Third, in global trade expert language, the character of the economy as a social sphere and the nature of the trading activity as a social activity are downplayed. This further reifies a de-historicized, amoral global trading system, even if this system is today widely acknowledged to be in deep need of reform. In sum, and as I argue in the concluding section, global trade expert language in its current iteration eradicates imagination about alternative roles that trade can play in moving toward more sustainable and equitable global orders.

Conclusion

In this chapter, I argued that global trade expert language plays a social role in constituting trade policy communities, because the ability to speak the language signals an individual's belonging to the global elite of trade policymakers and experts. Relying on previous scholarship, I suggested that this is a factor that can not only impart trade political actors with legitimacy, but also performs a gate-keeping function by delegitimizing those who refuse to use the language. This hypothesis lends itself to further empirical scrutiny in order to verify whether it holds outside the trade political communities that Del Felice, Hannah, and I have studied.

In addition, I cited anthropological and feminist scholarship working on other areas of global governance expertise which found that speaking expert language affects the individual's sense of identity, rationality and appropriate political action. This observation remains untested in the realm of trade policy. Such research would nonetheless provide important insights to strive for more detailed examinations of the knowledge/language nexus in trade policy.

I further claimed that global trade expert language posits states and commodities as the key subjects of global trade. As a result, human and environmental prerogatives not only occur as second-order or unprofessional concerns, but the role of agency in global trade relations is also obscured. While I have built this contention on my reading of the *Dictionary of Trade Policy Terms* as one authoritative source of global trade expert language, the finding merits verification across a broader range of sources, potentially including not only deliberately compiled reference works, but official documents from trade institutions, negotiating minutes, press releases on trade issues, and so forth. Such further findings might prove useful in the quest for theoretical frameworks to establish who benefits from global trade expert language.

Overall, my analysis raised an important dilemma: global trade expert language is the dominant vernacular through which political claims must be expressed in order to resonate with policymakers and experts in the field. At the same time, under global trade expert language in its current iteration, human realities are not what global trade is about. Instead, states and commodities prevail as the conceptual units on which our understandings of trade political reality rest. As the WTO director-general acknowledged in his above-cited remarks to the 2014 Public Forum, this limits our ability to provide the often-requested "thinking outside the box" for tackling contemporary global problems.

However, my chapter also reveals the need to differentiate two political questions in the search for new ideas. One broader political question is whether the mere existence of expert language is appropriate. For those who respond in the positive, the subsequent question is whether the current constitution of expert language is appropriate. In this regard, Massey provides room for cautious optimism when she affirms that language changes over time, and that "it can—through political work—be changed."[78] As Eagleton-Pierce shows in Chapter 7, marginalized trade political actors can bring challenges to the established language. Anecdotal evidence further suggests that counter-interpretations are already part and parcel of contestations among trade policymakers and experts.

As mentioned above, the "bicycle theory" is one of the most common and pervasive metaphors in global trade expert language. The *Dictionary* defines it as "the proposition that the multilateral trading system must keep moving forward through successive liberalizing rounds and agreements if it is to remain liberal. On this analogy, the system would fall over like a bicycle if long gaps between liberalizing moves were to permit protectionist sentiments and actions to become dominant."[79] In Chapter 1, Wilkinson critiques the bicycle theory as "creat[ing] an imperative around the perpetuation of a particular kind of liberalization—one that primarily benefits [the] core interests [underpinning the trade regime] while at the same time offering only limited prospects for those on the periphery—that has resulted in the conclusion of successive trade bargains that have been deeply asymmetrical." However, during my interview in May 2013, a South African trade official asked in relation to the argument that the Doha Round must progress in order for the global trading system to maintain relevance:

> Do you need to have this trade bicycle all the time? Ask a cyclist, do you need to have to be pedaling all the time? Sometimes you just stop, rest, check your bike, change the tires, you don't need to be pedaling the whole time. You wreck the bike and the cyclist, the members, is going to be exhausted. You can't perpetually just keep on cycling, you will fall over from exhaustion and the bike will be wrecked.[80]

The South African trade official's remarks, although informally made, indicate that global trade expert terminology is neither immune to interpretational challenges, nor immutable. In sum, there is reason for trade policymakers and experts, in Cohn's words, to "give careful attention to the language we choose to use—who it allows us to communicate with and what it allows us to think as well as say."[81]

Notes

1 WTO, *Glossary*, 2014, http://wto.org/english/thewto_e/glossary_e/glossary_e.htm.
2 Walter Goode, *Dictionary of Trade Policy Terms* (Cambridge and Geneva: Cambridge University Press and World Trade Organization, 2003).
3 Studies in the political economy of trade that engage questions of discourse include Celina Del Felice, "Power in Discursive Practices: The Case of the STOP EPAs Campaign," *European Journal of International Relations* 20, no. 1 (2014): 145–67; Matthew Eagleton-Pierce, *Symbolic Power in the World Trade Organization* (Oxford: Oxford University Press, 2012); Jane Ford, *Trading Cultures: A Social Theory of the WTO* (Basingstoke: Palgrave Macmillan, 2003); Erin Hannah, "NGOs and the European Union: Examining the Power of Epistemes in the EC's TRIPS and Access to Medicines Negotiations," *Journal of Civil Society* 7, no. 2 (2011): 179–206;

Rorden Wilkinson, "Language, Power and Multilateral Trade Negotiations," *Review of International Political Economy* 16, no. 4 (2009): 597–619; Rorden Wilkinson, "Of Butcheries and Bicycles: The WTO and the 'Death' of the Doha Development Agenda," *The Political Quarterly* 83, no. 2 (2012): 395–401; and Rorden Wilkinson, *What's Wrong with the WTO and How to Fix It* (Cambridge: Polity Press, 2014).

4 Wilkinson, "Language, Power and Multilateral Trade Negotiations"; Wilkinson, "Of Butcheries and Bicycles"; and Wilkinson, *What's Wrong with the WTO and How to Fix It.*

5 Eagleton-Pierce, *Symbolic Power in the World Trade Organization.*

6 Michael Barnett, "The UN Security Council, Indifference, and Genocide in Rwanda," *Cultural Anthropology* 12, no. 4 (1997): 555.

7 Carol Cohn, "Sex and Death in the Rational World of Defense Intellectuals," *Signs* 12, no. 4 (1987): 708.

8 In addition to my academic work in political economy and international law, I have gained work experience in the Directorate General for Trade of the European Commission, in the International Trade Centre and in an international consultancy company specializing in customs law.

9 Doreen Massey, "Vocabularies of the Economy," in *After Neoliberalism? The Kilburn Manifesto*, ed. Steward Hall, Doreen Massey and Michael Rustin (London: Soundings a Journal of Politics and Culture, 2013), 6–7.

10 Andreas Bieler and Adam Morton, "The Deficits of Discourse in IPE: Turning Base Metal into Gold?" *International Studies Quarterly* 52, no. 1 (2008): 103–128.

11 Del Felice, "Power in Discursive Practices," 145–167; Erin Hannah, *NGOs and Global Trade: Non-State Voices in EU Trade Policymaking* (London: Routledge, forthcoming); Silke Trommer, *Transformations in Trade Politics: Participatory Trade Politics in West Africa* (London: Routledge, 2014).

12 Director-General Roberto Azevêdo's statement to the Opening Session of the WTO Public Forum 2014, 1 October 2014, Geneva.

13 Trommer, *Transformations in Trade Politics.*

14 West African trade official cited in Trommer, *Transformations in Trade Politics*, 102.

15 Del Felice, "Power in Discursive Practices," 155.

16 Hannah, *NGOs and Global Trade.*

17 Barnett, "The UN Security Council, Indifference, and Genocide in Rwanda," 555.

18 Cohn, "Sex and Death in the Rational World of Defense Intellectuals," 703.

19 General Agreement on Trade in Services.

20 Trade-Related Aspects of Investment Measures.

21 Rules of Origin.

22 Subsidies and Countervailing Measures.

23 Sanitary and Phytosanitary Measures.

24 Technical Barriers to Trade.

25 Dispute Settlement Understanding.

26 Free trade agreements.

27 Regional trade agreements.

28 Preferential trade agreements.

29 Trans-Pacific Partnership.

30 Transatlantic Trade and Investment Partnership.
31 South African Customs Union.
32 South African Development Community.
33 North American Free Trade Agreement.
34 Central America Free Trade Agreement.
35 European Free Trade Association.
36 Most favored nation.
37 Special and differential treatment.
38 Generalized System of Preferences.
39 Non-tariff barriers.
40 Non-agricultural market access.
41 WTO members: Argentina, Bolivia, Brazil, Chile, China, Cuba, Ecuador, Egypt, Guatemala, India, Indonesia, Mexico, Nigeria, Pakistan, Paraguay, Peru, Philippines, South Africa, Tanzania, Thailand, Uruguay, Venezuela and Zimbabwe. Taken from WTO, *Groups in the Negotiations*, www.wto.org/english/tratop_e/dda_e/negotiating_groups_e.htm.
42 WTO members: Antigua and Barbuda, Barbados, Belize, Benin, Bolivia, Botswana, Côte d'Ivoire, China, Congo, Cuba, Dominica, Dominican Republic, El Salvador, Grenada, Guatemala, Guyana, Haiti, Honduras, India, Indonesia, Jamaica, Kenya, Korea, Republic of, Madagascar, Mauritius, Mongolia, Mozambique, Nicaragua, Nigeria, Pakistan, Panama, Peru, Philippines, Saint Kitts and Nevis, Saint Lucia, Saint Vincent and the Grenadines, Senegal, Sri Lanka, Suriname, Tanzania, Trinidad and Tobago, Turkey, Uganda, Venezuela, Zambia and Zimbabwe. Taken from WTO, *Groups in the Negotiations.*
43 WTO members: Angola, Antigua and Barbuda, Bangladesh, Barbados, Belize, Benin, Botswana, Burkina Faso, Burundi, Côte d'Ivoire, Cambodia, Cameroon, Cape Verde, Central African Republic, Chad, Congo, Cuba, Democratic Republic of the Congo, Djibouti, Dominica, Dominican Republic, Egypt, Fiji, Gabon, Gambia, Ghana, Grenada, Guinea, Guinea-Bissau, Guyana, Haiti, Jamaica, Kenya, Lao People's Democratic Republic, Lesotho, Madagascar, Malawi, Maldives, Mali, Mauritania, Mauritius, Morocco, Mozambique, Myanmar, Namibia, Nepal, Niger, Nigeria, Papua New Guinea, Rwanda, Saint Kitts and Nevis, Saint Lucia, Saint Vincent and the Grenadines, Samoa, Senegal, Sierra Leone, Solomon Islands, South Africa, Suriname, Swaziland, Tanzania, Togo, Trinidad and Tobago, Tunisia, Uganda, Vanuatu, Zambia and Zimbabwe; WTO observers: Afghanistan, Bahamas, Bhutan, Comoros, Equatorial Guinea, Ethiopia, Liberia, Sao Tomé and Principe, Seychelles, Sudan, Yemen; not WTO members or observers: Cook Islands, Eritrea, Kiribati, Marshall Islands, Federated States of Micronesia, Nauru, Niue, Palau, Somalia, South Sudan, Timor-Leste and Tuvalu. Taken from WTO, *Groups in the Negotiations.*
44 WTO members: Argentina, Brazil, Egypt, India, Indonesia, Namibia, Philippines, South Africa, Tunisia and Venezuela. Taken from WTO, *Groups in the Negotiations.*
45 WTO members: Benin, Burkina Faso, Chad and Mali. Taken from WTO, *Groups in the Negotiations.*
46 WTO members: Argentina, Australia, Bolivia, Brazil, Canada, Chile, Colombia, Costa Rica, Guatemala, Indonesia, Malaysia, New Zealand,

Pakistan, Paraguay, Peru, Philippines, South Africa, Thailand and Uruguay. Taken from WTO, *Groups in the Negotiations.*

47 Canada, the EU, Japan and the United States.

48 EBA stands for Everything But Arms and is the EU's preferential scheme for the group of least developed countries. It provides duty-free, quota-free access to the EU market in all sectors except arms and armament, but initially excluded bananas, sugar and rice for a phase-in period of five to eight years.

49 UNCTAD is the United Nations Conference on Trade and Development, set up in 1964.

50 "Methods used by customs authorities to allocate a value to imported goods for the purpose of striking the correct import duty." Taken from Goode, *Dictionary of Trade Policy Terms*, 114.

51 "The need to obtain a permit for importing a product." Taken from Goode, *Dictionary of Trade Policy Terms*, 222.

52 "Goods passing through at least one other country between manufacture and reaching their final destination." Taken from Goode, *Dictionary of Trade Policy Terms*, 446.

53 "Supports for agriculture considered to distort trade and therefore subject to reduction commitments." Taken from Goode, *Dictionary of Trade Policy Terms*, 22.

54 "The existence of a causal link between increased imports and serious injury or the threat of serious injury to domestic industry producing like or directly competitive products which can be used to impose safeguards." Taken from Goode, *Dictionary of Trade Policy Terms*, 73.

55 "Any type of business or professional establishment within the territory of a member of the GATS for the purpose of supplying a service." Taken from Goode, *Dictionary of Trade Policy Terms*, 83.

56 "The import outside of the manufacturer's or distributor's authorized channel of a product with an intellectual property content from another country where the product has been lawfully placed on the market by the owner of the intellectual property right, or with the owner's consent." Taken from Goode, *Dictionary of Trade Policy Terms*, 327.

57 "Action taken by a country to restrain imports from a country that has increased a tariff or imposed other measures adversely affecting its exports." Taken from Goode, *Dictionary of Trade Policy Terms*, 364.

58 "Members of the WTO may apply food safety, animal health and plant health regulations to their international trade, but they must not use them to discriminate arbitrarily or unjustifiably between members in similar conditions. The WTO Agreement on Sanitary and Phytosanitary Measures sets out rules for achieving this. It encourages members to harmonize measures and to base them on international standards, guidelines and recommendations where these are available. If members wish to maintain higher standards, they must carry out risk assessments. A risk assessment can be an evaluation of the likelihood of the introduction or spread of a pest or disease in the light of the sanitary and phytosanitary measures applied. It can also be an evaluation of the potential for adverse effects on human or animal health arising from the presence of additives, contaminants, toxins or disease-causing organisms in food, beverages or feedstuffs. Risk assessment must take into account available scientific evidence,

relevant processes and production methods, relevant inspection, sampling and testing methods, prevalence of specific diseases or pests, existence of pest- or disease-free areas, relevant ecological and environmental conditions, and quarantine or other treatment. An assessment of the economic factors involved is also required with the objective of minimizing negative trade effects if measures are taken." Taken from Goode, *Dictionary of Trade Policy Terms*, 367.

59 Comparative advantage is usually attributed to David Ricardo. It proposes "that a country is more likely to export goods that it can produce relatively efficiently." See full entry in Goode, *Dictionary of Trade Policy Terms*, 79.

60 Factor endowment is a theoretical concept associated with factor proportion theory, attributed to Eli Heckscher and Bertil Ohlin. The Heckscher-Ohlin theorem "states that countries will export those goods whose production is relatively intensive in the factors with which they are well endowed." See full entry in Goode, *Dictionary of Trade Policy Terms*, 177.

61 Trade diversion is an analytical tool for the assessment of the impact of free trade areas and customs unions. It is based on Jacob Viner's theoretical proposition that "a share of the increased trade experienced by participants [to the free trade area or customs union] is merely due to a redirection of their trade, and not increased trade due to the arrangement." See full entry in Goode, *Dictionary of Trade Policy Terms*, 435.

62 Benjamin Cohen, "The Political Economy of International Trade," *International Organization* 44, no. 2 (1990): 261–81; Paul Krugman, *Ricardo's Difficult Idea*, 1998, http://web.mit.edu/krugman/www/ricardo.htm.

63 Barnett, "The UN Security Council, Indifference, and Genocide in Rwanda," 557.

64 Cohn, "Sex and Death in the Rational World of Defense Intellectuals," 704.

65 Cohn, "Sex and Death in the Rational World of Defense Intellectuals," 704.

66 Barnett, "The UN Security Council, Indifference, and Genocide in Rwanda," 557.

67 Cohn, "Sex and Death in the Rational World of Defense Intellectuals," 711.

68 For an account, see Pedro Roffe, Geoff Tansey and David Vivas-Eugui, *Negotiating Health: Intellectual Property and Access to Medicines* (London: Earthscan, 2006); and Benjamin Coriat, Fabienne Orsi and Cristina d'Almeida, "TRIPS and the International Public Health Controversies: Issues and Challenges," *Industrial and Corporate Change* 15, no. 6 (2006): 1033–62.

69 Office of the United Nations High Commissioner for Human Rights and World Health Organization, *The Right to Health*, Fact Sheet 31 (Geneva: United Nations, 2008).

70 WHO, *The Right to Health* (Geneva: WHO, 2014), www.who.int/mediacentre/factsheets/fs323/en/.

71 WTO, *Declaration on the TRIPS Agreement and Public Health* (2001), www.wto.org/english/thewto_e/minist_e/min01_e/mindecl_trips_e.htm.

72 Goode, *Dictionary of Trade Policy Terms*, 2.

73 Cohn, "Sex and Death in the Rational World of Defense Intellectuals," 711–2.

74 Stuart Hall, "The Great Moving Nowhere Show," *Marxism Today* (November/December 1998): 9–14.

75 Goode, *Dictionary of Trade Policy Terms*, 339.
76 Goode, *Dictionary of Trade Policy Terms*, 339.
77 I would like to thank Tim Rhys for his helpful clarifications of geological concepts.
78 Massey, "Vocabularies of the Economy," 3.
79 Goode, *Dictionary of Trade Policy Terms*, 55–6.
80 Personal interview with Brendan Vickers, Department for Trade and Industry, Pretoria, South Africa, 30 May 2013.
81 Cohn, "Sex and Death in the Rational World of Defense Intellectuals," 690.

Part II

The substance of expert knowledge

The power of law and econometrics in knowledge production

4 Expertise through experience

Inequality and legitimacy in the juridification of international trade disputing[1]

Joseph Conti

- **Legal capacity for disputing**
- **Legitimacy and legal capacity**
- **In-house expertise**
- **Private legal services**
- **Legal assistance**
- **How practical expertise matters for disputing**
- **Conclusion**

Between 1986 and 1994, the Uruguay Round of negotiations between members of the General Agreement on Tariffs and Trade (GATT) produced the agreement establishing the World Trade Organization (WTO). The partial juridification of dispute settlement, which extended the formal right to all member countries to have trade grievances reviewed by impartial panels, has been described as historically unprecedented.[2] GATT members anticipated that the juridification of disputing would enhance the credibility and stability of the multilateral system.[3] This was based on the normative expectation, consistent with the legitimacy claims of law in general, that the trade rules would apply universally and impartially to all WTO members. This could only be fully realized, however, if member countries acquired the necessary expertise for effective disputing. Indeed, the greater legalism of disputing, and increased complexity of trade rules in the WTO agreements, have generated an imperative for member countries to make deep investments in legal capacity as a condition for effective use of the WTO dispute system. How expertise relevant to disputing is produced, mobilized and maintained over time thus appears critical to realizing the normative expectations about the legitimacy claims of the WTO derived from its juridification. Some feared that the persistence of inequalities in legal capacity may lead to "long term structural imbalances,"[4] with low-capacity countries disadvantaged in disputing.

Yet, little attention has been paid to actual perceptions of legitimacy held by practitioners as an *empirical*, rather than normative, problem related to the processes of disputing.

This chapter provides a qualitative account of how the acquisition and maintenance of expertise related to WTO disputing affects perceptions of the legitimacy of the WTO among trade practitioners. Practitioners constitute a primary audience and "legitimacy community"[5] for the WTO dispute system. They are "on the front line" in assessing the validity of the WTO's juridical procedures and play a central role in translating those outcomes, including their appropriateness, to politicians and other interests. This study reveals that practitioners view the system as legitimate due to the *possibilities* it creates for the acquisition of practical experience and expertise, and thus the potential for the realization of equality before the law. This is the case even while inequalities are simultaneously exacerbated due to escalating demands for investments in legal capacity and difficulties building and maintaining it over time.

This chapter proceeds by first providing an overview of scholarship about WTO legal capacity and its relationship to the credibility of the WTO system. The second section delves deeper into legal authority and the perceptual bases of legitimacy claims. The third section examines practitioner accounts of the production of expertise and the central role of in-house experts in using the system. Then alternative modes of mobilizing expertise, including the hiring of counsel and utilization of the Advisory Centre on WTO Law (ACWL) are detailed along with their implications for countries lacking significant legal capacity. Despite shortcomings, these modes of expertise are critical to the perceived legitimacy of the WTO, as are examples of the successful deployment of expertise by developing countries, as described in the final section. The ability to mobilize the disputing system effectively, however, may be frustrated not only by the challenges associated with the acquisition of relevant expertise, but also by the role of market power in the implementation phase of disputing, indicating the structural limits of investments in legal capacity for producing equality before the law.

Legal capacity for disputing

Dispute participation is unequally distributed across member countries. As of the beginning of 2013, 66 of 159 WTO member nations had ever participated in a dispute and of these the United States and Europe are the most frequent, participating in about 42 percent of disputes.[6] In contrast, of 454 total disputes, low-income countries were complainants in 28 and respondents in 24.[7] Seeking to explain differences in participation levels, another study constructed a probabilistic model of dispute initiation, built in part on the well-established empirical correlation between economic size and trade volume.[8] This demonstrated that trade volume is highly correlated with diversity of trade partners and both trade volume and diversity are predictive of higher rates of WTO dispute initiation. However, the model also underestimated the number of disputes initiated by the United States, Canada, and Europe, and overestimated the participation of Japan and most other WTO members, including developing countries. Explaining this discrepancy suggests attention to how legal capacity influences patterns of disputing.

Legal capacity is more than a team of lawyers but also includes a bureaucratic apparatus for determining governmental obligations, engaging in disputes, and managing legal, political and financial relationships with the private sector.[9] Where early attempts to model legal capacity on WTO disputing relied on unsatisfactory proxies, such as per capita gross domestic product or counts of Geneva-based trade delegation staff, Busch et al. developed a legal capacity index derived from a survey of WTO trade delegations that is predictive of WTO complaints about anti-dumping investigations (a sub-set of WTO disputes).[10] Their measure includes assessments of personnel turnover, specialized governmental dispute settlement agencies, private sources of financial support for disputing and the representation of delegations at regular WTO meetings.

Others have highlighted the effects of participation in disputing on subsequent participation. Direct participation has its largest effects early in the disputing process, with prior experience in a dispute predictive of subsequent dispute initiation.[11] At advanced stages, differences in legal capacity appear to diminish in significance.[12] Prior experience also shapes the strategies of disputants in deciding to escalate a dispute from the initial consultation phase to adjudication by a panel of trade experts. When the respondent to a dispute is more experienced than the complainant, the dispute is more likely to be litigated before a WTO Panel than when the complainant is more experienced, where the dispute is more likely to be resolved without adjudication.[13] Disputing experience enhances abilities to identify trade grievances, acquire evidence, formulate strong legal reasoning, meet filing deadlines, and endure the duration and expense of disputing while maximizing those costs for opponents. Repeated participation creates advantages vis-à-vis infrequent participants using the disputing process.

Research on the facets of legal capacity raises the question of the specific mechanisms through which countries develop legal capacity and how it might change over time. I address that question by showing how legal capacity is based in the expertise of individuals, which is acquired through direct experience in WTO disputing. The apparatus of legal capacity mobilizes human experience, skills, and knowledge in the form of expertise over time.

Legitimacy and legal capacity

Legitimacy is a subjective evaluation of the appropriateness of a social order, involving a belief that certain people, rules or institutions ought to be obeyed. Recourse to law asserts a distinct claim to legitimacy rooted in values realized by rationalized systems of rules that create expectations about who shall legitimately hold authority and how that authority should be exercised. By legalizing the disputing process of the WTO and making commitments that were difficult to reverse, member states sought to enhance the legitimacy of decision making about trade while limiting the influence of protectionist forces, particularly in powerful countries like the United States.[14]

The legitimacy claims of law—that it is impartial, universally applied, and governs relevant social circumstance—also require the development of experts and expertise. Specialized knowledge distinguishes between qualified legal actors and unqualified laymen, shaping the professional monopoly of lawyers and its distinctive legitimacy claims.[15] The distinctiveness of expert legal knowledge creates obstacles for those seeking qualification as a legal actor, thus preventing the devaluation of legal work, but it also creates obstacles for those needing to mobilize the law.

How expertise is acquired, maintained, and deployed affects whether the practice of law enhances or undermines legitimacy claims embedded in the recourse to law. If the practices engaged in the name of law are perceived by relevant legitimacy communities as occurring within the parameters of law's key values of equality and impartiality, then they are likely to be perceived as appropriate. However, expertise can also operate as a site for the production of inequality, and risk the delegitimization of law, to the degree to which expertise permits some parties to dominate legal processes over time. If expertise is too unequally distributed, the legitimacy of law is likely to suffer because it will be perceived as contradicting law's core values.

This risk of de-legitimation is relevant for considering the implications of developing countries' abilities to mobilize the WTO dispute system effectively. Alter noted: "International politics is rarely fair. But the reforms of the dispute settlement process created an expectation that power would be equalized by having disputes resolved by law."[16] It might be expected, given inter-state inequality, that the WTO would be perceived by those working in the WTO legal system as illegitimate due to how those lacking legal capacity are limited in their ability to participate, and the relatively greater expense and difficulty when they do. However, when treated as an empirical question, the legitimacy perceptions of practitioners work in subtle but distinctively different ways from what the normative expectation would predict. For practitioners, the legitimacy of the WTO is linked, not to the persistence of unequal capacities to mobilize WTO law, but to the possibilities of gaining, maintaining and deploying expertise, and the potential juridification creates for countries with low levels of legal capacity to gain experience.

In-house expertise

In the analysis that follows, I rely on interviews with well-placed WTO practitioners, WTO dispute documents, news reports and reports issued by the WTO, international organizations, and member country governments. I conducted 30 semi-structured interviews with practitioners from Argentina, Brazil, Canada, Costa Rica, the European Communities, Mexico, and the United States. Interviewees included senior legal counsel in trade delegations, ambassadors to the WTO as well as a former Appellate Body chair, WTO Secretariat staff in several divisions, and private attorneys.

A recurrent theme in the interviews is that experience matters for expertise. For example, this attorney in the Appellate Body Secretariat of the WTO said:

> because it's not simply about being smart. Like with any sort of judicial system, being smart is part of it, but part of it is knowing how it works. Knowing what type of questions to ask, knowing how to ask questions, knowing they don't like it when you give 'this' type of answer.[17]

"Knowing how it works" requires taking part in the action and learning the informal dimensions of the process, such as how to ask the right questions. Expertise is practical knowledge that includes diplomatic context and stakes. For instance, this Geneva-based private attorney remarked:

> the biggest mistake that young attorneys make coming [here] is thinking that the law says 'this' and 'this' is what is going to happen. No. There's a lot of nuance in the system … [That is] something you learn by just dealing with the delegations; something that you learn by seeing how the negotiations work. And there are vested interests throughout this whole system. If I change one practice in the US, people lose their jobs, and politicians lose their seats … The whole system has layers and layers and layers of sensitivity.[18]

Legal experience entails familiarity with process, political contexts and diplomatic sensitivities. This is beyond facility with legal requirements, which may also be complex. Interviewees noted the growing complexity of WTO rules and the disputes invoking them.[19] Uncertainties in the written law can also be a challenge, given the "constructive ambiguities" intentionally embedded in the treaty language to facilitate compromises among negotiators.[20] Confronting such ambiguities requires not only knowledge of the written law but also knowledge of the history and intent of the agreements if a practitioner is to develop reasonable expectations about how disputing will transpire.

It takes time working directly in Geneva, taking part in actual disputes to acquire this form of practical knowledge. For countries that do not participate regularly, it can be difficult to manage a dispute effectively. For instance, there are differences in the abilities of the United States compared with many poorer states, derived from repeated engagement with the processes of disputing:

> The United States is the most experienced party in the dispute settlement system … They've seen how it works a hundred times. They have a better feel for the system … [When] Barbados wants to bring a case against the US, even if they hire an outside law firm to do the work for them, they've never been in a panel hearing. They don't know how to play the game.[21]

Familiarity with disputing is derived from direct, practical experience taking part in trade disputes which has taught members how to "play the game." This confirms the importance of serial participation for the acquisition and maintenance of expertise over time and the advantages that accrue to repeat players. Critically, this informant argues that even the ability to hire legal representation does not fully compensate for a lack of in-house expertise, as some level of expertise is required to identify a grievance and to manage legal representatives throughout the process.

Differences in expertise manifest in Panel and Appellate Body hearings and have implications for the abilities of member countries to manage their disputes. For instance, an American counsel asserted that sometimes trade delegations from developing countries present arguments that are weak or not well developed:

> Where you see that more is some of the Third World-ish countries and even the Second World-ish countries. Sometimes they don't have people that are sophisticated, or sometimes their arguments are a little too squishy, kind of like, "that's not fair," more than, "that's not the obligation." You might see [panelists] helping them along, to stay in the game.[22]

This informant noted how expertise is unequally distributed across member nations with the locus of inequality in the personnel appearing before the Panel and the character of their argumentation. In practice, however, WTO law mixes with diplomacy, as when panelists help "Third World-ish" countries to "stay in the game." Such assistance from panelists is rooted in diplomatic norms of international trade and less in the formal rules. Again noting the unequal distribution of expertise between member countries, the same official contrasted the sometimes, "squishy" presentation of arguments by some poorer countries with the United States as a litigant:

> I'm the United States for God's sake. I'm rarely going to be in a circumstance where I've got nothing or I have very little.[23]

This informant, and other interviewees, asserted that the United States is always prepared with the staff, resources, organization and the expertise to handle any sort of dispute.[24] A senior counsel from the European Commission (EC) affirmed the importance of sophisticated personnel and described the implications of personnel changes for different countries:

> The key players have continuity … because people don't all move at the same time … I mean, you have transitions, you have people prepared … So for the big players it's not a real challenge. It may be that one guy was really effective at networking is replaced by someone who is more on the lawyer side and … less on the cocktail side and therefore gets less information in the next year—in the first year. At the end of the day, that does not make a big difference for the key players because [we have] full ammunition back home.[25]

Major players ensure continuity by fostering staff sizes large enough that rotations can occur without undermining the overall operation, by taking steps to prepare for transitions, and by maintaining full stocks of "ammunition" in the form of experienced practitioners in the home country. The respondent also noted the importance of the "cocktail side" of WTO expertise, reaffirming that in the context of the WTO expertise is more than knowledge of the written law, but includes the diplomatic work of building and maintaining social and professional networks useful for gathering information and managing disputes. However, for smaller trade delegations, routine personnel rotations may have serious implications:

> For smaller delegations, that may make a difference. I've seen that with certain developing countries where a country was quite well represented in Geneva and suddenly [they] change and [where] the person in charge is supposed to do not only dispute settlement but [intellectual property rights], rules and so on, but this guy … is more interested by [intellectual property rights] and rules and therefore misses completely the dispute settlement meetings.[26]

Smaller delegations risk losing accumulated expertise when rotating their personnel. Legal capacity, as a bureaucratic apparatus, must contain redundancies in experts to avoid losing expertise over time. This also suggests the difficulties of building legal capacity, particularly when such efforts can be readily undermined by personnel changes.

Practical experience is important and highly valued by practitioners for the specialized knowledge that it generates, which is rooted in the quasi-juridical character of WTO law, the strong role of diplomatic norms in disputing, and informal professional networks, in addition to facility with complicated rules. Some level of in-house expertise is necessary even if a trade delegation contracts with private legal services. Practitioners revealed that individuals are the repositories of experiential learning. In order to maintain acquired expertise over time, institutional resources and organizational capacity must be established that ensure multiple redundancies in practitioners who have direct experience with WTO disputing. The experiential source of expertise indicates the importance of serial participation for acquiring and maintaining it over time. Practitioners emphasized that those who participate are able to learn from the process and enhance their capabilities; indeed, participation is the only way to do so.

Private legal services

Prior to the WTO, private lawyers were, in practice, excluded from routine participation in GATT disputes. A series of WTO rulings[27] in the late 1990s, however, eliminated this informal prohibition on private attorneys so long as they were accredited to a member nation's trade delegation. In explaining its decision to permit private attorneys in the *EC—Bananas III* dispute, the Appellate Body noted the absence of formal prohibitions on private lawyers in the treaty texts as well as how access to such legal representation would facilitate the participation of member countries, particularly developing countries.[28] Thus concern for equal access to law encouraged a market in legal services for trade delegations.

As with in-house experts, most private attorneys derived their expertise from direct experience working in trade delegations prior to entering private practice. As this private attorney described, those lacking such work experience are initially disadvantaged:

> A lot of people that work with trade law have worked with governments in some capacity. It is the only way you get inside the WTO or the GATT and see what's happening inside, so it's a tremendous advantage. There are a lot of people here who don't have that experience and it's really a problem for them.[29]

The availability of for-hire legal representation with direct experience with WTO disputing provides opportunities for countries without extensive legal capacity to engage in the disputing process. To the degree that private legal services can compensate for in-house expertise, they appear as a countervailing tendency against the advantages accrued by frequent participants with institutional investments in legal capacity. The evidence, however, suggests that practitioners do not view private representation as fully compensating for a lack of in-house expertise, as explained by this private attorney:

> If you have effective legal representation and you are a developing country you are going to be able to pursue your interests more effectively. But for developing countries, what I always say, is that what you want to do is develop your own people in-house as well because the mistake is to look at WTO just as dispute settlement. It is a negotiating machine as well ... But, yes, private attorneys are a leveler. It's not the best solution for developing countries but it is an interim step until they have the resources and the experience to have their own lawyers in-house, which I think is ideal.

> Because the learning curve is high … And we see that for developing country members, to acquire this knowledge takes time. And it's not something that happens in a year. [And then] there's the whole area … of the diplomatic sensitivity that you need as well.[30]

Private legal representation provides the expertise necessary for effective disputing. However, governments face the imperative of remaining in control of their international relations, including the processes of disputing. The diplomatic concerns in disputing often exceed the mandate of private attorneys hired for a specific dispute, even though those lawyers are sensitized to those concerns. It takes time to develop in-house expertise, too. Despite the limitations, private counsels are perceived as enabling participation by low-capacity countries, creating potential for heightened engagement with the system.

Private legal services are expensive, even for many governments. For instance, in Antigua and Barbuda's dispute against the United States over Internet gambling[31] the legal fees for private attorneys were estimated at over US$1 million[32] and paid for by the Antiguan and British gambling industries.[33] According to interviewees, the high cost of legal representation far exceeded what the United States paid to defend itself with its in-house teams of lawyers.[34]

Relatively few firms offer legal services for WTO disputes and most of these firms are located in the United States or Europe. For instance, on the 2006 list of "who's who" in the broad category of international economic law, only 39 of 147 prominent attorneys were located outside Europe or the United States, and only 19 were located in the developing world.[35] An official from Argentina noted: "In Argentina there are not many attorneys in the private sector that really know about the WTO."[36] Another attorney described the dilemma faced by a developing country when trying to hire a private law firm for WTO work:

> There are very few trade law litigation lawyers that exist in the world. A lot of them are concentrated in Washington, DC, or New York, or Brussels, some may be in London … In the developing world there's very few lawyers … So it's very difficult to find somebody from your own national capital—if you are a developing country—who knows the ins and outs of WTO dispute litigation. Second, and if you are lucky enough to have the resources then it might not be that difficult to find a law firm … Then again, as a developing country you would have to always think: if they're a US law firm, and if the US is your opponent in your case, then might that necessarily have some sort of indirect conflict of interest?[37]

The domination of global legal markets for trade disputes by large firms located primarily in Europe or the United States diminishes their appeal for developing countries.

Private legal services are employed in a variety of different ways, due to their expense, availability of in-house expertise, and how the government would like to present itself.[38] For instance, some officials reported that their delegation maintains relationships with private attorneys so they can solicit advice when needed.[39] Private lawyers described playing a number of different roles: they may be accredited to a trade delegation and participate directly before panels and the Appellate Body, or they may be limited to providing supporting services, such as the preparation of documents or the provision of legal advice.[40] It may be desirable to have attorneys present at certain points in a dispute, while at other times, particularly when diplomatic concerns are paramount, governments may opt to represent themselves. Some interviewees reported that, at times, panelists might be more lenient on delegations relying on their own resources; at other times, standards for procedure may be elevated when attorneys are present.[41] That situation, however, may be reversed at the Appellate Body where time pressures are greater, juridical procedure more institutionalized, and there is less deference to parties that are not prepared or not well versed in the relevant legal questions.[42]

In sum, the market for private legal representation for WTO disputes enhances the abilities of countries lacking their own stock of experienced practitioners to manage disputes effectively. The ability of private attorneys to provide such services is usually based in their own direct experience in WTO affairs, reaffirming that individuals are the primary repositories of experiential learning. However, private expertise comes at a cost, which is prohibitive for governments and is usually dependent upon substantial private sector organization and financial support.[43] Moreover, practitioners reported that the need for in-house expertise was, in part, due to the diplomatic features of disputing and the imperative that governments maintain control over their foreign relations.

Whether private representation contributes to the building of legal capacity likely depends on how the relationship between the trade delegation and the private attorneys is structured. Regular contact with private experts, such as in the provision of legal advice, could be expected to enhance a delegation's understanding of WTO law and disputing processes. If hiring private legal services facilitates an initial foray into disputing, the likelihood of subsequent participation increases.[44] As such, recourse to private counsel can be seen, as interviewees noted, as an effective "interim" step towards amassing in-house expertise, and the market for private attorneys is perceived as enhancing the legitimacy of the system.

Legal assistance

Some countries lacking legal capacity can seek free or cut-rate legal advice and representation. Some attorneys provide sliding scale or pro bono legal services to developing countries as part of their perceived professional duties as lawyers.[45] Such services are not well documented and it is difficult to assess the extent of their use. The WTO, and some nongovernmental organizations, such as the Agency for International Trade Information and Cooperation and the South Centre, facilitate technical training for developing country personnel or programs intended to transfer skills and knowledge to developing countries.

The ACWL, an intergovernmental treaty organization founded in July 2001, operating in Geneva with nine staff attorneys, provides regular training courses and offers internships for lawyer trainees to work in the ACWL office. The main goal of the ACWL, however, is to address unmet legal needs of poor countries by providing subsidized legal services. It was launched with the aim of enhancing the credibility of the WTO by improving the abilities of all members to participate in it. In describing their mission, the ACWL website declares:

> To take full advantage of the opportunities offered by the WTO … a country must make a significant investment in knowledge … WTO Director-General Pascal Lamy has said that 'by ensuring that the legal benefits of the WTO are shared among all Members, the ACWL contributes to the effectiveness of the WTO legal system, in particular its dispute settlement procedures, and to the realisation of the WTO's development objectives.'[46]

The ACWL is widely respected and was frequently mentioned by interviewees, emphasizing its importance for developing countries. For instance, this Indian attorney reported:

> it's been the default law firm for us. It's available. It's in town. It's much cheaper—much cheaper—than a US law firm, and it has good lawyers, possibly [some] of the best in the world.[47]

The ACWL provides expertise on an ongoing basis. As described by this official, while India possesses a highly competent bureaucracy for WTO matters, like many other countries, it lacks domestic supply of lawyers knowledgeable about the many complexities of WTO law. Encouraging the development of this field of law within India is of major concern, but in the meantime, the Geneva delegation makes use of the ACWL and considers their services an asset to their legal efforts.

The ACWL is ideal for countries that are unable or unwilling to divert resources away from more critical areas of public action for the purposes of developing legal capacity or paying for lawyers.[48] A survey of delegations that had used the ACWL's services rated the quality of their services as superior to that of private firms, "because ACWL works on WTO issues all the time and has therefore built up a lot of expertise."[49] Most of its attorneys have worked as in-house experts for governments as well as in private practice. Its directors have acted as trade diplomats for members of the GATT/WTO, and its management board, while not directly involved in the provision of legal advice, comprises trade diplomats with extensive experience with the GATT/WTO. ACWL efforts to work with and educate representatives of trade delegations have increased the confidence of clients that "the system works and that small countries can also be successful in cases against large countries like the USA," and that they were able to be successful because of the ACWL's relatively low costs compared to private firms.[50] In a similar way, an official from Brazil, which is not a member of the ACWL, nonetheless observed that the ACWL assists countries lacking both legal capacity and the resources to fund private lawyers:

> It's an initiative very helpful for countries which don't have the resources to allocate to creat[ing] a specialized unit for trade dispute settlement matters, and which must allocate such resources to other more important and more urgent areas of public action. And the alternative is to have recourse to private lawyers [and] this depends on the availability of resource in the private sector.[51]

The ACWL works to enable countries lacking in-house expertise to understand the implications of WTO rules and navigate the WTO legal system. It does this both by direct legal representation and training, but also through familiarizing infrequent participants with how WTO law works in practice. As such, for practitioners from countries that use the ACWL as well as for those who do not, the ACWL enhances the legitimacy of the WTO. For instance, this former ambassador to the WTO asserted that:

> the WTO really wouldn't work very well if poorer countries couldn't make the rules work to their advantage when they were in

> the right ... And of course, there's the Advisory Centre on WTO Law ... That was an initiative borne out by a number of individuals in different governments, both developed and developing. [We] had to find a way of making the dispute settlement system work for the smaller and weaker and poorer countries as well as for the rich countries. And it's been pretty successful.[52]

In sum, the advantages of in-house expertise are derived from practical experience with the WTO legal system and its mix of law and diplomacy. Individuals acquire this expertise and then operate from within governments, international organizations, and law firms. Private legal services and legal assistance from the ACWL are alternative paths to mobilizing expertise for member states without in-house staff. While for-hire legal services are expensive, legal assistance through the ACWL is particularly helpful for relatively poor countries' abilities to raise their claims and gradually build up necessary expertise. The existence of these alternative routes for securing expertise is vital for perceptions of the system's legitimacy among practitioners. Practitioners have clearly linked the need for upgrading the expertise of low-capacity countries to the credibility of the system and perceived the system as legitimate because it offers mechanisms for acquiring expertise.

How practical expertise matters for disputing

The opportunities for developing countries created by the juridification of trade to contest the policies of more powerful trading partners bolsters the credibility of the system among practitioners. Actually doing so, however, requires overcoming the challenges of acquiring expertise. Even when successful in WTO litigation, many countries face significant hurdles in translating their legal victories into substantive compliance. Rich countries often retain the ability to limit their costs stemming from successful developing country litigation due to the difficulties associated with employing WTO compliance measures.

Challenges to the powerful require access to expertise

In 1995, Costa Rica initiated a dispute over safeguard duties imposed by the United States on imports of men's cotton underwear.[53] Both the review Panel and the Appellate Body ruled that the US measures were inconsistent with their WTO obligations. By the middle of 1997, the measures expired and the United States effectively complied, despite an extremely well-organized and -financed textile industry in the United States.

A Costa Rican official described the dispute system as "wonderful" and cited this case and others as evidence that the WTO legal system is fair, even favorable to smaller and poorer countries. He then contrasted this with the old system of disputing unfair trade practices of the United States—meeting with a low-level bureaucrat in a windowless room at the State Department. The WTO was clearly an improvement. He said:

> if the system works in favor of a small country of 4 million people and [does so in] front of the United States and in front of the EC, [then it] demonstrates that it is a matter of using the tools that are there.[54]

By utilizing the "tools" of disputing—WTO law and procedures for disputing—Costa Rica effectively challenged the United States. For practitioners, the ability to participate in WTO disputing enhances the legitimacy of the WTO.

Brazil's investments in legal capacity have enabled it to become a major player at the WTO,[55] successfully challenging the trading practices of the United States over cotton[56] and the EC over sugar.[57] Among practitioners, the possibility of disputing against Brazil is taken very seriously.[58] The Brazilian example demonstrates how a country can invest in participating, enabling its personnel to gain know-how through direct participation, as the basis upon which legal capacity may be institutionalized.

These investments by Brazil have not only enhanced its status within the WTO, but also the credibility of the WTO itself:

> [The cotton and sugar disputes] are very important for the WTO, not for Brazil, for the US, and the other countries involved, but for the WTO. They are very crucial and historical in the sense that they are a critical step towards the full integration of agriculture into the normal trade rules of the multilateral system.[59]

This official argued that these disputes called attention to the inequalities in global agriculture trade and moved the WTO system closer to addressing an important source of global inequality. The issue remains unresolved. Nonetheless, for practitioners, the ability of Brazil to mobilize the dispute system effectively enhances the legitimacy of the system, as it shows how juridification can foster equality before the law and result in greater influence of developing countries in the governance of the global trading system.

The limits of expertise in the face of market power

While evidence of the successes of Antigua, Costa Rica and Brazil demonstrates the possibility of developing countries effectively mobilizing the WTO legal system, it is less clear that legal victories lead to substantive compliance in specific instances. It did in the case of Costa Rica. It has not yet for either Antigua's or Brazil's disputes with the United States. Both Brazil and Antigua have received authorization to retaliate against the United States. As yet, neither has done so.

The Dispute Settlement Understanding, which governs the dispute process, provides that, failing a resolution of a dispute, the complaining party may seek authorization to "suspend concessions" granted through the WTO agreements by selectively raising tariffs or invoking other protectionist measures on imports from the responding country. The non-compliant party will suffer terms of trade that penalize its failure to remedy its trade practices.

Non-compliance is less of an option for poorer states that are more vulnerable not only to WTO mechanisms for inducing compliance, but also to extra-legal pressures.[60] An Argentine official described this dynamic:

> Developing countries don't have much option but to comply. Maybe we delayed a little bit, but in the end, we knew we had no option but to comply because the pressure of eventual retaliations on us is strong. But, the problem is with the compliance by big trade partners like the US and EC, and in that sense, we are a little bit disappointed, because—I do not dare to say that it's a total lack of compliance, but it's a concern—it's a concern.[61]

This interviewee described how major players have greater latitude in both threatening and implementing WTO-authorized retaliation. In only one instance has a developing country actually retaliated, even though several have been authorized to do so.[62] The economic leverage that is at the center of the compliance measures tends to work only when the complaining party has significant market leverage over the responding party and consequently places many developing countries at a significant disadvantage.[63] As a result, large trading countries are more likely to litigate with an expectation of full compliance while less affluent members, especially when disputing the trade policies of countries upon whose markets they are dependent for access, must weigh the value of something less, but which might still be quite important.[64]

The acquisition of expertise and the institutionalization of legal capacity cannot overcome the structural inequality of the compliance measures. This is recognized as a problem by some, such as this private attorney, who remarked: "the biggest problem is after you win a case. Then the system kind of grinds to a halt, because you have to go back if the country doesn't [comply]."[65] While these two factors have enabled some countries to manage the disputing process effectively, they are not sufficient to overcome differences in market power in the latest stages of the disputing process.

Conclusion

Expertise is central to legal capacity, which is required for effective use of the WTO dispute settlement system. Individuals acquire it through direct participation in disputing processes because the relevant know-how is more than knowledge of the formal law, but also entails familiarity with the diplomatic features of the disputing process. Acquiring expertise and building legal capacity enhances a country's ability to identify grievances and manage disputes. Countries may seek the aid of private counsel or legal assistance, yet neither of these modes of mobilizing expertise can ensure substantive compliance. The experiential basis of expertise means that serial participation is the primary route to building expertise. This creates an advantage for countries able to participate repeatedly. Combined with the increasing complexity of WTO law and processes for disputing, serial participation by high-capacity countries exacerbates the difficulties facing low-capacity countries attempting to acquire expertise.

The ability of poorer countries to use the system and to acquire expertise, even while disadvantaged or based on interim measures, provides a powerful rationalization for the WTO as it stands. Where legitimacy claims derived from juridification suggest that persistent inequalities in legal capacity would risk delegitimizing the system, practitioners instead emphasize how they learn over time. The legitimacy claims embedded in the juridification of the WTO—that its laws and procedures are universal and impartial—resonates with practitioners' sense of the possibilities, however difficult to realize over time, for producing and mobilizing expertise. The experiential basis of expertise, and the alternative modes of mobilizing it, thus serves to obscure the mitigating effects of market power and how serial participation by major players replicates inequalities in the practical ability to use the law. Law's claim to legitimacy does not actually require equality all of the time, but only in the breach, and participation in the system by low-capacity countries helps secure the legitimacy of the disputing system among practitioners.

From the vantage point of small and developing countries a rule-bound system of trade is arguably preferable to a global trading system organized around power politics, even if the juridification of trade creates new modalities of inequality. This raises the question of whether it is possible to better realize legitimacy claims derived from the juridification of trade and the expertise that it entails. The relationship between law and power is complex and not without contradiction. Minimally, however, it is clear that a more fully equitable international legal system requires broad access to the relevant expertise for mobilizing the law. This means that the global rule of law cannot be reduced to the rule of lawyers: the relevant legal expertise is unequally distributed and, more generally, the professional monopoly over legal work is premised on forms of social closure (i.e. complexity, experiential expertise) that create obstacles to equitable access to justice. If the goal of juridification is to realize not only the legitimacy of law, but also equality in its practical use (because this analysis demonstrates how legitimacy and equity may diverge), ad hoc means of supplying developing countries with the relevant expertise, such as private or pro bono legal services, will have to be supplanted with institutional reform. Setting aside big questions of whether increased liberalism and reduced policy space are in fact desirable for all countries, developing countries could be more effective in the existing trade regime through institutional reforms that shift the burden of legal capacity to the WTO and wealthier members of the WTO system.

Reforms might include empowering the WTO Secretariat to initiate disputes over systemic problems and grievances of least developed countries; WTO financial support for developing country legal training in home-country law schools, as well as Geneva-based internship programs; direct WTO support for the ACWL and other legal assistance organizations; and deeper institutionalization of the service commitments of private trade attorneys through a WTO bar.[66] Moreover, it is also necessary to increase the effectiveness of the WTO's compliance measures for countries with weak market power. A WTO compliance ombudsman to assist developing countries in determining the adequacy of compliance by trading partners to the decisions of the Appellate Body may also help. The significance of market power in securing compliance could be reduced by permitting cash transfers in lieu of punitive tariffs as the mechanisms of enforcement.[67] These suggestions are merely starting points for rethinking the relationship between legal expertise and the legitimacy of the WTO system, and the prospects of implementing them are daunting.

Questions about how law, and expert use of it, contributes to the legitimacy of international regimes are not restricted to the WTO. Increased reliance on law for claims to legitimacy, as indicated in the proliferation of international courts, generates demand for expertise and appears to foster the global expansion of the legal profession. These practices require ongoing study, as the particular configurations of law, legal practices, and practitioners make critical differences to the legitimacy of international economic governance.

Notes

1 This chapter is based on an earlier article, "Producing Legitimacy at the World Trade Organization: The Role of Expertise and Legal Capacity," *Socio-Economic Review* 8, no. 1 (2009): 131–55.
2 Kenneth W. Abbott, Robert O. Keohane, Andrew Moravcsik, Anne-Marie Slaughter and Duncan Snidal, "The Concept of Legalization," *International Organization* 54, no. 3 (2000): 401–19.
3 Judith L. Goldstein and Richard H. Steinberg, "Negotiate or Litigate-Effects of WTO Judicial Delegation on US Trade Politics," *Law & Contemporary Problems* 71, no. 1 (2008): 257–82.
4 Gregory Shaffer, "How to Make the WTO Dispute Settlement System Work for Developing Countries: Some Proactive Developing Country Strategies," in *Towards a Development-Supportive Dispute Settlement System in the WTO*, ed. Victor Mosoti (Geneva: International Centre for Trade and Sustainable Development, 2003), 15.
5 Julia Black, "Constructing and Contesting Legitimacy and Accountability in Polycentric Regulatory Regimes," *Regulation & Governance* 2, no. 2 (2008): 137–164.
6 Kara Leitner and Simon Lester, "WTO Dispute Settlement 1995–2012—A Statistical Analysis," *Journal of International Economic Law* 16, no. 1 (2013): 257–67.
7 Leitner and Lester, "WTO Dispute Settlement," 258.
8 Henrik Horn, Petros C. Mavroidis and Hakan Nordstrom, "Is the Use of the WTO Dispute Settlement System Biased?" Discussion Paper no. 2340 (London: Centre for Economic Policy Research, 1999).
9 Marc Busch, Eric Reinhardt and Gregory Shaffer, "Does Legal Capacity Matter? A Survey of WTO Members," *World Trade Review* 8, no. 4 (2009): 559–77.
10 Busch et al., "Does Legal Capacity Matter?" 559–77.
11 Christina Davis and Sarah Bermeo, "Who Files? Developing Country Participation in GATT/WTO Adjudication," *Journal of Politics* 71, no. 3 (2009): 1033–49.
12 Marc Busch and Eric Reinhardt, "Developing Countries and General Agreement on Tariffs and Trade/World Trade Organization Dispute Settlement," *Journal of World Trade* 37, no. 4 (2003): 719–35.

13 Joseph A. Conti, "Learning to Dispute: Repeat Participation, Expertise, and Reputation at the World Trade Organization," *Law & Social Inquiry* 35, no. 3 (2010): 625–62.
14 Goldstein and Steinberg, "Negotiate or Litigate-Effects of WTO Judicial Delegation on US Trade Politics," 257–82; Nitsan Chorev, *Remaking US Trade Policy: From Protectionism to Globalization* (Ithaca, NY: Cornell University Press, 2007); and Alec Stone Sweet, "Judicialization and the Construction of Governance," Faculty Research Series Paper 75 (New Haven, Conn.: Yale Law School, 1999), http://digitalcommons.law.yale.edu/fss_papers/75.
15 Pierre Bourdieu, "The Force of Law: Toward a Sociology of the Juridical Field," *Hastings Law Journal* 38, no. 5 (1986): 805–53.
16 Karen Alter, "Resolving or Exacerbating Disputes? The WTO's New Dispute Resolution System," *International Affairs* 79, no. 4 (2003): 788.
17 Interview with an attorney, WTO Appellate Body Secretariat, Geneva, 25 May 2004.
18 Interview with a private attorney, Geneva, 9 April 2006.
19 Interview with an Argentine official, Geneva, 19 April 2006; interview with a Costa Rican official, Geneva, 11 April 2006; and interview with an EC official, Brussels, 20 April 2006.
20 Joseph A. Conti, "The Good Case: Decisions to Litigate at the World Trade Organization," *Law & Society Review* 42, no. 1 (2008): 145–82.
21 Interview with an attorney, WTO Appellate Division, Geneva, 25 May 2004.
22 Interview with a US official, Washington, DC, 3 March 2005.
23 Interview with a US official, Washington, DC, 3 March 2005.
24 Interview with a Costa Rican official, Geneva, 11 April 2006; interview with a US official, Washington, DC, 4 March 2005.
25 Interview with an EC official, Brussels, 20 April 2006.
26 Interview with an EC official, Brussels, 20 April 2006.
27 WTO, *EC—Regime for the Importation, Sale and Distribution of Bananas (EC–Bananas IIII)*, WT/DS27, Panel report, circulated 22 May 1997; WTO, *Indonesia–Certain Measures Affecting the Automobile Industry (Indonesia-Autos)*, WT/DS54/15; WT/DS55/13; WT/DS59/13; WT/DS64/12, Panel report, circulated 2 July 1998; WTO, *Korea–Taxes on Alcoholic Beverages (Korea—Alcoholic Beverages)*, WT/DS75; and WT/DS84, Panel report, circulated 17 September 1998.
28 WTO, *EC—Bananas III*, WT/DS27/AB/R, paragraph 12.
29 Interview with a private attorney, Geneva, 9 April 2006.
30 Interview with a private attorney, Geneva, 9 April 2006.
31 WTO, *United States-Measures Affecting the Cross-Border Supply of Gambling and Betting Services (US—Gambling)*, WT/DS285, Panel report, circulated 10 November 2004.
32 Paul Blustein, "Against All Odds: Antigua Besting US in Internet Gambling Case at WTO," *The Washington Post*, 4 August 2006.
33 Bradley S. Klapper, "WTO Clears $21m in Sanctions Vs. US," *Associated Press*, 21 December 2007.
34 Interview with a Canadian official, Geneva, 3 April 2006.
35 *The International Who's Who of Trade & Customs Lawyers*, fifth edition, 2006, on file with author.

36 Interview with an Argentine official, Geneva, 11 April 2006.
37 Interview with an attorney, Geneva, 26 May 2004.
38 Interview with private attorneys, Washington, DC, 28 February 2005, and Geneva, 9 April 2006.
39 Interview with a Brazilian official, Geneva, 20 May 2005; interview with an Indian official, Geneva, 19 May 2005.
40 Interview with private attorneys, Washington, DC, 28 February 2005, and Geneva, 9 April 2006; and interview with a former ambassador to the WTO, Geneva, May 2005.
41 Interview with a private attorney, Washington, DC, 28 February 2005, and Brussels, 21 April 2006; and interview with a US official, Washington, DC, 3 March 2005.
42 Interview with a private attorney, Brussels, 21 April 2006.
43 Gregory Shaffer, *Defending Interests: Public-Private Partnerships in WTO Litigation* (Washington, DC: Brookings Institution Press, 2003).
44 Davis and Bermeo, "Who Files?" 1033–1049.
45 Interview with private attorneys, Geneva, 9 April 2006, and Washington, DC, 28 February 2005.
46 ACWL, "The ACWL's Mission," www.acwl.ch/e/about/about_us.html.
47 Interview with an Indian official, Geneva, 19 May 2005.
48 Interview with a Brazilian official, Geneva, 20 May 2005.
49 Nora Plaisier and Paul Wijmenga, *Evaluation of Trade-Related Technical Assistance, Three Geneva-Based Organisations: ACWL, AITC and QUNO*, Policy and Operations Evaluation Department (IOB) Working Document (The Netherlands: IOB, 2004): 23.
50 Plaisier and Wijmenga, *Evaluation of Trade-Related Technical Assistance*, 26.
51 Interview with a Brazilian official, Geneva, 20 May 2005.
52 Interview with a former ambassador to the WTO, Geneva, May 2005.
53 WTO, *United States—Restrictions on Imports of Cotton and Man-Made Fibre Underwear (US–Underwear)*, WT/DS24, Panel report, circulated 8 November 1996.
54 Interview with a Costa Rican official, Geneva, 11 April 2006.
55 Gregory Shaffer, Michelle Ratton Sanchez, Barbara Rosenberg and Hakan Nordstrom, "The Trials of Winning at the WTO: What Lies Behind Brazil's Success," *Cornell International Law Journal* 41, no. 2 (2008): 383–501.
56 WTO, *United States—Subsidies on Upland Cotton (US—Upland Cotton)*, WT/DS267, Panel report, circulated 8 September 2004.
57 WTO, *European Communities—Export Subsidies on Sugar (EC—Export Subsidies on Sugar)*, WT/DS266, Panel report, circulated 15 October 2004.
58 Interview with an Argentine official, Geneva, 19 April 2006.
59 Interview with a Brazilian official, Geneva, 20 May 2005.
60 Pilar Zejan and Frank L. Bartels, "Be Nice and Get Your Money: An Empirical Analysis of World Trade Organization Trade Disputes and Aid," *Journal of World Trade* 40, no. 6 (2006): 1021–47.
61 Interview with an Argentine official, Geneva, 19 April 2006.
62 William J. Davey, "Compliance Problems in WTO Dispute Settlement," *Cornell International Law Journal* 42, no. 1 (2009): 119–28.
63 Marco Bronckers and Naboth van den Broek, "Financial Compensation in the WTO: Improving the Remedies of WTO Dispute Settlement," *Journal of International Economic Law* 8, no. 1 (2005): 101–26.

64 Conti, "The Good Case," 145–82.
65 Interview with a private attorney, Washington, DC, 28 February 2005.
66 Joseph A. Conti, *Between Law and Diplomacy: The Social Contexts of Disputing at the World Trade Organization* (Stanford, Calif.: Stanford University Press, 2011).
67 Conti, *Between Law and Diplomacy.*

5 Numbers

The role of computable general equilibrium modeling in legitimizing trade policy

Clive George

- **Wrong numbers**
- **Quantifying the theory of comparative advantage**
- **Equilibrium in question**
- **Missing numbers**
- **Blinded by trivia**
- **Why negotiate?**
- **The bigger picture**
- **Conclusion**

No trade policy proposal is complete without some numbers. In launching negotiations on the proposed Transatlantic Trade and Investment Partnership (TTIP) between the European Union (EU) and the United States, Britain's Prime Minister David Cameron announced that it "could add as much as £100 billion to the EU economy, £80 billion to the US economy, and as much as £85 billion to the rest of the world."[1] For President Barack Obama the deal "would support hundreds of thousands of jobs on both sides of the ocean."[2] Numbers lend substance to qualitative arguments. Economists provide them. If their analysis says that a proposed policy will boost the economy by some definable number, this may be regarded as sufficient justification for the policy.

When numbers are used properly they provide valuable information for decision making, but they can be subject to manipulation and multiple interpretations. As Jerome Himmelstein observes, "they are easy to abstract from the messy processes through which human beings produce them, and once reified they take on the appearance of pure, objective, undeniable nuggets of fact."[3] This is especially so when the numbers are generated by a computer, widely revered for its supposed independence from human subjectivity.[4]

We are all heavily dependent on numbers in our everyday lives. How much does something cost? How much change should I get? What weight of flour do I need for baking this cake? What volume of water, how many eggs? In general, we trust the numbers we are given. When the pump says it has delivered 20 liters of gas (petrol) we believe it. When a prime minister tells us he will deliver £100 billion we tend to believe that too, subconsciously imagining a team of weights and measures inspectors checking his numbers as rigorously as they have checked the pump.

In the numerical sciences the equivalent of the weights and measures inspector is the whole scientific community. An individual physicist may not always be totally objective and honest in designing an experiment and reporting its results, but the profession as a whole can be trusted to exercise sufficient discipline, through peer review or otherwise, to maintain its own integrity. Our trust in the scientific system, and in the engineering profession that makes use of it, is such that all but a very few of us can get on an airplane without giving a second thought to whether the wings might fall off. Public trust in the economics profession is similar—or at least it was, until the wings of the global economy fell off in 2008.[5]

Although we all make use of numbers and tend to trust them, our understanding of them is often limited. Few people have any idea how an aeronautics engineer calculates the stresses in an airplane's wings as it flies through a thunderstorm. However, most of us are aware of the wind tunnels and test beds that are used to check the calculations, if necessary to destruction. Fewer are aware that no such thing exists for an economic calculation. The theoretical numbers that are used to support trade policy suffer from the same problem as many other branches of mainstream economics: they cannot be tested in the real world. By Karl Popper's philosophical reasoning, that makes much of mainstream economics an exercise in pure mathematics, not a science.[6]

Wrong numbers

Lack of understanding can easily lead to misinterpretation, whether or not a number truly represents reality. Joel Best tells the story of a paper submitted by one of his graduate students which opened with an eye-catching quote from a professional journal, claiming that "every year since 1950, the number of American children gunned down has doubled."[7] Suspecting that the student had made a mistake in copying the quote, Best checked the source, to find exactly that statement. Intrigued, he checked back to the document used by the author of the journal article. The wording was only slightly different, but crucially so: "the number of American children killed each year by guns has doubled since 1950." A factor of two between 1950 and 1995, the year the journal was published, is believable. The misquote is not. On the highly conservative assumption that the number of victims in 1950 was just one, we need only multiply two by two 45 times to discover that the number of American children killed by guns in 1995 would have been over 35 trillion.

Misinterpretation of the numbers provided by trade economists has yet to reach that scale, but it can be quite dramatic. In promoting the proposed EU–US deal to the European American Chamber of Commerce in New York, Europe's Trade Commissioner Karel de Gucht claimed that it would "deliver a growth boost to the European and American economies of roughly 0.5 percent."[8] If that were true it would be quite impressive, bearing in mind the difficulty both economies currently have in achieving any growth at all. However, in failing to understand the numbers provided by his economists, Commissioner De Gucht overstated his case by at least a factor of ten. The most optimistic of the scenarios examined in their computable general equilibrium (CGE) trade model projected a one-off increase in Europe's gross domestic product (GDP) of roughly 0.5 percent (David Cameron's £100 billion), accruing over a ten-year period.[9] This equates to a growth boost not of 0.5 percent, but of 0.05 percent, for ten years only. However, it was Commissioner De Gucht's number that was picked up by the BBC, which reported EU estimates that the proposed deal would "boost annual GDP growth by 0.5%."[10] Joel Best calls such numbers "mutant statistics"—distorted versions of the original figures which then get propagated.[11]

Even economists who are quite skeptical about the benefits of free trade have made the same mistake in interpreting their results. In an analysis of the impact on developing countries of the current World Trade Organization (WTO) negotiations, the authors described a single one-off increase in GDP of 0.10 percent as "a modest addition of 0.10 percent to GDP growth each year."[12] When the article was subsequently re-published as a chapter in a book the error was corrected.[13] However, the authors still argued that the gain was worth much more than a tenth of a percent because it would grow at compound interest to become ten times as much in ten years' time. If that were true, the same would also apply to the other 99.9 percent, leaving the impact still no more than a tenth of a percent.

This eagerness to present the results of CGE calculations in the most favorable possible light is readily seized by trade negotiators. When the current round of WTO negotiations were launched at Doha in 2001, the European Commission (EC) asked a group of us at the University of Manchester to undertake a series of independent studies of the proposals, known as Sustainability Impact Assessments.[14] In one of our many discussions with Europe's negotiators, it was argued that the benefit would be worth much more than the half percent projected by one of the models, since the extra would be received every year forever. That may be true, but it is still only half a percent.

Even the £100 billion quoted by Prime Minister Cameron for the EU-US proposal was potentially misleading. One hundred billion is a large number—so large that most people will be impressed by it. Any number bigger than 100,000 falls into that category. As Joel Best puts it, "a million, a billion, a trillion—what's the difference? They're all big numbers."[15] To understand such numbers they need to be put in context. £100 billion (or €120 billion) is a half of one hundredth of the size of the EU economy. A tenth of that, the projected annual increment to the economy of 0.05 percent, is a half of one thousandth of it. If Britain's prime minister had chosen to put his very big number in context, it would have seemed less big. Similarly misleading claims have been made about the importance of the hundreds of billions of dollars calculated to be available from the WTO negotiations.[16] The hundreds of billions shrink rapidly when expressed as a percentage of GDP, giving figures somewhere between 0.25 and 0.50 percent. This is analogous to a single pay rise of that size, phased over the ten years or more that it takes for the changes to have effect.[17]

The value of the proposed EU-US deal would have seemed even less big if the officials advising the commissioner and prime minister had been less selective in their choice of numbers. It is common for advocates to choose selectively which numbers they report,[18] while researchers or their sponsors generally select a small subset of data to include in their press releases.[19] For the EU-US trade deal the numbers quoted were for the most part optimistic of the scenarios used in the model. The least optimistic (and perhaps more realistic) scenario gave projections of one-fifth the size of those quoted, i.e. a boost to economic growth not of 0.5 percent, nor 0.05 percent, but 0.01 percent.

Quantifying the theory of comparative advantage

Some trade models can be extremely useful, particularly in alerting policymakers to the dangers inherent in their proposals. Partial equilibrium models serve this purpose, by providing an estimate of the changes in imports, exports and domestic production that would result from reducing import taxes (tariffs) in a particular economic sector. If imports are projected to rise and exports to fall, but only by a small proportion of total production, this may be deemed acceptable in return for a more advantageous deal in some other sector. However, if the model projects that the domestic industry would be all but wiped out, the trade negotiator will need to exercise more caution. CGE models can provide similar information for every economic sector in the entire global economy, albeit with less precision. That is not their prime purpose. Their advantage over other models is that they can provide numbers for the overall impact on the economy, such as those quoted by Mr Cameron and misquoted by Mr De Gucht.

Are they accurate numbers? They can never be tested, so we can never be sure. The best we can do is test the logic on which they are based and the validity of the data they use. The logic of a general equilibrium trade model is broadly similar to that of David Ricardo's theory of comparative advantage, developed in the early nineteenth century.[20] As far as it goes, Ricardo's logic is fairly sound, although it does not go very far. If one country (Portugal in his example) can produce two types of goods (wine and cloth) more cheaply than another (England), its investors will still benefit from trading in those goods. If Portugal produces wine more cheaply than it does cloth, it can make savings by shifting all of its production into wine, and exporting it to England in return for imports of cloth. Ricardo felt the need for numbers to support his argument, but could do no better than a hypothetical example. It was not until the 1980s that powerful low-cost computers made it possible to solve the general equilibrium equations through which his theory of comparative advantage could be quantified.

Ricardo's argument made no allowance for transport or other trade costs, and assumed no international movement of capital. Either of these, by his own admission, could negate the theory. Also, his analysis of the benefits of trade applied only to investors, whose profits would increase by the amount saved in labor costs. Employees would gain nothing, or even lose. In the same book, Ricardo presented his labor theory of value—subsequently seized upon by Marx—which argued that in the absence of other factors, a free market would reduce wages to subsistence level, irrespective of whether goods were traded internationally. Despite these limitations, Ricardo's theory is still widely regarded as the fundamental argument in favor of free trade. CGE models aim to overcome its problems, but have their own limitations.

In an audit of the EC's management of trade policy, the European Court of Auditors found that the Commission had not appropriately assessed all the economic effects.[21] It identified inherent limitations and weaknesses in the CGE models and datasets used, such that they were only suitable for simulation and not for forecasting. In particular, it described the simulation of long-run effects as tenuous. In its reply, incorporated into the Court's report, the EC acknowledged that the models have limitations, but described them as "the most robust and relevant methodological approaches available in the economics profession for trade policy analysis," using datasets that are "widely accepted worldwide by virtually all similar international organizations such as the WTO, World Bank, OECD [Organisation for Economic Co-operation and Development], UN [United Nations], IMF [International Monetary Fund] and the US government."[22] In other words, irrespective of their limitations, the use of CGE models for trade policy analysis is solidly entrenched within the mainstream economics profession and in the establishments that use the findings.

Equilibrium in question

The very concept of equilibrium analysis has been subject to severe criticism since its inception. Friedrich Hayek accepted that it has a useful function to perform, "but when it comes to the point where it misleads some of our leading thinkers into believing that the situation which it describes has direct relevance to the solution of practical problems, it is high time that we remember that it does not deal with the social process at all."[23] Keynes, in relation to his observation that "in the long-run we are all dead," is said to have remarked, "equilibrium is blither."[24] As Steve Keen observes, a real-world economy is certain not to be in equilibrium, and virtually every challenge to mainstream economic theory has called upon it to abandon the concept.[25]

In equilibrium theory, the "long run" is however long it would take the real economy to adjust from one supposed equilibrium state to another. In a trade model the first of these two states represents the current situation, while the other incorporates the proposed changes to tariffs and other trade parameters. The analysis does not attempt to simulate the intervening period of adjustment, during which unneeded production facilities close, new ones are planned and then built, land is put to new uses, and people who become surplus to requirements in one economic sector seek employment in another. The model provides only an indication of the eventual outcome once the imagined equilibrium conditions have been restored.

Such models are limited in what they are capable of modeling, and require many simplifying assumptions and approximations.[26] In some cases these may be reasonably valid, yielding a useful indication of magnitude for some of the effects. However, they fail to address some of the most significant effects, and give results for others that can be highly dubious. The models were developed at a time when tariffs for manufactured goods and agricultural produce were high, in order to evaluate the impact of reducing or removing them. Subsequent rounds of trade liberalization have reduced these tariffs considerably, so that the focus of negotiations has moved on to other areas, such as non-tariff barriers for goods, similar barriers to trade in services, and wider issues such as intellectual property rights and freedom of investment. For all of these, the available data are sparse and the barriers are generally qualitative rather than quantitative. For input to a computer model the available information has to be converted into numbers, typically in the form of imaginary tariffs that the modeler considers to have an equivalent effect. This makes the analysis even less reliable than it is for goods.

Even for tariff reductions, the model results are only approximate and are heavily dependent on the input data. In the lead-up to the WTO negotiations in Cancún in 2003, benefits of US$500 billion to the developing world were widely quoted. By the next round of negotiations, in Hong Kong two years later, it was hard to find estimates as high as $100 billion.[27] The difference, of a factor of five, was due mainly to the release of an updated version of the database used by most of the models.

In principle, the level of uncertainty in the output of a trade model can be evaluated within the model itself, by obtaining a reliable measure of uncertainty for each item of input data, adapting the algorithms to evaluate variances as well as mean values, and presenting a best estimate of uncertainty alongside each of the results. This is standard practice for any mathematical model whose results are crucial, such as in the design of a nuclear facility. However, it is rarely done, if ever, for trade economics models. The models' users never ask for it to be done, perhaps because they prefer not to know how far from the truth the results might be. A rough indication of the uncertainty that still remains in the more recent analyses can be obtained from the spread of results from different studies. Plus or minus 50 percent at a tolerable level of confidence is typical. In some cases the variations are bigger than the number itself, such that a number predicted to be positive could easily be negative. Even greater errors can result from invalid assumptions in the models. When the equations are used outside their range of validity the numbers they produce become completely meaningless.

Missing numbers

Although the inherently unrealistic assumptions of equilibrium analysis limit the validity of the results for overall economic impact, some of the more detailed numbers produced by CGE models are more meaningful. Irrespective of whether an equilibrium state is ever reached, when a country reduces import tariffs in one economic sector in return for a trading partner reducing them in another, trade between the two will almost certainly increase, and domestic production in both countries will rise in one of the two sectors and fall in the other. In order to estimate the overall economic impact of a proposed trade agreement, a CGE trade model must also calculate these production changes. In every case, a small change in overall economic performance depends on much larger changes in imports and exports, while in many cases the changes in domestic production are just as large.

While the advocates of a trade agreement are keen to quote numbers for the overall effect, they are usually more reserved in quoting the details. In launching negotiations on the TTIP, President Obama announced that it would increase exports, without mentioning that it would also increase imports. This was duly picked up by the BBC, again mentioning the exports but not the imports.[28] The EC's press release gave the numbers, or rather, one of the numbers.[29] It quoted the EC's economic study in saying that EU exports to the United States would go up by a highly impressive 28 percent. It failed to mention that EU imports from the United States were projected to go up by an even more impressive 37 percent.

In this case, the changes in domestic production projected by the CGE model were much smaller than the changes in trade flows, because the two economies have similar structures and most sectors were expected to experience rises of similar magnitude in both exports and imports. By contrast, the WTO negotiations embrace countries with very different economic structures, and changes in production are much larger. In consequence, the effects on employment are much larger. Most CGE trade models assume full employment both before and after the changes, and take it as a given that workers will move from sectors that decline to those that expand. No analysis is done of how those changes might take place. In practice, it may be many years, if ever, before the people who become surplus to requirements in one sector find employment in another. This can result in significant impacts on overall unemployment levels, as well as on individual people's lives, particularly when the production changes are large.

According to the modeling studies reviewed in the Sustainability Impact Assessment of the WTO Doha Development Agenda, the removal of all tariffs and subsidies for manufactured and agricultural goods would give a global economic welfare gain of less than 0.5 percent.[30] The associated shifts in production calculated by the models were far larger.[31] In India, clothing production was projected to go up by nearly 40 percent, in Indonesia by nearly 30 percent and in China by over 20 percent. What goes up, goes down somewhere else. The clothing sector was projected to decline by around 20 percent in the new member states of the EU, by 15 percent in the United States, by 18 percent in Mexico and by 25 percent in the Middle East and North Africa. Production of electronic equipment would go up by 10 percent in Mexico and down by more than 10 percent in most of the rest of Latin America. Total agricultural output would go up by about 20 percent in Australia and New Zealand, by 34 percent in Brazil and by 12 percent in the rest of Latin America. It would go down in Japan by about 18 percent and in the EU by 12 percent. Among individual agricultural products, oilseed production would rise by 70 percent in South Africa and 24 percent in the rest of sub-Saharan Africa. It would go down by 70 percent in Mexico and by 46 percent in the United States. Sugar was projected to go up by around 50 percent in Central America and by 47 percent in East Africa, while going down by 59 percent in Japan and by 43 percent in the EU.

The actual effects are likely to be a lot smaller than this once the Doha Round is eventually concluded, because the trade measures that are finally agreed will be a lot smaller than the full liberalization evaluated through these models. However, the same would apply to the overall economic benefit. If the estimate of production changes were reduced from a few tens of percent to a few percent, the expected benefit would fall from less than half a percent to nearly nothing.

Blinded by trivia

Before the 2008 crisis, the US and European economies both grew at over 2.5 percent a year for over three decades, amounting to about 30 percent in each decade.[32] According to the EC's CGE model, the TTIP would boost the US and EU economies, at most, by a mere 0.5 percent in a decade. This may be worth having, but if the United States and Europe are to restore their normal rates of economic growth, where are they going to get the other 29.5 percent from? The "biggest bilateral trade deal in history"[33] would, according to the model, yield a mere sixtieth of what is needed.

CGE models of the WTO's Doha Development Agenda yield similar results for developing countries, giving an average gain of around

0.5 percent, accruing over a period of about a decade. For the whole three decades between 1962 and 1992 South Korea's GDP grew by over 100 percent per decade. The other tiger economies of Southeast Asia were not far behind, while China's growth from 1982 to 2012 was over 120 percent per decade. On that basis, even if Doha were capable of delivering the full liberalization assumed, its 0.5 percent gain would not be worth bothering with.

In reality, the rapid economic growth achieved in all these countries was heavily dependent on their increasing participation in international trade. However, CGE trade models get nowhere near explaining why. Being rooted in equilibrium analysis, they are incapable of addressing the inherently dynamic nature of economic development. Some models incorporate what are referred to as dynamic features within the static equilibrium framework, but typically go no further than to modify the assumed relationships between income, savings, investment and capital stock.[34] They do not address the structural factors, which transformed South Korea from one of the poorest countries in the world to among the richest in the space of a few decades.

The development of South Korea and the other Asian tigers echoes that of Japan in the Meiji revolution, of the United States and the rest of Europe when they were catching up with Britain before that, and of Britain itself when establishing its global economic dominance in the eighteenth and nineteenth centuries.[35] All adopted the approach that has become known as the developmental state, in which heavy state intervention steers the structure of the economy out of sectors with low added value per employee and into others with high added value. In Britain, which led the way through trial and error, the country's newly emerging manufacturing industries, as well as the merchant fleet that shipped their products and raw materials around the world, were heavily protected from foreign competition until the country was well on the way to achieving its global dominance. The rest of Europe, America, Japan and the newly industrializing countries of East Asia all did much the same until their manufacturing industries were strong enough to compete internationally.[36] Most of the trade liberalization measures in South Korea and Taiwan were introduced in the 1980s, two decades after they had embarked on their dramatic transformations towards becoming fully developed industrial economies.[37] The smaller "tiger" economies of Singapore and Hong Kong used similarly interventionist policies in the early stages of their development.[38]

This kind of structural transformation is difficult to achieve, involving a wide range of policy measures tailored to a country's specific circumstances, and often in the face of strong opposition from powerful interest groups, both internally and internationally. However, even interventions that are much more modest can produce rates of growth far in excess of those projected by equilibrium models. Conversely, when trade liberalization is accompanied by inappropriate policies or no state intervention at all, the impact can again be far larger than the CGE projections, but in the opposite direction.

This is most strikingly apparent in countries that suffer from the "resource curse," obeying the law of comparative advantage to the letter, with no barriers to exports of oil or diamonds, and no barriers to importing everything else. Statistical analyses of the relationship between a country's endowment of exportable natural resources and its success in increasing the incomes of the poor show an inverse correlation.[39] The richer the country is in these resources, the poorer are its people. Countries such as Norway have escaped the curse through government interventions specifically designed to avoid it. Elsewhere, military dictators, absolute monarchs, warring warlords, and the most skillful of entrepreneurs get very rich indeed by following the mantra of free trade, without having to invest in the skills and earning power of the rest of the people. No mathematical model can conceivably capture such effects.

While the CGE trade models favored by mainstream economics provide the numbers that politicians need for promoting their policies, they fall a long way short of evaluating the actual impacts of those policies.

Why negotiate?

If the real world were as simple as the mathematical equations used in a CGE model there would be no need for trade negotiations; the analysis of a proposed agreement would yield an optimal solution in which no country experiences a net loss and all maximize their net gains. The solution is simple. The optimum occurs when every country removes all its barriers to free trade. If any country choses not to join, it would not deter the rest. The biggest gains to each country come from the unilateral removal of its own barriers, no matter what the others do. As Paul Krugman has pointed out, if the conventional economic argument in favor of free trade were the only consideration, there would be no WTO and no trade negotiations.[40]

In reality, these economic calculations play little or no role in the development of a country's negotiating position. They clearly show that America and Europe would benefit from removing all their agricultural subsidies and import barriers, irrespective of other countries' actions. Yet they will not do it, other than through minor concessions given in return for other countries responding to their requests. The same calculations show that those countries would benefit just as much from doing what they are asked, even without the concessions. They too will not do it, unless they can get something in return. Each party uses the calculations of net economic benefit liberally in its efforts to win public support and to influence the policies of other parties, but hardly at all in developing its own—other factors are far more important.

Trade barriers are introduced for a wide variety of reasons. Social and environmental reasons include preserving the character of rural areas, ensuring the security of food supplies, promoting equitable income distribution, protecting consumers from health or safety risks, conserving the natural environment, generating government revenues for social, environmental or other expenditure, or, just as commonly, responding to the demands of powerful interest groups. Economic reasons generally relate to a country's long-term goals for its economic development, which will often far outweigh the shorter-term costs of forgoing cheap imports or subsidizing domestic production.

All of these are essentially political issues, for which any policy decision must balance the different interests of the various socio-economic groups affected. The claim that a decision is based on the numbers produced by a mathematical model effectively precludes any analysis of real conflict, power relations, and social transformation.[41] The numbers hide conflicts rather than solving them, and mask the politics under a cloak of apparent inevitability.

The bigger picture

In a thinly disguised glimpse of the political realities of international affairs the EU's *Lisbon Strategy for Growth and Jobs* committed Europe to becoming "the most dynamic and competitive knowledge-based economy in the world."[42] The strategy had no need to state the obvious corollary, that for Europe to be the most competitive, some other economy had to be the least competitive. The official review of the strategy, chaired by former Netherlands Prime Minister Wim Kok, reinforced the message. It noted that while the *Lisbon Strategy* was about achieving Europe's vision of what it wants to be and what it wants to keep, "competitor countries and regions are moving on as well, threatening Europe's position in the global economic league table."[43] Again the corollary was obvious. For Europe to preserve its position at or near the top, it would have to ensure that others remained at the bottom. China was identified as a particular threat, having "begun to compete not only in low but also in high value-added goods," while in the service sector "India's challenge is no less real."

The *Lisbon Strategy* formed the basis of the EU's subsequent trade strategy, *Global Europe: Competing in the World.*[44] This made no mention of any of the numbers generated by trade economics models. It focused instead on efforts to persuade China, India, Brazil, and other low- and middle-income countries to remove their remaining barriers to European exports and investment, while granting Europe unrestricted access to their resources of raw materials. This objective, subsequently confirmed in the updated trade strategy,[45] bears a marked resemblance to how European countries got to the top of the global economic league table in the first place. It has nothing to do with equilibrium theory, and everything to do with economic structures and power relations.

While trade agreements between high-income countries and the developing world have been described as "strengthening the already powerful and further weakening the weak,"[46] the true motivations for the Euro-American TTIP are open to conjecture but could be similar. Some commentators regard the deal as a charter for deregulation and the capture of power by transnational corporations.[47] Others see it as an attempt by the United States and Europe to restore their traditional dominance of the international economic system, which has come under threat from lack of progress in the Doha Round and increasing competition from China, India and other rising economic powers.[48] Whatever the true motivations, the miniscule gains calculated by trade economics models are barely relevant.

Conclusion

The fact that the European Court of Auditors has recognized the limitations of CGE models, and has criticized the European Commission for its over-reliance on them, is cause for hope that bureaucrats and politicians will begin to get the message too. Further hope comes from the EC's chief scientific advisor, who accuses the Commission of twisting facts to fit its political agenda and has come up with proposals that might make it harder.[49]

Meanwhile, the economics profession is itself beginning to change, albeit slowly, partly in response to the 2008 crisis, partly through the efforts of a growing body of heterodox economists, and partly through pressure from its own junior members. In some universities economics students have demanded that their professors reintroduce topics such as the history of economic thought and political economy into their curricula.[50] Today's mathematically minded professors will eventually retire, to be replaced by a new generation who, we might hope, will take on the task of restoring the discipline to its former status as a true social science.

Should this happen, it will still not stop politicians seeking evidence to support their policies, nor from masking the true reasons for those policies. This stifles debate on the issues surrounding those policies, and may result in governments marching steadily on towards disaster. In the case of trade policy, any attempt to maintain Western economic hegemony in the face of the rising might of China and the other emerging powers is unlikely to have any more than short-term effect, which would come at the price of pushing the world into a bipolar state of strategic confrontation amounting to a new cold war and worse.

Perhaps the biggest hope of avoiding such a fate is that a combination of legislative inertia and civil society opposition on both sides of the Atlantic will prevent the EU–US negotiations from achieving any more than a face-saving deal with minimal effect. This might be enough to persuade Western governments to consider the alternative, of drawing the emerging powers into the debate on how the future world should be governed, rather than insisting on the rightness of their own model. From there it is not hard to imagine a reconstituted World Trade Organization seizing the initiative again, to launch a renewed Development Agenda that, unlike the Doha Development Agenda, is truly worthy of the name.

Notes

1 Office of the Press Secretary, *Remarks by President Obama, UK Prime Minister Cameron, European Commission President Barroso, and European Council President Van Rompuy on the Transatlantic Trade and Investment Partnership, Lough Erne, Northern Ireland* (Washington, DC: The White House, 17 June 2013).
2 Office of the Press Secretary, *Remarks by President Obama*, 1.
3 Jerome L. Himmelstein, "How the Mass Media Use Numbers to Tell a Story: The Case of the Crack Scare of 1986," *Numeracy* 7, no. 1 (2014): Article 2.
4 Theodore M. Porter, *Trust in Numbers: The Pursuit of Objectivity in Science and Public Life* (Princeton, N.J.: Princeton University Press, 1995).
5 In relation to the 2008 crisis, Joseph Stiglitz has observed, "[i]f economics is a science, it is presumably to be judged by its ability to predict. It has, by and large, failed that test." See Joseph E. Stiglitz, "An Agenda for Reforming Economic Theory," presented at the Institute for New Economic Thinking's (INET) conference, Cambridge, 9 April 2010.
6 Karl Popper, "The Logic of Scientific Discovery," in *Popper Selections*, ed. David Miller (Princeton, N.J.: Princeton University Press, 1985).

7 Joel Best, *Damned Lies and Statistics: Untangling Numbers from the Media, Politicians, and Activists* (Berkley, Calif.: University of California Press, 2011), 1.
8 Karel de Gucht, "The Transatlantic Trade and Investment Partnership," speech to the *European American Chamber of Commerce, New York* (Brussels: European Commission, 21 May 2013).
9 Centre for Economic Policy Research (CEPR), *Reducing Trans-Atlantic Barriers to Trade and Investment* (London: CEPR, 2013).
10 "EU 'Growth Boost from US Free-trade Deal'," BBC, 3 March 2013, www.bbc.co.uk/news/business-21647540.
11 Best, *Damned Lies and Statistics.*
12 Santiago Fernandez de Córdoba, Sam Laird and David Vanzetti, "Trick or Treat? Development Opportunities and Challenges in the WTO Negotiations on Industrial Tariffs," *The World Economy* 28, no. 10 (2005): 1375–1400.
13 Sam Laird, David Vanzetti and Santiago Fernandez de Córdoba, "Smoke and Mirrors: Making Sense of the WTO Industrial Tariff Negotiations," Policy Issues in International Trade and Commodities Study Series No. 30 (New York and Geneva: UNCTAD, 2006).
14 C. George and C. Kirkpatrick, "Sustainability Impact Assessment of Trade Agreements: From Public Dialogue to International Governance," *Journal of Environmental Assessment, Policy and Management* 10, no. 1 (2008): 67–89.
15 Best, *Damned Lies and Statistics*, 20.
16 Mark Weisbrot and Dean Baker, "The Relative Impact of Trade Liberalization on Developing Countries," in *The Development Imperative: Toward a People Centered Approach*, ed. Eric Hershberg and Christy Thornton (New York: Social Science Research Council, 2005).
17 Frank Ackerman, "The Shrinking Gains from Trade: A Critical Assessment of Doha Round Projections," GDAE Working Paper No. 05-01 (Medford, Mass.: Global Development and Environment Institute, Tufts University, 2005).
18 Best, *Damned Lies and Statistics.*
19 Himmelstein, "How the Mass Media Use Numbers to Tell a Story."
20 David Ricardo, *On the Principles of Political Economy and Taxation*, third edition 1821 (Kitchener, Ont.: Batoche Books, 2001).
21 European Court of Auditors, *Are Preferential Trade Arrangements Appropriately Managed?* Special Report No. 02 (Luxembourg: Publications Office of the European Union, 2014).
22 European Court of Auditors, *Are Preferential Trade Arrangements Appropriately Managed?* 2.
23 Friedrich A. Hayek, "The Use of Knowledge in Society," *American Economic Review* 35, no. 4 (1945): 519–30.
24 George L.S. Shackle, *Epistemics and Economics: A Critique of Economic Doctrines* (London: Cambridge University Press, 1972), 223.
25 Steve Keen, *Debunking Economics* (London: Zed Books, 2011).
26 Serban Scrieciu, "How Useful are Computable General Equilibrium Models in Sustainability Impact Assessment?" in *Impact Assessment and Sustainable Development: European Practice and Experience*, ed. Clive George and Colin Kirkpatrick (Cheltenham: Edward Elgar, 2007).
27 Ackerman, "The Shrinking Gains from Trade," 3.

28 Duncan Bartlett, "EU and US 'in Biggest Trade Deal'," BBC, 17 June 2013, www.bbc.co.uk/news/business-22943170.
29 European Commission, "European Union and United States to Launch Negotiations for a Transatlantic Trade and Investment Partnership," Press release memo 13-95 (Brussels: European Commission, 2013).
30 Colin Kirkpatrick, Clive George and Serban Scrieciu, *Sustainability Impact Assessment of Proposed WTO Negotiations: Final Global Overview Trade SIA of the Doha Development Agenda: Final Report* (Manchester: Institute for Development Policy and Management, University of Manchester, 2006).
31 Clive George, *The Truth About Trade* (London: Zed Books, 2010).
32 The historical growth rates in this section are calculated from the inflation-adjusted data in World Bank, *World Development Indicators* (Washington, DC: World Bank, 2014), http://databank.worldbank.org/data/. At non-adjusted current prices the growth rates were even higher.
33 As described by David Cameron, see Office of the Press Secretary, *Remarks by President Obama.*
34 Joseph F. Francois, Bradley McDonald and Hakan Nordström, "Liberalization and Capital Accumulation in the GTAP Model," GTAP Technical Paper No. 7 (West Lafayette, Ind.: Center for Global Trade Analysis, Purdue University, 1996).
35 Ha-Joon Chang, *Kicking Away the Ladder: Development Strategy in Historical Perspective* (London: Anthem Press, 2002).
36 Chang, *Kicking Away the Ladder.*
37 Dani Rodrik, *The Global Governance of Trade as if Development Really Mattered* (New York: UNDP, 2001).
38 Mari Pangestu, "Industrial Policy and Developing Countries," in *Development, Trade, and the WTO: A Handbook*, ed. Bernard M. Hoekman, Aaditya Mattoo and Philip English (Washington, DC: World Bank, 2002); and United Nations Industrial Development Organization (UNIDO), *Industrial Development Report 2002/2003* (New York: UNIDO, 2002).
39 Jeffrey D. Sachs and Andrew M. Warner, *Natural Resource Abundance and Economic Growth* (Cambridge, Mass.: Harvard Institute for International Development, 1995).
40 Paul Krugman, "What Should Trade Negotiators Negotiate About?" *Journal of Economic Literature* 35, no. 1 (1997): 113–120.
41 Tony Lawson, "Mathematical Modelling and Ideology in the Economics Academy: Competing Explanations of the Failings of the Modern Discipline?" *Economic Thought* 1, no. 4 (2012): 3–22.
42 European Council, "Working Together for Growth and Jobs: A New Start for the Lisbon Strategy," communication from President Barroso in agreement with Vice-President Verheugen, COM(2005)24, 2 February 2005, 3.
43 European Communities, *Facing the Challenge: The Lisbon Strategy for Growth and Employment: Report from the High Level Group*, Report from the High Level Group chaired by Wim Kok (Luxembourg: Office for Official Publication of the European Communities, November 2004), 20.
44 European Commission, "Global Europe: Competing in the World—A Contribution to the EU's Growth and Jobs Strategy," communication from the Commission to the Council, the European Parliament and the Committee of the Regions, COM(2006)567, Brussels, Belgium, 4 October 2006.

45 European Commission, *Trade, Growth and World Affairs: Trade Policy as a Core Component of the EU's 2020 Strategy*, COM(2010)612 (Brussels, Belgium, 2010).
46 Friends of the Earth International (FoE), *Global Europe: The Tyranny of "Free Trade," the European Way* (Amsterdam: FoE Secretariat, 2008).
47 John Hilary, *The Transatlantic Trade and Investment Partnership: A Charter for Deregulation, an Attack on Jobs, an End to Democracy* (Brussels: Rosa Luxemburg Stiftung, 2014); and Dean Baker, "The US–EU Trade Deal: Don't Buy the Hype," *The Guardian*, 15 July 2013.
48 Pierre Defraigne, *Questioning the Transatlantic Trade Partnership* (Brussels: College of Europe Foundation, 2013); Kim Bizzarri, *A Brave New Transatlantic Partnership* (Brussels: Seattle to Brussels Network, 2013); Uri Dadush, "Don't Buy the Hype on the Transatlantic Trade Deal," *Carnegie Endowment*, 1 March 2013, http://carnegieendowment.org; and Marc Venhaus, "The Transatlantic Trade and Investment Partnership as a New Strategy to Marginalize Emerging Powers," in *The Transatlantic Colossus: Global Contributions to Broaden the Debate on the EU–US Free Trade Agreement*, ed. Daniel Cardoso, Philani Mthembu, Marc Venhaus and Miguelángel Verde Garrido (Oktoberdruck, Berlin: Berlin Forum on Global Politics, Internet & Society Collaboratory and FutureChallenges.org, 2013).
49 EurActiv, "EU Twisting Facts to Fit Political Agenda, Chief Scientist Says," 27 May 2014, www.euractiv.com (accessed 27 May 2014).
50 The International Student Initiative for Pluralism in Economics has established a worldwide student movement promoting the reform of economics teaching: www.isipe.net/open-letter.

6 The double movement of law and expertise

Andrew Lang

- **Economic expertise in the application of the Subsidies Agreement**
- **The sufficiency of scientific evidence in SPS disputes**
- **Cultures of objectivity**
- **Conclusion**

In assessing the role of expert knowledge in global trade politics, it can be useful to distinguish broadly between three different sites or stages in which expertise is deployed and contested. For these purposes, we can, for the moment, imagine trade negotiations according to the traditional—and for these purposes perfectly functional—model of self-interested bargaining between states. Following this model, the first stage at which expertise is deployed is during the formulation of trade policy preferences at the level of the state. The role of expertise in this domain should be self-evident: it is impossible for decision makers to make judgments about the objectives that can and should be pursued through trade policy without explicit or implicit recourse to a complex mix of expert knowledges—from the formal doctrine of the trade economist, to the intuitions of the experienced trade diplomat, the professional knowledge of the sectoral regulator, to the quantitative expertise of the economic statisticians, among many others. Here, expert knowledges frame the choices available to decision makers, provide information about the likely consequences of their choices, and provide the terms in which decision makers formulate their overall strategic objectives, as well as the tactical means used to achieve them.

The second stage is the negotiation itself. Here, expertise of all sorts again structures the encounter in a variety of ways. Most obviously, the expertise of the experienced trade negotiator—as evidenced not only in the tactics deployed but also in the turns of phrase, behavioral instincts and even bodily postures—can clearly influence the process of negotiations, and perhaps even their outcome. Furthermore, the knowledge and opinions offered by outside experts—perhaps officials from the WTO Secretariat, opinion leaders from think tanks, international organizations, or universities—can, in some cases, help to break negotiating deadlocks using their epistemic authority to build consensus behind particular negotiating proposals. Here, the deployment of expertise is part of the art of persuasion, so central to even the hardest of hard-edged negotiations.

It is the third stage, however, on which I want to focus attention in this chapter. This stage occurs after the conclusion of formal negotiations, once a legal text has been agreed, and the hard work of interpreting and applying it begins. How might we imagine expertise working in this domain? What is the relationship between the text of the law and the bodies of expertise that were engaged during the process of its production?

It is quite common to imagine the relationship between legal texts and certain expert knowledges in terms of the former in some sense *encoding* the latter. There is a certain common sense to this view, and for many purposes it is perfectly adequate. The treaty text is, as I have just said, the product of a contest between different expertise and knowledge claims: it follows that the content of the text will, to some degree, reflect the dominant forms of knowledge and expertise at play in the negotiating context. Thus, Ruggie's famous story about the embedded liberal foundations of the General Agreement on Tariffs and Trade (GATT) 1947 shows convincingly how the shape of the legal text emerging from post-war negotiations reflected the particular form of economic liberal ideology shared by the most important GATT trading nations at the time.[1] More prosaically, the Subsidies Agreement, about which I will say much more in a moment, is often described as being in some sense based on a set of economic insights about the market-distorting effect of subsidies, as well as on a broader economic ideology that devalorizes industrial policy. Indeed, the entirety of international trade law is commonly said to be built on Ricardian trade economics and the doctrine of comparative advantage.

The argument that I want to make in this chapter is that the process of encoding—by which I refer broadly to the process of implicitly or explicitly basing a legal text on a body of expert knowledge—is a more complex and contradictory process than is often thought. For clarity, I need to distinguish this claim from two other arguments with which it might be confused. One of them begins with the observation that a treaty text emerging from trade negotiations never reflects simply the encoding of a single consensus body of expertise. Rather, it always represents a complex and potentially unstable mix of expertise, often in tension, and often compromised. This observation leads us to reject the encoding model for being too simple, and for failing to acknowledge the multiple forms of expertise that remain in play and in tension within a single body of law. This objection has great force, and is undoubtedly valid, but it is not the claim that I want to make in this chapter.

A second line of argument might point to the indeterminacy of both the treaty text, and the body of expert knowledge on which it is based, to highlight the choices that remain open in the application of both in particular contexts. From this point of view, the encoding model is objectionable because it mistakenly treats legal text as rigid, and it fails to register the ways in which the contest between types of expertise continues to be waged in the context of legal interpretation and application. Again, this claim is perfectly true, and it is one that I have made before, but I do not want to repeat it here.

The third claim, which is the subject of this chapter, is different. It is this: even if we assume for the sake of argument that the process of encoding is unitary, complete, and unambiguous—though we know it is not—the mere fact of encoding a body of expertise in law works simultaneously in two opposite directions. On the one hand, and most obviously, it enables a form of decision making in which a body of expert knowledge is simply "applied" in the course of the legal resolution of a dispute. On the other hand, however, it equally and just as importantly enables a form of decision making that does precisely the opposite—which marks its distance from the body of expert knowledge on which it is based, and self-consciously adopts positions contrary or orthogonal to it. We cannot understand the role of expertise in the interpretation and application of international economic law, I argue, unless we appreciate the extent to which it is necessarily and inherently characterized by this "double movement." In the next two sections, I offer two illustrations of this double movement, before offering an explanation and interpretation of it in the concluding part.

Economic expertise in the application of the Subsidies Agreement

The first illustration comes from the jurisprudence under the World Trade Organization's (WTO) Agreement on Subsidies and Countervailing Measures (SCM Agreement). Although this agreement is a relatively recent one, it builds on a series of disciplines on industrial and other subsidies developed gradually over the first 50 years of the post-war trading system. The GATT 1947 itself contained only relatively loose provisions on subsidies in Article XVI, consisting of a notification requirement coupled with an obligation to "discuss … the possibility of limiting the subsidization" with those trading partners suffering "serious prejudice" as a result of the subsidies in question.[2] In addition, flexibility to provide subsidies to domestic producers was maintained through an exemption from the national treatment obligation in Article III:8(b). Partially offsetting these permissive provisions was Article VI:3, which permitted GATT contracting parties to impose countervailing duties on subsidized imports, subject to certain procedural safeguards. The notion of a "subsidy," however, was nowhere defined.

In 1955, further obligations on export subsidies were added to Article XVI. The new Paragraph 4 envisaged that agreement would be reached to abolish all export subsidies on non-primary products by 1958, and provided for a "standstill" for existing subsidy programs until then.[3] In relation to primary (mainly agricultural) products, contracting parties agreed that they should "seek to avoid the use" of export subsidies, and not to use them in a manner that would result in their having a "more than equitable share of world trade" of the product in question.[4] While these amendments still did not address the definitional issue, in 1960, during the negotiations designed to put GATT Article XVI: 4 into effect, a Working Party produced an illustrative list of measures that could reasonably be treated as export subsidies, in the absence of a general definition of the concept.[5]

The Tokyo Round saw the adoption of the Subsidies Code, a new and, at the time, important agreement signed by 23 GATT contracting parties. It contained a more categorical prohibition of export subsidies, some elaborated disciplines on domestic subsidies, and new constraints on the unilateral imposition of countervailing duties. However, this was superseded some 16 years later by the SCM Agreement itself, negotiated during the Uruguay Round, and coming into force in 1995.[6] The SCM Agreement contained, for the first time, a general definition of the concept of a "subsidy": under Article 1.1 of the agreement, a subsidy is deemed to exist, where: (i) there is either a "financial contribution" by a government or public body, or any form of "income or price support"; and (ii) a "benefit is thereby conferred" on the recipient. Such subsidies are only subject to the disciplines contained in the agreement if they are "specific."[7]

As regards substantive disciplines, the SCM Agreement continued the separate treatment of export and domestic subsidies found in earlier texts. On one hand, export subsidies and so-called domestic content subsidies were prohibited outright, though there was an exemption for agricultural subsidies, which were addressed in a separate agreement.[8] On the other, domestic subsidies were "actionable" under the agreement only if they cause, or threaten to cause, "adverse effects to the interests of other Members"—a concept that is elaborated in considerable detail in Articles 5 and 6. In respect of both actionable and prohibited subsidies, the injured member was given a choice of remedies: to bring a complaint to the dispute settlement body seeking removal of the subsidy; and/or unilaterally to impose countervailing duties on the subsidized import to offset the effect of the subsidy.[9] Part V of the agreement then imposed a series of important procedural and substantive limits on the use of such countervailing duties.

What, then, does the SCM Agreement have to tell us about the relationship between law and expertise? It will come as no surprise that in many of the cases brought under this agreement, panels and the Appellate Body have used techniques and concepts drawn from economics to help them to interpret its terms. For example, I noted above that a measure only constitutes a subsidy for the purposes of the SCM agreement if it confers a "benefit" on its recipient. A central question in the application of the agreement, then, is whether a "benefit" exists, and what its magnitude is. But in comparison to what? In response to this question, the Appellate Body has made clear that the market is the yardstick by which a "benefit" is to be identified and measured.[10] As a result, the Appellate Body has found itself on some occasions required to define the relevant market for the purposes of a benefit analysis. Since certain strands of economics offer a well-developed set of tools, concepts, and techniques for the purpose of market definition, it is hardly surprising that we see the Appellate Body turn to economic expertise in its jurisprudence on this question. For instance, in the 2013 decision in *Canada—Feed-in Tariffs* (*FIT*), the Appellate Body used the concepts of demand-side substitutability and supply-side substitutability to help it decide that the wholesale market for renewable energy in Ontario was distinct from that of wholesale electricity more generally.[11] Certain parts of its judgment are, in their form, very similar to standard economic analyses of market competition:

> supply-side factors suggest that windpower and solar [photovoltaic] (PV) producers of electricity cannot compete with other electricity producers because of differences in cost structures and operating costs and characteristics. Windpower and solar PV technologies have very high capital costs (as compared to other generation technologies), very low operating costs, and fewer, if any, economies of scale. Windpower and solar PV technologies produce electricity intermittently (depending on the availability of wind and sun) and cannot be relied on for base-load and peak-load electricity. Differences in cost structures and operating costs

> and characteristics between windpower and solar PV technologies, on the one hand, and other technologies, on the other hand, make it very unlikely, if not impossible, that the former may exercise any form of price constraint on the latter. In contrast, conventional generators produce an identical commodity that can be used for base-load and peak-load electricity. They have larger economies of scale and exercise price constraints on windpower and solar PV generators.[12]

In subsequent paragraphs, the Appellate Body also deployed the traditional economic notions of positive and negative externalities to support its argument that electricity from different sources ought to be treated differently.[13]

Another example can be taken from the 2008 Appellate Body decision in *US—Cotton (21.5)*, in which Brazil challenged a variety of different measures taken by the US government to support the domestic production and export of cotton. One of the key issues in that case was whether the payment of certain price-contingent subsidies to US cotton farmers caused "significant price suppression" under Article 6.3(c) of the SCM Agreement. The argument was that such payments affected farmers' planting decisions, which in turn lowered world prices through increased supply. In considering this question, the Appellate Body made it clear that techniques borrowed from economics would often be helpful in determining causation:

> Given the focus on production and price effects, an analysis of price suppression would normally include a quantitative component. There is some inherent difficulty in quantifying the effects of subsidies, because, as we have indicated, the increase in prices, absent the subsidies, cannot be directly observed. One way to undertake the analysis is to use economic modeling or other quantitative techniques … [which] provide a framework to analyze the relationship between subsidies, other factors, and price movements.[14]

The role of the Panel, the Appellate Body has noted, is to assess the evidentiary value of the models in question and, to the extent that they are considered convincing to a Panel, they are often in practice sufficient to dispose of the legal question of price suppression under Article 6.3(c).[15] A similar attitude was adopted in *EC—Large Civil Aircraft*, in which the Appellate Body suggested that the counterfactual analysis necessitated by Article 6.3 "requires the adjudicator to undertake a modeling exercise as to what the market would look like in the absence of subsidies."[16] As a result of such comments, it is now not uncommon for parties to engage in considerable technical argument concerning the appropriate economic models to use, the validity of the assumptions on which they are based, their applicability, application to the case at hand, and so on.[17]

The Appellate Body decision in *EC—Aircraft* is also noteworthy in this context for the way in which it interprets the legal concept of "export contingency" by reference to certain distinctions drawn from the economic notion of a market distortion. The standard of "export contingency" is not met, the Appellate Body suggests, "merely because the granting of the subsidy is designed to increase a recipient's production, even if the increased production is exported in whole." It is also not met simply because "the granting of the subsidy may, in addition to increasing exports, *also* increase the recipient's domestic sales." Rather,

> we consider that the standard for *de facto* export contingency under Article 3.1(a) and footnote 4 of the *SCM Agreement* would be met when the subsidy is granted so as to provide an incentive to the recipient to export in a way that is not simply reflective of the conditions of supply and demand in the domestic and export markets undistorted by the granting of the subsidy.[18]

In order to prove its case, then, a complainant may provide evidence of historical sales, or if no historical sales data are available, "the comparison could be made with the performance that a profit-maximizing firm would hypothetically be expected to achieve in the export and domestic markets in the absence of the subsidy."[19]

It is true that in all of these examples the Appellate Body applied certain economic concepts in ways to which some economists might object. All of the decisions referred to above have been criticized on that basis.[20] But the point I wish to make is simply that in these illustrations, the Appellate Body is interpreting the law so that, to speak loosely, it becomes something of a vehicle for economic forms of expertise and analysis. Economic concepts are used to give meaning and color to legal concepts. The application of a legal provision is, in practical terms, largely governed by the determination of certain facts through economic analysis—whether it be product scope of the market, the causal impact of the measure in question, the magnitude of price effects, or something else—and gives the tools of economic expertise the primary role in the determination of such facts. This is, it seems to me, mostly what people have in mind when they talk about a body of law as "based on" certain economic precepts, or "encoding" certain economic concepts or principles, and it is a very familiar jurisprudential mode.

However, there is also at the same time an apparently contradictory mode of argumentation in the jurisprudence under the SCM Agreement, which pushes in exactly the opposite direction. This mode begins with the opposite claim that the incorporation of economic concepts into law transforms their nature: they become *legal* concepts, the defining feature of which is precisely their (potential) divergence from their economic counterparts. In this mode, the questions of market definition and causation are not primarily factual matters, but legal questions, for which economic expertise may be helpful, but very far from determinative. When arguing in this mode, judges and interpreters foreground their departures from economic expertise and perceptions, and indeed see their function as, in part, cutting short potentially endless debates between and among economic experts about the adequacy and accuracy of any particular analysis, by reference to an alternative set of self-consciously legal techniques, including the deliberate production of legal fictions.

Examples of this mode of reasoning can be found in precisely the same cases as those referred to above. I noted, for example, that the Appellate Body had recourse to economic techniques to define the product scope of the relevant market in the *Canada—FIT* case, but in a subsequent step of the argument, the Appellate Body performed precisely the opposite move, reframing the argument so as to highlight the differences between the economic and legal concepts of "the market." One of the claims made by the complainants in that case was that the prices paid to such suppliers of renewable energy under long-term contractual arrangements were higher than they would have received under market conditions, and thus constituted a subsidy. A benchmark market price was needed, therefore, to determine whether or not the price did indeed constitute a subsidy. However, here a difficult question arose: should the benchmark price be calculated taking the government-mandated energy-supply mix as given, or should it be calculated without such a constraint? Clearly, if the government-mandated supply mix were ignored, there was a subsidy—there was no argument that a market for renewables simply would not exist in the absence of such a government mandate.

The Appellate Body found that it had to take the supply mix as given. The reasons given had to do with the idiosyncrasies of electricity markets, the Canadian experience with electricity liberalization, and especially the sovereign right of WTO members to organize their electricity markets:

> Government intervention in favor of the substitution of fossil energy with renewable energy today is meant to ensure the proper functioning or the existence of an electricity market with a constant and reliable supply of electricity in the long term … Although [a government-defined supply mix] has an effect on market prices, as opposed to a situation where prices are determined by unconstrained forces of supply and demand, it does not exclude *per se* treating the resulting prices as market prices for the purposes of a benefit analysis under Article 1.1(b) of the SCM Agreement. Thus, where the government has defined an energy supply-mix that includes windpower and solar PV electricity generation technologies, as in the present disputes, a benchmark comparison for purposes of a benefit analysis for windpower and solar PV electricity generation should be with the terms and conditions that would be available under market-based conditions for each of these technologies, taking the supply-mix as a given.[21]

It is true that much of the economic evidence tendered by the parties related to markets that did not contain such a government-defined supply mix, and which more closely approximated a textbook "free market" in electricity. However, based in significant part on its understanding of the limitations of its mandate and institutional role, the Appellate Body did not see itself as having the freedom to adopt the textbook free market as its benchmark, nor even real-life markets that approximated it. Instead, then, the Appellate Body draws a clear line between legal notions of the "market" in a benchmark analysis under the SCM Agreement, and that which is deployed in economic analysis. The Appellate Body emphasizes that they are, in the final analysis, distinct and mutually irreducible concepts.

Another example of a similar move comes from the *Brazil—Aircraft* case. One of the questions in that case was whether certain elements of Brazil's export financing program were protected by the wording of item (k) of the Illustrative List of Export Subsidies, which defined certain measures as export subsidies, but only where they are "used to secure a material advantage in the field of export credit terms." Brazil argued that the payments in question were not in fact used to secure an advantage, but instead merely to offset Canada's subsidies to its own aircraft industry, as well as to reduce an artificial disadvantage which Brazilian companies faced given the "Brazil risk" that the market priced into credit terms for such companies (in part on account of economic policies of the Brazilian government itself).[22] This argument potentially raised complex problems of economic analysis. Was the relevant market distorted by the practices in question? If so, how might a more accurate market price be constructed from existing economic evidence? However, the Panel avoided such problems easily, simply noting the absence of any *express* textual support for Brazil's position in the SCM Agreement, and thereby short-circuiting potentially complicated economic analysis:

> In no case is it suggested that whether or not a benefit exists would depend upon a comparison with advantages available to a competing product from another Member … Nor can we find any suggestion in either Article 3.1(a) of the SCM Agreement or the Illustrative List of Export Subsidies that whether a measure is a prohibited export subsidy should depend upon whether the measure merely offsets advantages bestowed on competing products from another Member.[23]

For good measure, the Panel went on to note that "there is no hint that a tax advantage would not constitute an export subsidy simply because it reduced the exporter's tax burden to a level comparable to that of foreign competitors."[24] This was so, even though such questions would matter tremendously if one were to assess the competitive effects of the subsidy from an orthodox economic perspective, with a view to correcting market distortions or leveling the competitive playing field. Again, it seems that the legal notion of a subsidy is self-consciously and explicitly distinguished from its economic counterpart, with barely any need for explanation.

Brazil subsequently amended its measure, so that the interest rate payments in question were tied to a market benchmark related to the prevailing US Treasury Bond ten-year rate, plus an additional spread of 20 basis points. The problem here was whether this rate represented a reasonable approximation of what a commercial actor in the market might ask. Again, though, the need to assess complicated economic evidence on this question was avoided through the use of a fictional benchmark referred to in the text of the agreement. Given the express reference in item (k) of the Illustrative List to "international undertaking[s] on official export credits," the Panel (following an earlier Appellate Body ruling[25]) determined that one appropriate benchmark would be the relevant Organisation for Economic Co-operation and Development (OECD), Commercial Interest Reference Rate, as calculated according to the methodology set out in Article 16 of the OECD Arrangement.[26] Aware that this reference rate may or may not correspond to a "true" market rate, the Panel made it clear that it was open in principle for Brazil to prove that lower rates were actually commercially available on the market—even if in practice the prevalence of government involvement in this sector made finding appropriate commercial comparators almost impossible.[27]

The same self-conscious adoption of a fictional or partial benchmark can be seen in some of the Panel decisions in the *Softwood Lumber* litigation. One issue that famously arose in that litigation was whether the domestic Canadian market for stumpage provided an appropriate benchmark, given the thorough degree to which it was structured and affected by government action. In *US—Softwood Lumber III*, the Panel explicitly eschewed economists' preferred benchmark of a "hypothetical undistorted or perfectly competitive market."[28] Without contesting the substantive claim that the domestic market was in some sense fundamentally distorted, the Panel noted that "if the drafters of the SCM Agreement had wanted to exclude the use of market prices in case of price suppression due to the government's involvement, they would have explicitly provided so, but they have not."[29] A subsequent Panel noted, significantly, "we do not believe that it would be appropriate for this Panel to substitute its economic judgment for that of the drafters."[30] It is true that this approach was subsequently revised by the Appellate Body, which found textual support for the rejection of such a distorted benchmark in certain circumstances. However, the Appellate Body still drew a clear line between the legal benchmark defined in the text of the agreement, and the sort of market benchmark used in economic analysis.[31]

In all of these cited instances, then, the benchmarks used represented explicitly "distorted" markets, or fictions that bore no necessary connection to any known market, as their basis to define, characterize, or determine the effects of the measures in dispute. This is, in crucial aspects, precisely the opposite of the mode of argumentation described above, in which law acts as a vehicle for economic concepts and techniques. Here, the incorporation of a concept such as the "market" into law fundamentally changes its character: the act of encoding it in law is precisely what allows the adjudicators in the above disputes to depart from purely economic understandings of the concept, and to construct their own fictional markets which purport to have validity and relevance only within the legal context in which they arise. However, before reflecting a little on the significance of this, I want to demonstrate a similar phenomenon at work in a different jurisprudential context, though still within the field of WTO law.

The sufficiency of scientific evidence in SPS disputes

Like the SCM Agreement, the Agreement on the Application of Sanitary and Phytosanitary Measures (SPS Agreement) was the product of the Uruguay Round of negotiations, and entered into force in 1995. At the time, it was considered by all accounts a relatively minor and highly technical agreement, addressing only a very specific set of issues raised by a relatively minor set of trade restrictive measures, namely sanitary and phytosanitary (SPS) measures. SPS measures are, speaking broadly, those food safety and quarantine measures that WTO members use to protect their territories from pests, diseases, and other health risks that enter through importation of foreign goods. The agreement itself contains a fuller and more precise definition of the measures to which it applies:

[An SPS measure is a]ny measure applied:

a to protect animal or plant life or health within the territory of the Member from risks arising from the entry, establishment or spread of pests, diseases, disease-carrying organisms or disease-causing organisms;
b to protect human or animal life or health within the territory of the Member from risks arising from additives, contaminants, toxins or disease-causing organisms in foods, beverages or feedstuffs;
c to protect human life or health within the territory of the Member from risks arising from diseases carried by animals, plants or products thereof, or from the entry, establishment or spread of pests; or
d to prevent or limit other damage within the territory of the Member from the entry, establishment or spread of pests.

A special new treaty to deal specifically with these measures was thought necessary because the general obligations and exceptions contained in the GATT 1947 had proven in the prior decades too vague and poorly suited to the context of disputes over SPS measures. The Preamble to the SPS Agreement therefore notes explicitly that it is designed "to elaborate rules for the application of the provisions of GATT 1994 which relate to the use of sanitary or phytosanitary measures, in particular the provisions of Article XX(b)."

As a result, many of the provisions contained in the SPS Agreement go well beyond those contained in the GATT 1947. Article 3, for example, obliges WTO Members to "base their sanitary or phytosanitary measures on international standards, guidelines or recommendations," subject to certain caveats. Article 5.5 contains a requirement that WTO Members must "avoid arbitrary or unjustifiable distinctions in the levels it considers to be appropriate in different situations"; while Article 5.6 provides that SPS measures must not be "more trade-restrictive than required to achieve their appropriate level of sanitary or phytosanitary protection, taking into account technical and economic feasibility."

For the purposes of the present argument, however, the most important provisions are those that require SPS measures to have a scientific basis. Article 2.2 provides that:

> Members shall ensure that any sanitary or phytosanitary measure is applied only to the extent necessary to protect human, animal or plant life or health, is based on scientific principles and is not maintained without sufficient scientific evidence, except as provided for in paragraph 7 of Article 5.

Article 5.1 elaborates further that members "must ensure that their sanitary or phytosanitary measures are based on an assessment, as appropriate to the circumstances, of the risks to human, animal or plant life or health" posed by the imports in question, with the following two paragraphs detailing the sorts of factors that ought to be taken into account in risk assessment. Article 5.7 provides for a limited and temporary carve-out where relevant scientific evidence is "insufficient" to perform an adequate risk assessment.

These science-based provisions have proven the most significant of the obligations contained in the SPS Agreement. They have been litigated in every dispute so far brought under the SPS Agreement. Parties invariably spend a great deal of time arguing about the persuasiveness and adequacy of the scientific evidence that underpins the measure at issue. Their relevance for the purposes of this chapter is clear: at least on the face of the text, there is an obvious sense in which the SPS Agreement provides pride of place to scientific expertise, using it as the primary measure by which to distinguish protectionism from legitimate SPS measures. In a move which for Jasanoff represents a globalization of a particularly American culture of objectivity,[32] it appears to draw on the epistemic authority of science for an objective, external standpoint from which to resolve SPS disputes. As such, it has been described as the "most ambitious technocratic achievement of the Uruguay Round,"[33] and represents a good example of what I have referred to above as the encoding in law of non-legal (scientific) expertise.

However, this is by no means the complete picture. In a perceptive analysis of the 2006 Panel decision in *EC—Approval and Marketing of Biotech Products*—a challenge brought by the United States, Argentina, and Canada to the European Union's (EU) system for the approval of genetically modified crops and food—Bonneuil and Levidow describe what they see as the "paradox" of the jurisprudence under the SPS Agreement. On one hand, they note, the *Biotech* case was all about the nature and extent of scientific evidence of risks associated with genetically modified products. More than 1,000 pages of text—including submissions from parties, and the report itself with its annexes—was dedicated, they observe, to summarizing and discussing the scientific evidence and expert opinions put forward by both parties. On the other, however:

> the Panel hardly refers to scientific arguments in its findings, which instead emphasize the defendant's procedural failures, and the Panel's conclusions are strictly fashioned as a legal interpretation. Moreover, the Panel avoids any substantive judgment on whether or not the defendant's procedures were based on scientific evidence of risk.[34]

Thus, the Panel found against one aspect of the EU's approval system on the basis that it led to an undue delay in decision-making procedures. It found further that EU member state measures were non-compliant with Article 5.1 on the basis that the documents on which they were based did not meet the formal requirements of a "risk assessment" as defined in Annex 1. It also found that Article 5.7 was inapplicable simply by referring to the fact that the EU itself had carried out its own risk assessment to show that existing evidence was sufficient to perform a risk assessment. All of these grounds for decisions, Bonneuil and Levidow note, permitted the Panel to avoid taking a position on questions of disputed scientific knowledge, even as the legitimacy of the judgment rested in some real sense on its "'science-based' imprimatur."[35]

This paradox represents an illustration of the double movement, which, in my view, characterizes the jurisprudence under the science provisions of the SPS Agreement as a whole. On one side, there are many occasions in the jurisprudence in which the line between scientific and legal judgments becomes blurred. The views of scientific experts on matters of risk are taken to be more or less determinative of the legal question of whether there is a violation of the relevant SPS provision. The legal burden of proof is not clearly distinguished from the scientific burden of substantive persuasion, and legal objectivity is effectively equated with scientific rigor and adherence to scientific standards of truth. On the other side, however, and sometimes even in the same cases, Panels and the Appellate Body are at pains to draw a clear line between legal and scientific issues, to emphasize that legal standards of sufficiency of scientific evidence are *different from* those pertaining in scientific communities, to note that a finding of a violation of the SPS Agreement is *not* the same thing as a determination about the nature and extent of risk, and to draw a clear distinction between the role of the adjudicator and that of the scientific expert.

One of the best illustrations of this dynamic comes from the twists and turns of the jurisprudence on the standard of review applicable under Articles 2.2 and 5.1 of the SPS Agreement.[36] The first case to deal with this question was *EC—Hormones*, in which the Appellate Body somewhat hedged its bets. On one hand, the Appellate Body noted, the standard of review is not "*de novo* review as such," which would place the Panel in the same position as the risk assessor, requiring it to form its own view as to the substantive merits of scientific dispute brought before it. On the other hand, however, nor was the appropriate standard that of "total deference," which would of course undermine the operation and objectives of the Agreement as a whole. The appropriate standard, it opined, was found in Article 11 of the Dispute Settlement Understanding (DSU), namely, an "objective assessment of the facts." In practice, this turned out in that case to be a relatively deferential standard. Thus, the Appellate Body famously made clear in its decision that WTO members have the right to rely on minority scientific opinion without having that decision called into question in a WTO tribunal. What matters, the Appellate Body said, was merely that this minority opinion came from a "qualified and respected source," and that it reasonably supported the SPS measure in question.[37] Thus the technique of defining the standard of review was deployed to shift the terms of argument, from the scientific question of whether the evidence was persuasive or correct, to the legal question of whether it was sufficient for the purposes of the SPS Agreement, taking into account the *institutional* issue of "the balance established in [the SPS Agreement] between the jurisdictional competences conceded by the Members to the WTO and the jurisdictional competences retained by the Members for themselves."[38]

In a number of subsequent cases, however, legal and scientific judgments were not so clearly distinguished. Perhaps the best example is *Japan—Apples*, in which a core question was whether the importation of apples (especially mature, symptomless apples) was likely to lead to the introduction of fire blight into the Japanese ecosystem. The Panel found that this was unlikely, primarily on the basis of the opinion of the independent experts called to give evidence before it:

> we note, in light of the elements placed before us by the parties, as well as in light of the comments of the experts appointed by the Panel, that the scientific evidence suggests a negligible risk of possible transmission of fire blight through apple fruit …
>
> We further recall the opinion of the experts that due to the development of new scientific research tools, in particular DNA-based methods, they were more confident than ever before that there was only a negligible chance of fire blight being transmitted through apple fruit …
>
> Nonetheless, we note that even if the scientific evidence before us demonstrates that apple fruit is highly unlikely to be a pathway for the entry, establishment and spread of fire blight within Japan, it does suggest that some slight risk of contamination cannot be totally excluded. The experts all categorized this risk as "negligible" …[39]

Importantly, the Panel appeared to think that it followed immediately from this conclusion that the measure was "maintained without sufficient scientific evidence" for the purposes of Article 2.1. For a number of commentators, this decision came close to the *de novo* review prohibited by the Appellate Body in *EC-Hormones*.[40] Whether or not that is true, at the very least we can say that the foundation of the decision was in the scientific determination of facts, and that in practice the Panel's finding of a legal violation flowed almost automatically from the scientific opinions given before it.

In *US/Canada—Continued Suspension*, both sides of the double movement were clearly visible. Here, it played out as a disagreement over the appropriate standard of review between the Panel and the Appellate Body. The Panel, in a famous statement, set out a standard of review, which on its face appears to place the legal adjudicator in a similar position to that of the scientific assessor:

> Although the Panel is not carrying out its own risk assessment, its situation is similar in that it may benefit from hearing the full

> spectrum of experts' views and thus obtain a more complete picture both of the mainstream scientific opinion and of any divergent views … [On some points], a larger number of experts expressed opinions and, sometimes, they expressed diverging opinions. While, on some occasions, we followed the majority of experts expressing concurrent views, in some others the divergence of views were such that we could not follow that approach and decided to accept the position(s) which appeared, in our view, to be the most specific in relation to the question at issue and to be best supported by arguments and evidence. As we have told the parties and the experts during these proceedings, this Panel is not composed of scientists.[41]

In context, the claim that the "Panel is not composed of scientists" at the end of the quotation should be understood not as a way of drawing a boundary between legal and scientific expertise, but rather as articulating an attitude of deference to scientific expertise on crucial determinations of fact. The Panel's statement, it seems to me, sets out a standard and process of review that, to a very large extent, locates the task of determining the legality of the measure in the determination of facts, in turn based heavily on opinions of scientific experts.

The Appellate Body in the same case, however, took a very different view:

> It is the WTO Member's task to perform the risk assessment. The panel's task is to review that risk assessment. Where a panel goes beyond this limited mandate and acts as a risk assessor, it would be substituting its own scientific judgment for that of the risk assessor and making a *de novo* review and, consequently, would exceed its functions under Article 11 of the DSU. Therefore, the review power of a panel is not to determine whether the risk assessment undertaken by a WTO Member is correct, but rather to determine whether that risk assessment is supported by coherent reasoning and respectable scientific evidence and is, in this sense, objectively justifiable.[42]

It reiterated its finding in the earlier *Hormones* case that WTO members are permitted to base their measures on divergent or minority opinion, as long as this minority opinion has "the necessary scientific and methodological rigor to be considered reputable science."[43] Once this criterion is met, the Appellate Body said, a Panel's task is to "assess whether the reasoning articulated on the basis of the scientific evidence is objective and coherent."[44] While the precise meaning of this text has proven nebulous, what is crystal clear is the function that the Appellate Body's test is playing here. It is a way of drawing a clear line between legal and scientific processes of review, such that the preponderance of scientific evidence on any particular point of fact becomes less significant to the resolution of the legal questions at hand, and the application of independent legal expertise more significant. In a move reminiscent of Bonneuil and Levidow's analysis of the *Biotech* Panel's judicial avoidance techniques, the Appellate Body in *Continued Suspension* found ultimately that in light of the Panel's misunderstanding of the appropriate standard of review, and in light of the inadequacy of the relevant evidence before it, it was not able to make a decision on the legality of the European measure before it.

The pendulum appears to have swung again in the relatively recent SPS case of *Australia—Apples.* Here, the Appellate Body reiterated its statement of the appropriate standard of review from *Continued Suspension*, but this time gave heavy emphasis to the final stage of the articulated review process, namely the question of "whether the reasoning articulated on the basis of the scientific evidence is objective and coherent."[45] At this stage of the analysis, the Appellate Body joined the Panel in conducting what looked very similar in substance to the sort of review conducted years earlier by the Panel in *Japan—Apples.* Virtually every assumption in every model used by the risk assessor was tested for its veracity and realism, and intermediate conclusions inferred from indirect evidence were tested for their logic, such that one is left with the overwhelming impression that the basis of the decision was simply that neither the Panel nor the Appellate Body found Australia's risk assessment substantively persuasive.[46]

Cultures of objectivity

From one perspective, the two stories I have just told are entirely unremarkable. One explanation of the SPS jurisprudence, for example, is simply that there are two (or more) different interpretations of the appropriate standard of review in play, and that the interpretive conflict is yet to be resolved in favor of one or the other. On this view, there is nothing particularly special about disagreements over the appropriate standard of review: they may be durable and very difficult to resolve, but this is hardly an unusual state of affairs in the life of the law. An insightful variant of this explanation is that offered by Bonneuil and Levidow, who (rightly) characterize the standard of review as "a flexible, discursive resource to be used tactically by the different actors" who seek to have certain issues characterized as either legal or scientific, as it suits the case they seek to make.[47] On this view, the twists and turns of the jurisprudence reflect the fact that the boundary between law and science is constructed and reconstructed in the context of each case: "each party and expert construct[s] different boundaries between science and law, as well as between the experts' role and judges' role" to suit their purposes.[48] The contest to define the standard of review, then, is one venue in which the contest between types of expertise continues to be played out after negotiations have finished, in the process of legal interpretation.

Furthermore, one perfectly serviceable explanation of the jurisprudence under the Subsidies Agreement may simply be that the Appellate Body's use of economic expertise depends entirely on the nature of the question it is addressing. That is to say, there are certain questions (such as the product scope of the relevant market in *Canada—FIT*) that economic concepts and techniques can and do answer well, but there are certain other questions (such as the appropriate institutional foundations of the market used for benchmarking purposes) to which economics is just poorly suited, and therefore cannot be used. The different approaches I described above to the use of economic expertise in subsidies cases, then, could reflect nothing more than the different questions that Panels and the Appellate Body have been required to answer in the cases before them.

As useful as these explanations are for some purposes, at the same time they also both miss something important. To suggest, as the second explanation does, that the differing uses of economic expertise in dispute settlement proceedings derives simply from the nature of the question at issue is to miss the fact that the framing of the "question at issue" is itself not entirely given, but rather emerges as part of the argumentative process. It is the result of choices made by Panels and the Appellate Body, not (just) a cause of them, and to view the SPS standard of review as nothing more than a site on which contests between legal and scientific expertise are played out—as the first explanation does—fails to register the extent to which the "double movement" I have described in the two vignettes above is *functional* for, and inherent to, the dispute settlement system, and indeed central to its mode of operation.

The interpretation I offer of the two vignettes above is, in the end, a very simple one. It is this: both subsidies and SPS disputes pose particularly difficult and, at some level, intractable problems for the international trading system. How does one distinguish between the legitimate exercise of a precautionary approach to risk regulation from an illegitimate or disguised restriction on imports? How does one draw a line between impermissible subsidies on the one hand, and other kinds of governmental measures that correct market failures or address pre-existing and unfair competitive disadvantages, on the other? One function of the dispute settlement system, I would suggest, is to resolve such issues "objectively" (a term I leave deliberately undefined for the moment). We know, of course, that objectivity is, in the ultimate analysis, not a characteristic of a particular procedure of decision making but a local, cultural-institutional achievement requiring the investment of significant resources to produce and maintain.[49] If this is true, then we might say that the function of the dispute settlement system is to provide a set of tools, resources, and techniques for *making objective* the resolution of subsidies and SPS disputes in any particular context.

Now, it is not hard to see that the demands of objectivity can be very different in very different circumstances. Where there is a body of economic or scientific expertise that for the moment is quiet, in the sense that a consensus provisionally exists within the relevant discipline that certain facts and epistemic framings may be taken to be uncontroversial, then the best tactic for achieving objectivity will be simply to borrow the hard-won (if provisional) objectivity of that disciplinary expertise. This is the first half of the double movement I described above, and we saw it at work in such cases as *Japan—Apples, US—Upland Cotton*, the *Aircraft* cases, and others. However, where the body of scientific or economic expertise has become destabilized, or is emerging in a highly politicized environment, then the demands of objectivity may be different. "Objectivity" in that context then comes to take on the hue of neutrality vis-à-vis the scientific controversies at issue. This is where the legal techniques of distinguishing legal from scientific questions, of carefully defining and circumscribing legal standards of review, of explicitly adopting legal fictions, are of most use in "making objectivity." This is the second half of the double movement, which we saw at work in the Panel decision in *EC—Approval and Marketing of Biotech Products*, in the Appellate Body decision in *US/Canada—Continued Suspension*, some parts of the Appellate Body decisions in *Canada—FIT*, and in the *Brazil—Aircraft* litigation.

This is what I mean when I say that "encoding" a body of economic or scientific expertise in a body of legal norms is a more complex and ambivalent move than is typically imagined. The point is that encoding expertise in law works precisely because it enables *both* halves of this double movement. We are of course familiar with the way that encoding enables a legal system to borrow the objectivity of the expertise on which it draws, but encoding *also* enables the legal system to establish its objectivity precisely by distinguishing itself from that expertise—by drawing a clear line between legal and economic/scientific questions. That this is inherent in the encoding process becomes obvious once we realize that the incorporation of (say) an economic concept into a legal text inherently and necessarily changes its character and positions it in a new context of meaning making: it becomes a *legal* concept, the defining feature of which is precisely its (potential) divergence from its economic counterpart. Furthermore, this is not an accidental effect of encoding, but central to its ability to produce objectivity in different ways, using different resources and techniques, as circumstances change. Encoding expertise works, then, somewhat paradoxically providing a set of techniques for making decisions which depart from the dictates of that expertise—and derive their legitimacy and objectivity from that departure.

It follows from this that what matters a great deal in determining how the system of WTO law works in these contexts is the culture of objectivity in which it is embedded. What kinds of choices tend to count as "neutral" or "impartial" in the context of the application of WTO law?[50] Conversely, what sorts of decisions tend to be treated as controversial or political or partial, and why? What, in other words, are the key markers of objectivity in the context of WTO legal decision making, and the intuitions and habits of thinking on which they are based?

Conclusion

It is the point of this chapter primarily to pose such questions, and to demonstrate their significance in understanding how expertise operates in the context of WTO law, rather than to answer them. Nevertheless, it is possible briefly to state a handful of the more obvious characteristics of the culture of objectivity at work in the operation of WTO law. First, most observers of the WTO dispute settlement system will agree that the Appellate Body often deploys a species of uncompromising, even rigid, textualism to demonstrate its impartiality and objectivity in sensitive cases—even where it might be argued that an interpretive approach based on the intentions of the drafters may lead to the opposite conclusion.[51] A case like *US—Gambling* is a clear example, though there are many others.[52] Second, an interpretive approach, which safeguards the regulatory autonomy of the respondent WTO member is also often deployed by Panels and the Appellate Body, particularly over the last decade, to signal its neutrality in relation to the contested values underlying the regulatory measure in question.[53] This is so despite the fact that such an approach is clearly non-neutral in the sense that it has the effect of allocating part of the costs of such measures on constituencies within the complaining member. Third, displays of institutional modesty are also an important element of the WTO's culture of objectivity. This may, for example, take the form of a refusal to make decisions about the interpretation of provisions of international law outside the narrow confines of WTO law,[54] or a refusal to adjudicate the legitimacy of a regulatory measure beyond assessing whether or not it is protectionist.[55] Fourth and finally, it is, I think, fair to say that decisions which privilege the status quo of existing markets—in the specific sense of leaving in place the institutional foundations on which markets are constructed—are more likely to be perceived as neutral and objective than the opposite. *Canada—FIT* is perhaps the best example of this norm at work.

It is, no doubt, a vain exercise to attempt to specify fully the culture of objectivity at work in any particular institutional context—one can be virtually certain that in most cases there will be multiple such cultures at play, and a great deal of fluidity over time. However, it does seem to me to be important to be attentive to the tools and techniques that are deployed in a particular legal-institutional context to achieve the effect of objectivity and neutrality, as they are so central to any complete explanation of the way in which law and expertise are co-articulated in the interpretation and application of a treaty text. This is particularly so, given that studies of the role of expertise in global trade politics have so far produced a number of fascinating accounts of the role of expert knowledges in processes of preference formation and negotiation, but somewhat fewer that focus on processes of legal interpretation and application.

Notes

1 John Gerard Ruggie, "International Regimes, Transactions, and Change: Embedded Liberalism in the Postwar Economic Order," *International Organization* 36, no. 2 (1982): 379–415.
2 General Agreement on Tariffs and Trade (GATT), 30 October 1947, Article XVI.
3 GATT, Article XVI: 4. As it happened, agreement proved impossible, however, and in the end only a subgroup of 17 industrialized countries reached an agreement in 1960.
4 GATT, Article XVI: 3.
5 Working Party Report on "Provisions of Article XVI: 4," adopted 19 November 1960, BISD, 9th Supplement (1961): 185.
6 WTO, *Marrakesh Agreement Establishing the World Trade Organization*, opened for signature 15 April 1994, 1867 UNTS 3 (entered into force 1

January 1995), annex 1A, Agreement on Subsidies and Countervailing Measures.

7 SCM Agreement, Article 1.2.
8 SCM Agreement, Article 3.1.
9 SCM Agreement, Article 10, footnote 35.
10 WTO, *Canada—Measures Affecting the Export of Civilian Aircraft* (*Canada—Aircraft*), WT/DS70/AB/R, Appellate Body Report, adopted 20 August 1999, paragraph 157.
11 WTO, *Canada—Certain Measures Affecting the Renewable Energy Generation Sector (Canada—Renewable Energy); Canada—Measures Relating to the Feed-in Tariff (FIT) Program (Canada—Feed-in Tariff Program)*, Appellate Body Report, adopted 24 May 2013.
12 WTO, *Canada—FIT*, paragraph 5.174.
13 WTO, *Canada—FIT*, paragraph 5.189.
14 WTO, *US—Subsidies on Upland Cotton Recourse to Article 21.5 by Brazil*, WT/DS267/AB/RW, adopted 20 June 2008, paragraph 356.
15 WTO, *United States—Subsidies on Upland Cotton (US—Upland Cotton)*, WT/DS267/AB/RW, Article 21.5, Appellate Body Report, adopted 20 June 2008, paragraph 357.
16 WTO,*European Communities—Measures Affecting Trade in Large Civil Aircraft*, WT/DS316/AB/R, Appellate Body Report, adopted 1 June 2011, paragraph 1110.
17 The EU advanced a calibrated model in the Panel proceedings in that case: Appendix VII.F.2, paragraph 61; see also Dominic Coppens, *WTO Disciplines on Subsidies and Countervailing Measures: Balancing Policy Space and Legal Constraints* (Cambridge: Cambridge University Press, 2014).
18 WTO, *European Communities—Measures Affecting Trade in Large Civil Aircraft*, paragraph 1045.
19 WTO, *European Communities*, paragraph 1047.
20 See, for example, Luca Rubini, "What Does the Recent WTO Litigation on Renewable Energy Subsidies Tell Us about Methodology in Legal Analysis? The Good, the Bad and the Ugly," EUI Working Paper (San Domenico di Fiesole, Italy: European University Institute, May 2014).
21 WTO, *Canada—Certain Measures Affecting the Renewable Energy General Sector (Canada—Renewable Energy)*, WT/DS412/AB/R, Appellate Body Report, adopted 24 May 2013, paragraph 5, 190. See also WTO, *Canada—Certain Measures Affecting the Renewable Energy General Sector (Canada—Renewable Energy)*, WT/DS412/R, Panel Report, adopted 24 May 2013, paragraph 7.308–313.
22 WTO, *Brazil—Export Financing Programme for Aircraft (Brazil—Aircraft)*, WT/DS46/R, Panel Report, adopted 20 August 1999, paragraphs 7.21–22.
23 WTO, *Brazil—Export Financing Programme for Aircraft (Brazil—Aircraft)*, paragraphs 7.24–25.
24 WTO, *Brazil—Export Financing Programme for Aircraft (Brazil—Aircraft)*, paragraph 7.25.
25 WTO, *Brazil—Export Financing Programme for Aircraft (Brazil—Aircraft)*, WT/DS46/AB/R, Appellate Body Report, adopted 20 August 1999, paragraph 182.
26 WTO, *Brazil—Export Financing Programme for Aircraft Recourse to Article 21.5 of the DSU by Canada (Brazil-Aircraft [21.5, Panel])*, WT/DS46/

RW, Panel Report, adopted, 4 August 2000, paragraph 6.84 and surrounding.

27 WTO, *Brazil—Export Financing Programme for Aircraft Recourse to Article 21.5 of the DSU by Canada (Brazil-Aircraft)*, WT/DS46/AB/RW, Appellate Body Report, adopted 4 August 2000, paragraph 64.

28 WTO, *United States—Preliminary Determinations with Respect to Certain Softwood Lumber from Canada*, WT/DS236/R, Panel Report, adopted 1 November 2002, paragraph 7.50.

29 WTO, *United States—Preliminary Determinations with Respect to Certain Softwood Lumber from Canada*, paragraph 7.52.

30 WTO, *United States—Final Countervailing Duty Determination with Respect to Certain Softwood Lumber from Canada*, WT/DS257/R, Panel Report, adopted 17 February 2004, paragraph 7.59.

31 WTO, *United States—Final Countervailing Duty Determination with Respect to Certain Softwood Lumber from Canada (US—Lumber IV)*, WT/DS257/AB/R, Appellate Body Report, adopted 17 February 2004, paragraphs 100–101.

32 Sheila Jasanoff, "The Practices of Objectivity in Regulatory Science," in *Social Knowledge in the Making,* ed. Charles Camic, Neil Gross and Michèle Lamont (Chicago, Ill.: University of Chicago Press, 2011), 307–36.

33 Cristophe Bonneuil and Les Levidow, "How Does the World Trade Organization Know? The Mobilization and Staging of Scientific Expertise in the GMO Trade Dispute," *Social Studies of Science* 42, no.1 (2012): 79.

34 Bonneuil and Levidow, "How Does the World Trade Organization Know?" 77.

35 Bonneuil and Levidow, "How Does the World Trade Organization Know?" 97.

36 See Sab Schropp, "Commentary on the Appellate Body Report in *Australia-Apples* (DS367): Judicial Review in the Face of Uncertainty," *World Trade Review* 11, no. 2 (2012): 171–221; and Lukasz Gruszczynski, *Regulating Health and Environmental Risks under WTO Law: A Critical Analysis of the SPS Agreement* (Oxford: Oxford University Press, 2010).

37 WTO, *European Communities—Measures Concerning Meat and Meat Products (Hormones) (EC—Hormones)*, WT/DS285/AB/R, Appellate Body Report, adopted 27 September 2005, paragraph 194.

38 WTO, *European Communities*, paragraph 115.

39 WTO, *Japan—Measures Affecting the Importation of Apples (Japan—Apples)*, Panel Report, adopted 10 December 2003, paragraphs 8.169–8.181.

40 See Schropp, "Commentary on the Appellate Body Report in *Australia-Apples* (DS367)," 171–221; and Gruszczynski, *Regulating Health and Environmental Risks under WTO Law.*

41 WTO, *Canada—Continued Suspension of Obligations in the EC—Hormones Dispute (Canada—Continued Suspension)*, Panel Report, adopted 14 November 2008, paragraph 7.411.

42 WTO, *EC—Hormones*, AB, paragraph 590.

43 WTO, *EC—Hormones*, paragraph 591.

44 WTO, *EC—Hormones*, paragraph 591.

45 WTO, *EC—Hormones.*

46 For a similar view, see Schropp, "Commentary on the Appellate Body Report in *Australia-Apples* (DS367)," 171–221.

47 Bonneuil and Levidow, "How Does the World Trade Organization Know?" 90.

48 Bonneuil and Levidow, "How Does the World Trade Organization Know?" 90.

49 Jasanoff, "The Practices of Objectivity in Regulatory Science."

50 See Cass R. Sunstein, "Lochner's Legacy," *Columbia Law Review* 87, no. 5 (1987): 873, for an argument that poses the same questions, for essentially the same reasons, in a different context.

51 See, for one among many examples, Sol Picciotto, "The WTO's Appellate Body: Legal Formalism as a Legitimation of Global Governance," *Governance: An International Journal of Policy, Administration, and Institutions* 18, no. 3 (2005): 477.

52 WTO, *United States—Measures Affecting the Cross-Border Supply of Gambling and Betting Services (US–Gambling)*, WT/DS285/R, Panel Report, adopted 20 April 2005.

53 See Andrew Lang, "Conclusion: After Neoliberalism?" in *World Trade Law after Neoliberalism: Remaining the Global Economic Order* (Oxford: Oxford University Press, 2013).

54 WTO, *EC—Measures Concerning Meat and Meat Products (EC—Hormones)*, Appellate Body Report, WT/DS26/AB/R, adopted 13 February 1998; WTO, *European Communities—Measures Affecting the Approval and Marketing of Biotech Products (EC—Approval of Marketing of Biotech Products)*, Panel Report, WT/DS291, 292, 293/R, adopted 21 November 2006.

55 Simon Lester, "Book Review: *World Trade Law after Neoliberalism*. By Andrew Lang," *Journal of International Economic Law* 15, no. 2 (2012): 701–7.

Part III

The agency of expert knowledge

The power of critical technicians, embedded NGOs, and organic intellectuals

7 Symbolic power and social critique in the making of Oxfam's trade policy research

Matthew Eagleton-Pierce

- **Social critique and trade politics**
- **The symbolic power of knowledge**
- **Oxfam's trade policy research through the lens of symbolic power**
- **Conclusion**

This chapter investigates the making of expert knowledge in relation to international trade policy and how such processes are intertwined with forms of power. Similar to other spheres of capitalism, our understanding of the power-knowledge nexus can help to inform questions of participation, agenda setting, and material outcomes within formal trade politics. A focus on such links can also shed light on how professional experts within this field often struggle over the sources and techniques of legitimation. In keeping with the aims of this book, to explore how authoritative claims on trade knowledge shape the topography of the (im)possible, the argument here probes the recent history of a particular organization: Oxfam International.

As one of the most recognizable voices in civil society, Oxfam offers an interesting illustration for how a critique of capitalism, rooted in a sense of social justice, can register a place in debates on trade policy. Within the space constraints here, the argument explores how Oxfam analysts carved out this position and, in particular, unpicks some of the core strategies and styles of such labor. In doing so, this chapter complements and enriches existing literature, not only in respect to the analysis of civil society groups in trade politics but, more broadly, our understanding of how alternative heterodox opinions can contest orthodox forms of knowledge.

To prosecute this enquiry, the chapter deploys a conceptual framework informed by the work of Pierre Bourdieu—specifically, his notion of symbolic power. By adopting this sociological optic, the argument aims to offer fresh insights into the social construction of linguistic authority within the policy *milieu* of trade politics. In particular, a Bourdieusian perspective targets the ways in which forms of power acquire recognition and, in doing so, can enlighten our understanding of the possibilities for agency within constrained social spaces.

The chapter is thus organized into three main sections. First, in an initial contextual discussion, the chapter situates the problem area in relation to the complex legacy of social critique within transnational trade policymaking. Second, the conceptual toolkit on symbolic power is outlined and unpacked, including broader empirical illustrations drawn from trade issues. In the third section, the framework on symbolic power is applied to explain the specific case of Oxfam's rise in trade policy debates. The chapter ends with some concluding remarks, including notable caveats to the larger argument and pathways for considering further research.

Social critique and trade politics

Since the first currents of socialism and the work of Marx, social critique has posed recurring problems for how capitalism is justified and practiced. Although such efforts are often limited, disorganized, or beset by setbacks and blockages in relation to larger "orthodoxies," this does not mean that the critique remains unworthy of analytical attention. On the contrary, as argued by Boltanski and Chiapello, critique can be conceived as a major (although by no means the only) "motor of change" in the evolution of the system.[1] Not only does social critique confront capitalism with troubling ethical questions, most prominently around themes of economic inequality and human exploitation, but also, through a period of reflection, experimentation, and potential incorporation, critique may inadvertently "give" new ideological resources to reinvigorate capitalism (or rather, capitalism "captures" and claims new ideas for itself). This means that the precise contribution of any critique often remains unclear and potentially incoherent, particularly in terms of how it inspires agents and the extent to which it may have any concrete impact. In other words, certain forms of critique often play an anxious dance between, on the one hand, a desire to be recognized by power and, on the other, a need to create a heterodoxy that can substantially challenge the orthodoxy.

The social space of policymaking on international trade presents an interesting object for dissecting this wider relationship between critique and capitalism. In broad terms, the period since the mid-1990s has seen the emergence of alternative voices who have unsettled, contested, or strongly rebuked how the political economy of trade has been both conceptualized and materially prosecuted. One can argue that the strengthening of an "augmented Washington Consensus"[2]—a vision that still contains the core "Victorian virtue" of "free markets and sound money,"[3] but now appeals to "second generation reforms" around matters of governance, institutions, and poverty reduction[4]—was a reaction to how neoliberalism had become a "damaged brand." Within such debates, the inequities that marked the transnational regulation of trade—with the distinctions between richer and poorer countries being one major axis—generated some of the most heated claims and counterclaims.[5] It needs to be underscored that this "force of critique"[6] took many forms and involved multiple agents, including initial efforts by developing country governments to contest World Bank and International Monetary Fund (IMF) reforms; austerity-related street protests and riots in different African and Latin American cities; the rise of the alter-globalization movement with its common appeal to "global justice"; and the expansion of critical research by professional experts, located within several areas of the social sciences, agencies of the United Nations, and the wider field of civil society.

In other words, the universe of potential arguments contained within the liberal "trade orthodoxy" or episteme[7] has undergone a change which has been provoked by contrarian voices. In order to better understand the historical evolution of trade politics, including assessing whose agency is articulated and how, we need to plot how substantial such change has been, both in theory and practice. As part of a larger investigation into this question,[8] this chapter addresses a particular focus on the ties between social critique and global trade politics: the cultivation of research-intensive, policy-facing groups. The immediate touchstone for this type of enquiry would be trade literature on non-governmental organizations (NGOs) or civil society actors. Here, authors have explored a number of worthy themes over the past two decades, including debates about NGO access to, and critiques of, World Trade Organization (WTO) negotiation processes, the relevant size of the "NGO community," and the specific impact of advocacy work on particular trade issues (such as in respect to access to medicines or agricultural concerns).[9]

Nonetheless, the precise relationship between knowledge, activism, and agency in the regulation of trade is still in need of further investigation. Erin Hannah's scholarship has offered one of the more astute readings of changes in this space. In Hannah's view, a "new brand of actor" has emerged over recent years: socially progressive "embedded NGOs" that "seek to re-embed global markets in broader social and environmental values."[10] Such agents "accept the basic tenets of free trade as essential for development and poverty alleviation," but try to highlight and empower vulnerable actors via detailed policy advice. For instance, the International Centre for Trade and Sustainable Development (ICTSD) is a good example of a so-called embedded NGO. As Hannah argues, such research-focused collectives "are central to the construction of conventional wisdom about the limits and possibilities of trade."[11]

A similar interest in the culture and policy impacts of ICTSD is also seen in Paul Mably's analysis.[12] Through a focus on the G33 coalition in the WTO, Mably argues that sympathetic ICTSD research on the G33 worked to "legitimize" the group and lend its members "a higher level of credibility" in trade negotiations. Thus, these studies help us to better grasp the making, and significance, of a specific type of professional critic common to the world of trade policy analysis.[13]

The argument of this chapter connects with such scholarship, but also seeks to offer a distinctive double contribution in theory and empirics. In respect to the former, the rest of the argument debates how enquiries into the nexus between knowledge and power in trade policy can be enhanced through a richer sociological analysis. This particular conceptual orientation has only been explored in limited ways within scholarship on trade politics. The deployment of Bourdieu's arsenal on symbolic power is designed to offer a corrective to such analytical lacunas, particularly through charting the struggles over legitimation that characterize the trade policy world.

In respect to the latter, the chapter concentrates on Oxfam International as a revealing case of research-intensive activism on trade policy. Oxfam's trade campaigns have received some dedicated academic inspection, particularly around its fair trade initiatives and its contribution to the "Making Poverty History" movement.[14] Nonetheless, there has been less attention on tracing the historical emergence of Oxfam's position in the trade policy field and how, in particular, it sought to improve its research outputs through a process of adaptation. Thus, this chapter aims not only to elucidate some features of this recent history, but to conduct the evaluation through the prism of symbolic power, to the details of which we can now turn.

The symbolic power of knowledge

In the broader study of world politics, the potential utility of Bourdieu as a theoretical inspiration has sparked increased interest in recent years, mirroring the appropriation of his ideas elsewhere in the social sciences. Bourdieu has been framed in light of the so-called "practice turn" in International Relations (IR), which has sought to conceive of political action in ways not captured by purposeful instrumental rationality (logic of consequences), norms (logic of appropriateness), or communicative action (logic of arguing).[15] This interest has been particularly strong among scholars who address the politics of international security and diplomacy.[16] Indeed, the extent to which Bourdieu has now "made it" in IR can be illustrated by special volumes dedicated to analyzing his work and how it can inform international political explanations.[17] However, notwithstanding these developments, so far at least, Bourdieu's concepts have rarely been used for enhancing our understanding of the politics of the world economy—a neglect that this chapter aims to address.

The application of the conceptual framework of symbolic power to the specific study of the research-intensive civil society groups on trade is certainly not an automatic move. However, this chapter suggests that Bourdieu's ideas do have merit and can enrich our understanding of political practice within this particular domain of capitalism. Bourdieu was a polyglot who studied philosophy and taught himself anthropology, before developing a significant corpus of sociological research. Rather than rigidly impose his concepts, he is treated here as an intellectual stimulus, not a prophet. A perspective on symbolic power brings forward a series of sub-concepts. With an eye on relational analysis, these "thinking tools" work together to form a larger theoretical design. By way of initial introduction, symbolic power offers a way to conceptualize how existing forms of power acquire legitimacy or, as Bourdieu would put it, pass as (mis)recognized. It places particular attention on how language, as a preeminent (although not the only) symbolic system, both reflects and constitutes power, to the extent that the notion of power is considered intertwined with the idea of legitimation.[18]

Following earlier arguments made elsewhere, this chapter argues that there are three major contributions of this perspective to the study of international trade politics.[19] First, such a framework offers new objects for investigation that are either discounted or underplayed in common debates on power in trade politics. Against the coercive, realist power vision, which tends to treat language either as some "ephemeral" feature of diplomatic tussles or as the dry preoccupation of lawyers, the idea of symbolic power can be deployed to explore the properties of the "linguistic market," a Bourdieusian expression for a bounded social space where only certain arguments acquire legitimacy. For the author of *Distinction*,[20] there is a panoply of linguistic methods that may be interlaced with power, but the role of classification systems is particularly important. Inspired by the classical anthropology of Durkheim and Mauss[21] and the philosophical anthropology of Cassirer,[22] Bourdieu argues that classifications of the social world matter because they may have a determining effect on many practices operating at lower levels of abstraction; indeed, this is often a stated goal. For instance, when applied to the WTO, one can point to many classifications that have a political significance across national institutions and territories, not only in reference to particular trade agreements but also in the form of generic identity categories (such as the taken-for-granted developed/developing/least developed country schema). At the same time, in a further effort to tease out why only certain ideas are legitimate in the linguistic market, Bourdieu uses the twin notions of orthodoxy and heterodoxy to probe critically how the conventional wisdom is framed, rather than to rarify the commonsense as an ordinary state of affairs.

Second, once power is understood to flow through language, the analysis of symbolic power can inform our understanding of core political processes. In terms of participation, a Bourdieusian approach works against the standard view of power as a scarce resource marshaled by an elite population. In contrast, he points to the diffuse, everyday practices of justificatory claim making which shape definitions of political practices and yet, crucially, are often not read as expressions of power (as historically defined). In other words, symbolic power is a kind of "denied" power in which the explicit declaration of self-interest is downplayed. This does not mean that privileged players are incapable of wielding such power in an intentional way (*à la* rational choice); rather, Bourdieu seeks to reveal how many practices would not be sustainable if they appeared to emanate from the pursuit of pure self-interest. Thus, agents need to cultivate symbolic power in order to insulate themselves from criticism. Such insights have consequences for how we plot change in trade talks, including enriching the analysis of coalitions[23] and the links between language and political mobilization.[24]

In respect to agenda setting, Bourdieu's concepts shed new light on old problems. Particularly relevant for the trade context are the ties he draws between law, politics, and methods of institutionalization. Law itself is symbolic power *par excellence*, a monumental body of knowledge that works to codify publically particular interests into the universal.[25] Such a point is admittedly captured in some uses of the notion of institutional power or in wider constructivist theorizing that has traced the legal legitimacy of WTO rules and norms.[26] However, the symbolic power framework can be distinguished by how deeply the politics of law are dissected, uncovering not only how interests are defended and distorted through law, but also via more subtle euphemisms and sleights of hand.[27]

Third, and related, it may appear that the competition over symbolic power acquires a degree of autonomy from the material world it supposedly represents. The trade policy game seems to turn upon itself, with players engrossed in the chips and prizes that they have intersubjectively valued. However, this depiction is only partially correct. The stakes for controlling symbolic power in the world economy are high because they shape the configuration and stabilization of particular material interests. For instance, as other authors have argued, the Uruguay Round settlement, which gave birth to the WTO, also consecrated legally justifiable rules which protect highly profitable corporate rents.[28] Thus, it should not be surprising that the actors who benefit from such material gains will seek to safeguard and consolidate the outcomes of the Uruguay Round (either in the WTO or other trade forums). In this example, the notion of symbolic power could enter as a conceptual device for examining three core problems: (i) to unmask how the historical genesis of such legal classifications was shaped by particular corporate entities; (ii) given the universalization of these rules and norms, to reveal how major business interests will likely have an upper hand in subsequent trade agendas; and (iii) to shed light on how the freedom of actors who are critical of dominant legal framings will be constrained by the classification struggles of the past. In sum, informed by a desire to expose social inequities and against liberal meliorist sensibilities, a Bourdieusian interpretation of materialism aims to uncover the often-elaborate forms of social labor used to conserve and transform capital.

The call by Bourdieu for an expanded definition of political and economic interest—ranging from calculating strategies to masked or even unconscious practices—also matters for addressing the relationship between compulsory power and symbolic power. In one crucial sense, my argument is not only that a vision of power that is fixated on materialism represents a narrow interpretation but, in addition, how a symbolic power framework can help us to better grasp under what conditions forms of materialism, including coercive acts, acquire added analytical meaning. For instance, actions of compulsory power are sometimes used to deal quickly with a threat that cannot be accomplished by more time-consuming and strenuous processes of symbolic power accumulation. The coercive move may be used to cut short or disfigure a rival process of legitimation, but one would need to examine the content of such symbolic power to understand why compulsory power was being exercised at that point in time. Equally, if following the deployment of compulsory power, a certain actor has a damaged reputation, it may be very necessary for them to rebuild their stock of symbolic power around an issue. Such episodes reveal that coercion is usually rare and expensive because of the fundamental need to appeal to different logics of legitimacy in capitalist relations, an historical trend that arguably has become more pronounced. Indeed, because of the importance of protecting symbolic power, the agent who has potential compulsory power may resort to exercising their dictates behind closed doors—that is, away from other audiences that could expose the contradictions and cruelty of such measures.

In essence, symbolic power is a different concept in how it allows for the durability and inertia of certain political relations and conditions of (mis)recognition, yet still facilitates scope for examining how agents actively remake the social world through historical tools of cognition. Importantly, the definition of symbolic power cannot be succinctly fixed and applied to all situations, but rather should be treated here as an "open concept" that acquires meaning through the labor of empirical research. Thus, in conversation with Wacquant, in a point Bourdieu often underscored, concepts are no good unless they are put into action in a "systematic fashion."[29] With this in mind, we can now turn to address how Bourdieu's sense of the symbolic power of knowledge can be applied to the study of Oxfam's activism on trade.

Oxfam's trade policy research through the lens of symbolic power

Oxfam International represents a pertinent example of the relationship between alternative thinking on trade politics and advocacy work. From its earliest activism on fair trade in the 1940s, to the larger "global justice" campaigns around the turn of the millennium, Oxfam has carved out a significant voice on many trade policy concerns. In one sense, when compared with other civil society groups and charities, Oxfam is unusual in terms of its size: in the 2012/13 year, for instance, the total income of the organization was €955 million, with over 10,000 permanent staff working in a confederative structure across 93 countries.[30] This geographical reach, fieldwork exposure, and deep legacy of engagements with policymaking processes at a variety of levels does, nonetheless, make Oxfam a good test of wider trends that have marked struggles between social critique and capitalism. Indeed, it will be suggested, notably in respect to certain campaigning techniques and presentation methods, that Oxfam representatives have been entrepreneurs in the cultivation of a particular activist subjectivity. With Bourdieu's symbolic power framework in mind, this section plots and dissects some of the learning strategies and practices that have characterized Oxfam's recent research on trade. In particular, to better reveal the distinctiveness of the symbolic power that has been cultivated around forms of trade analysis, the argument compares efforts pursued in the 1980s and early 1990s, with the subsequent period until the mid-2000s.

Within the 1980s, Oxfam's attention to trade policy was often intertwined with other economic issues, notably debt and aid, and how such problems contributed to hunger in Southern countries. In the wake of the Cambodian and Ethiopian crises, under the directorship of Frank Judd (1985–91), the group began to make further investments in research. Like today, these efforts were targeted at Oxfam's own supporters in order to help them understand the difficult issues under scrutiny which, in turn, would assist in fundraising strategies. In addition, the same research also aimed to be cogently packaged to political decision makers, an objective that required demonstrating empirical command of relevant issues.[31]

During the late 1980s, under the "Hungry for Change" campaign frame, Oxfam produced a number of reports that, in retrospect, formed a basic template for future research projects. We see here experimentation with a number of augmentation themes, of which three are notable. First, the idea of an occasional overview report is established, one that synthesizes together interconnected problems, before offering policy recommendations.[32] Second, a variety of types of evidence are marshaled within these reports in an effort to provoke and persuade the reader, including drawing upon Oxfam's own field officers, data from international organizations and other literature sources. In terms of methods, descriptive statistical analysis is given a prominent position, along with specific case study boxes and illustrative photos. Third, the use of catchy one-liners is included to add a degree of "flair" to publicity, often through encapsulating some sense of injustice, such as: "For every £1 the world contributed to famine relief in Africa in 1985, the West took back £2 in debt repayment."[33]

Nonetheless, when one turns to the actual subject matter of trade policy debated by Oxfam around this time, some insiders have expressed reservations about its content and effectiveness. In 1991, Kevin Watkins joined the group from the Catholic Institute of International Relations, rising from policy analyst up to the position of head of research. Over the next decade, Watkins proved a very significant research leader who sharpened Oxfam's attention on trade policy. One of the major lessons that Watkins took from the 1980s and 1990s, when the Uruguay Round was being negotiated, was that activists on trade politics were left significantly behind the main actions that shaped the agenda: corporate lobbying of Western governments.[34] As he expressed it: "When I joined Oxfam, NGO advocacy on trade was very limited both in terms of its ambition and approach."[35] Watkins was concerned that analysis tended to focus almost exclusively around terms of trade in agriculture and Organisation for Economic Co-operation and Development (OECD) surpluses which, while being important, overlooked the wider General Agreement on Tariffs and Trade (GATT) agenda around textiles, services, investment, and intellectual property.[36] At a higher level of abstraction, reflecting his own normative positioning, he was against more radical "anti-trade" or "anti-growth" reasoning heard within some quarters of Oxfam. Instead, Watkins suggested that "it was possible, within certain limits, if you could work the system effectively, to secure small gains in market access for developing countries."[37] It was this more moderate political disposition, one that called for dissecting and unpicking the trade orthodoxy and searching for new policy opportunities, that would characterize much of Oxfam's research in the 1990s and early 2000s.

As the WTO was established in 1995, Oxfam's trade policy research became increasingly focused around agendas emanating from Geneva. Along with a larger summary book, *The Oxfam Poverty Report*,[38] Watkins authored another substantive report on agricultural rules and food security,[39] while other researchers analyzed the North American Free Trade Agreement,[40] as well as the relationship between trade and the "new issues" of labor rights and the environment.[41] Nonetheless, in a common pattern that is witnessed elsewhere in the "NGO industry," political windows of opportunity strongly structure the direction and content of research activities. In this respect, the period surrounding the WTO Seattle Ministerial in 1999, which featured efforts to launch a new trade round of talks, provided the necessary moment to mobilize intellectual and activist energies. For instance, in terms of the volume of outputs, from 1999 to 2001, 26 publications focused on trade politics, including traditional topics such as agriculture, but also other concerns related to the WTO's institutional design, the access to medicines case, and gender issues. By contrast, in the entire period from 1980 to 1998, 19 publications featured trade discussions. A second window of opportunity pivoted around the following WTO ministerial conference, held in Cancún in 2003. In respect to the period from 2002 to 2004, Oxfam's trade policy-focused work increased even further, publishing a total of 75 pieces. In the context of shifting configurations of diplomatic power in WTO negotiations, including the notable activism of the G20 and G33 coalitions to contest the United States-European Union duopoly, this particular window marked the high-water mark of Oxfam's coverage on trade policy.[42]

The case of the West African cotton dispute can be highlighted here as an interesting piece of Oxfam-led activism that marked this latter period. The problem centered on a coalition of West and Central African (WCA) countries—Benin, Burkina Faso, Mali, and Chad—which began campaigning in 2003 at the WTO for the liberalization of cotton trade. In a nutshell, the problem concerned how these countries, as highly competitive cotton producers, tried to engineer greater access to third markets, particularly China, in order to enhance their market access opportunities. This quartet of countries argued, however, that such export potential was being impeded by highly subsidized US cotton farmers, whose own competitiveness was artificially inflated. The issue quickly became a contentious lightning rod and absorbed a considerable portion of the WTO's negotiating energy, including spawning a major, related dispute settlement case by Brazil against the United States.[43]

Oxfam, along with a network of other civil society players, played a significant role in the very creation of "African cotton" as a political problem that needed WTO attention. Although it is often tricky to identify the precise significance of these contributions and how, in particular, WCA officials interpreted their activism, it is safe to say that the initiative would not have been the same without such input. In the first place, the work of Watkins needs to be credited with mainstreaming the empirical connection between US cotton subsidies and WCA livelihoods. His 2002 report, *Cultivating Poverty*—backed by strong statistical analysis, a political critique of US cotton policy, and quotes from WCA farmers—had a key impact in terms of increasing information awareness.[44] As *Cultivating Poverty* became more widely read and cited, Oxfam's Geneva-based advocacy team plotted how cotton could be articulated in the WTO context. In particular, researchers such as Céline Charveriat and Romain Benicchio consulted with lawyers and analysts based at ICTSD, a major research hub on trade policy mentioned earlier.[45] ICTSD became important in terms of building solidarity between African missions in Geneva, as well as connecting ambassadors with other relevant actors, such as a Senegal-based network called Environment and Development Action in the Third World.[46] By the end of 2004, following a decision from WTO members that cotton would be addressed "ambitiously, expeditiously, and specifically,"[47] Oxfam produced two further cotton-specific reports in an effort to maintain political momentum around the issue.[48]

To return to the conceptual ambitions on symbolic power, what can be learnt about Oxfam's research strategies around trade policy? Three themes are worth further exploring. First, demonstrating command of what is legitimate knowledge remains the *sine qua non* for professionals in this social world. All critiques that are developed by Oxfam authors are thus founded upon an understanding of "orthodox" trade knowledge or, to be precise, the particular "sanctified" knowledge that is relevant to the problem under scrutiny. The symbolic power associated with this knowledge may embrace a range of theories, principles, modes of reasoning, agendas, and histories that are attached to the trade policy game. Oxfam reports will often tap into, and play with, many of these forms of symbolic power in an effort to sway the reader and demonstrate credibility. For instance, at the disciplinary level, economics and law have been the major academic fields that have provided education or, in more prescriptive terms, training, in the subject of international commercial exchange. In other words, these disciplines have stood as the "admission gateways," to invoke a term with a Bourdieu inflection, that aspiring experts have to pass through in order to acquire a (or the most) legitimate right to speak on trade. In the most profound sense, economists and lawyers draw upon, in both conscious and implicit ways, the pre-existing legitimacy associated with such canonical bodies of knowledge. This combined stock of symbolic power—when one considers its historical construction over centuries, its transnational reach from Western centers of power to "emerging" or marginalized locations and, in particular, its incorporation into rules and customs of modern statehood—is monumental and resists easy summation.[49]

Given that almost all other policy-facing knowledge producers on trade—from government officials, to experts within international organizations, to academic consultants—build their arguments through the prism of economic and legal theories, the Oxfam analyst who rejects this foundation of symbolic power would likely have a very short career (indeed, given competitive entry conditions, they would probably never be hired). To recall, therefore, this point concurs with Bourdieu's larger argument that symbolic power is partly constructed in an effort to protect agents from forms of criticism. For instance, in the aforementioned Oxfam literature, one often sees an engagement with precise legal rules or economic modeling of the effects of certain agreements. Under Watkins's leadership, in a point confirmed by others who have walked in his footsteps, the empirical "standard" of Oxfam's research has improved when compared with the 1980s and early 1990s,[50] but the meaning of "improvement," in this respect, is partially a judgment on the capacity to understand "the legitimate vision of the social world and its divisions."[51] Within this particular space of civil society professionals, the accumulation of symbolic power involves mastering the principles of legitimacy that shape the parameters and substance of the policy game, a process which, in turn, gives all players a sense of shared identity. In short, only those who speak in the legitimate tongue—who know their Pareto from their Kaldor-Hicks in efficiency criteria, their amber box from their blue box in agricultural domestic support, or their mode one from their mode four in services negotiations—may pass through the entrance gates and fight for the symbolic and material prizes that await.

Once this process of persuasion is underway, a second theme of relevance can begin: the incorporation of a heterodox critique to distinguish the Oxfam opinion from orthodox speakers. Such strategies of positionality in the intellectual marketplace are crucial for attracting attention and maintaining institutional status. In keeping with the historical legacy of social critiques of capitalism, the Oxfam writer is traditionally imbued with a social justice sensibility, including a capacity to unearth and trace forms of human suffering beneath the veneer of orthodox knowledge. In this sense, pure forms of economic and legal knowledge are not the only sources of symbolic power that are nurtured by Oxfam authors to mount their trade campaigns. We also see explicit and tacit appeals to other systems and techniques of legitimation, notably Christian values of care and compassion for "distant suffering" beyond the West. In some instances, the object of critique is clear, such as in the *Cultivating Poverty* report where the policies of the US government are strongly attacked.[52] At other times, carving out a heterodox critique on trade policy is more delicate or limited in scope. Regardless of the precise level of ambition, Oxfam analysts frequently target the tensions, inconsistencies and contradictions expressed in orthodox formulations of trade practice. In the words of Luc Boltanski and Eve Chiapello, they are found "tightening up" the "tests of justification"—that is, to make whatever is the test under scrutiny ("WTO is good for development," "WTO enables fair negotiations," etc.) "stricter."[53] Such activity may not accomplish its objectified goal—the removal of a certain agenda or set of rules—but could instead complicate and, importantly, slow down particular policymaking processes.

A final theme of importance would build upon this analysis of alternative sources of symbolic power, but address the style, rather than the precise analytical substance, of such publications. In a visual, screen-based culture, where the Internet serves as a major channel of political communication and images of all kinds can be digitally manipulated, the stylistic packaging of Oxfam's arguments has arguably become more significant. One could also include under this theme the attention to publication titles, headlines and other one-liners that are often penned in an exciting prose designed to grab the attention of audiences. Such trends in presentation methods are obviously systemic and now inform the contemporary public relations of countless organizations beyond Oxfam. However, one pioneering feature of Oxfam's reports centers on the use of select quotes (along with photographs) from the field, whereby the voice of a farmer or producer helps to justify the overall argument. In particular, such quotes help to form an opposition between, on the one hand, economic and legal "scientific" knowledge (such as in the form of statistics, models, rules and customs of trade) and, on the other hand, the "common layperson" who exists "on the ground," removed from "higher-level" professional and expert politics. These quotes of the marginalized poor are often positioned near the beginning of Oxfam reports. As elements within an argumentation scheme, they sometimes exist in a tense or ambiguous relationship with the subsequent analysis: either as enlightening the sterilized scientific knowledge with a human association or, in other contexts, seeming to stand apart as the "true" and "most authentic" source of revelation. It is also worth noting that such symbolic features are not without controversy when seen through postcolonial eyes, reflecting a larger "commodity diversity" emotive feel that is common to the current liberal episteme.[54]

Conclusion

This chapter has sought to shine a brief spotlight on some of the strategies pursued by Oxfam's trade-focused research through the conceptual prism of symbolic power. By way of conclusion, and as a pathway for further research, three caveats need to be made. First, a richer understanding of the location of Oxfam analysts in the trade policy field can only be adequately grasped through an analysis of other knowledge producers—rivals and allies—who inhabit the same social world. This point was alluded to in the chapter, but a more detailed exploration would also unpick the working practices of orthodox-leaning experts, such as those who move within the WTO Secretariat, the World Bank or, more diffusely, policy-facing economists and lawyers. At the same time, the sense of self that is cultivated by Oxfam researchers is also, in part, a product of distinguishing themselves from heterodox intellectuals who may have limited impact on the political world but, nonetheless, share a similar normative worldview. Through such analysis, one would, in Bourdieu's terminology, begin to chart and decipher the relationship between symbolic power, social space, and position taking.

Second, a deeper investigation into this area would, in addition to providing further context on the political economy, also reveal some of the internal tensions operating within Oxfam over the past three decades. Every external presentation of strategy—the choice of which trade problem to publicize, how to address the issue, how to mobilize constituents, or how to handle any subsequent criticism—will inevitably feature choices over direction in a constrained environment. Explaining such decision-making processes would help us to gain a perspective on the often-intense labor process involved in deploying symbolic power.

Third, through such objectified research, one will also hope to provide certain insights into the potential for more emancipatory forms of trade politics. To imagine substantive alternatives to the present configuration between material structures and symbolic structures, one must first understand how the orthodox-arguing universe constrains freedom of expression, including the imagination to think of alternatives. The collective labor of Oxfam researchers, in addition to other like-minded social movements interested in trade policy, stands as an interesting illustration of how contemporary social critique can push back against the justificatory boundaries of capitalism. One potential—although by no means invulnerable—general strategy would involve further exploring and testing of sources of symbolic power that are not easily captured by capitalism. For instance, as noted, Oxfam's appeals to social justice are partly informed by quasi-religious connotations, a sense of family life, or more general ideals of a "common humanity."

In other words, social critique derives its energy from revealing the roots of indignation, including cries for liberation, the removal of human suffering, and the unmasking of inauthentic persons and objects.[55] Here, reviving the notion of exploitation in relation to trade politics—in all its obvious and subtle forms—should be at the heart of an emancipatory vision. For sure, capitalism is always, at the same time, revising its answers to these demands, but a research agenda on global trade that casts an unflinching and critical gaze on such themes would probably be more robust and, at the same time, more problematic to those who benefit from existing forms of power.

Notes

1 Luc Boltanski and Eve Chiapello, *The New Spirit of Capitalism* (London: Verso, 2007), 27.

2 Dani Rodrik, *One Economics, Many Recipes: Globalization, Institutions, and Economic Growth* (Princeton, N.J.: Princeton University Press, 2007).
3 Paul Krugman, "Dutch Tulips and Emerging Markets: Another Bubble Bursts," *Foreign Affairs*, July/August 1995, 29.
4 Narcís Serra and Joseph E. Stiglitz, *The Washington Consensus Reconsidered: Towards a New Global Governance* (Oxford: Oxford University Press, 2008).
5 Jagdish Bhagwati, *In Defense of Globalization* (Oxford: Oxford University Press, 2004); William R. Cline, *Trade Policy and Global Poverty* (Washington, DC: Peterson Institute, 2004); and L. Alan Winters, Neil McCulloch and Andrew McKay, "Trade Liberalization and Poverty: The Evidence So Far," *Journal of Economic Literature* 42, no. 1 (2004): 72–115.
6 Boltanski and Chiapello, *The New Spirit of Capitalism*, 483.
7 Emanuel Adler and Steven Bernstein, "Knowledge in Power: The Epistemic Construction of Global Governance," in *Power in Global Governance*, ed. Michael Barnett and Raymond Duvall (Cambridge: Cambridge University Press, 2005), 294–318.
8 Matthew Eagleton-Pierce, *All the Trader's Men: Expertise and Power in World Trade* (forthcoming manuscript).
9 Peter van den Bossche, "NGO Involvement in the WTO: A Comparative Perspective," *Journal of International Economic Law* 11, no. 4 (2008): 717–49; Martina Piewitt, "Participatory Governance in the WTO: How Inclusive is Global Civil Society?" *Journal of World Trade* 44, no. 2 (2010): 467–88; and Hannah Murphy, *The Making of International Trade Policy: NGOs, Agenda-Setting and the WTO* (Cheltenham: Edward Elgar, 2010).
10 Erin N. Hannah, "The Quest for Accountable Governance: Embedded NGOs and Demand Driven Advocacy in the International Trade Regime," *Journal of World Trade* 48, no. 4 (2014): 459.
11 Hannah, "The Quest for Accountable Governance," 478.
12 Paul Mably, "Centralized Production: The Group of G33," in *The Politics of Trade: The Role of Research in Trade Policy and Negotiations*, ed. Diana Tussie (Ottawa: International Development Research Centre, 2009), 267.
13 Matthew Eagleton-Pierce, *Symbolic Power in the World Trade Organization* (Oxford: Oxford University Press, 2013).
14 Suzan Ilcan and Anita Lacey, "Governing Through Empowerment: Oxfam's Global Reform and Trade Campaigns," *Globalizations* 3, no. 2 (2006): 207–25; Susan Ariel Aaronson and Jamie Zimmerman, "Fair Trade? How Oxfam Presented a Systemic Approach to Poverty, Development, Human Rights, and Trade," *Human Rights Quarterly* 28, no. 4 (2006): 998–1030; and Craig Berry and Clive Gabay, "Transnational Political Action and 'Global Civil Society' in Practice: The Case of Oxfam," *Global Networks* 9, no. 3 (2009): 339–58.
15 Vincent Pouliot, "The Logic of Practicality: A Theory of Practice of Security Communities," *International Organization* 62, no. 2 (2008): 257–88; and Emanuel Adler and Vincent Pouliot, ed., *International Practices* (Cambridge: Cambridge University Press, 2011).
16 For instance, see Didier Bigo, "Pierre Bourdieu and International Relations: Power of Practices, Practices of Power," *International Political Sociology* 5, no. 3 (2011): 225–258; and Michael Williams, *Culture and*

Security: Symbolic Power and the Politics of International Security (London: Routledge, 2007).

17 Rebecca Adler-Nissen, ed., *Bourdieu in International Relations: Rethinking Key Concepts in IR* (Abingdon: Routledge, 2012).

18 Pierre Bourdieu, *Language and Symbolic Power* (Cambridge: Polity Press, 1991); Pierre Bourdieu, *Outline of a Theory of Practice* (Cambridge: Cambridge University Press, 1977); Pierre Bourdieu, *Pascalian Meditations* (Cambridge: Polity Press, 1997); Pierre Bourdieu, "Social Space and Symbolic Power," *Sociological Theory* 7, no. 1 (1989): 14–25; Pierre Bourdieu, "Symbolic Power," *Critique of Anthropology* 4 (1979): 77–85; Pierre Bourdieu, "The Economics of Linguistic Exchanges," *Social Sciences Information* 16, no. 6 (1977): 645–68; Pierre Bourdieu, "The Force of Law: Toward a Sociology of the Juridical Field," *Hastings Law Journal* 38 (1987): 805–53; and Pierre Bourdieu, "What Makes a Social Class? On the Theoretical and Practical Existence of Groups," *Berkeley Journal of Sociology* 32 (1987): 1–18.

19 Eagleton-Pierce, *Symbolic Power in the World Trade Organization.*

20 Pierre Bourdieu, *Distinction: A Social Critique of the Judgement of Taste* (London: Routledge, 1984).

21 Emile Durkheim and Marcel Mauss,*Primitive Classification* (Abingdon: Routledge, 2010 [1903]).

22 Ernst Cassirer, *An Essay on Man: An Introduction to a Philosophy of Human Culture* (New Haven, Conn.: Yale University Press, 1944).

23 Amrita Narlikar and Diana Tussie, "The G20 at the Cancun Ministerial: Developing Countries and their Evolving Coalitions in the WTO," *World Economy* 27, no. 7 (2004): 947–966.

24 Rorden Wilkinson, "Language, Power and Multilateral Trade Negotiations," *Review of International Political Economy* 16, no. 4 (2009): 597–619.

25 Bourdieu, "The Economics of Linguistic Exchanges."

26 Andrew T.F. Lang, "Reconstructing Embedded Liberalism: John Gerard Ruggie and Constructivist Approaches to the Study of the International Trade Regime," *Journal of International Economic Law* 9, no. 1 (2006): 81–116; and Andrew T.F. Lang, *World Trade Law after Neoliberalism: Re-imagining the Global Economic Order* (Oxford: Oxford University Press, 2011).

27 Bourdieu, "What Makes a Social Class?"; and Bourdieu, "The Economics of Linguistic Exchanges."

28 For instance, in the areas of agribusiness and intellectual property, see Jennifer Clapp, *Food* (Cambridge: Polity Press, 2012); Jennifer Clapp and Doris Fuchs, ed., *Corporate Power in Global Agrifood Governance* (Cambridge, Mass.: MIT Press, 2009); Susan K. Sell, *Private Power, Public Law: The Globalization of Intellectual Property* (Cambridge: Cambridge University Press, 2003); and Carolyn Deere, *The Implementation Game: The TRIPS Agreement and the Global Politics of Intellectual Property Reform in Developing Countries* (Oxford: Oxford University Press, 2009).

29 Wacquant, in a point made within Pierre Bourdieu and Loïc J.D. Wacquant, *An Invitation to Reflexive Sociology* (Chicago, Ill.: University of Chicago Press, 1992), 96–7.

30 Oxfam International, *Oxfam Annual Report 2012–13* (Oxford: Oxfam International, 2013).

31 Maggie Black, *A Cause for Our Times: Oxfam the First 50 Years* (Oxford: Oxford University Press, 1992).
32 For instance, see Nigel Twose, *Cultivating Hunger: An Oxfam Study of Food, Power & Poverty* (Oxford: Oxfam, 1984); and John Clark, *For Richer for Poorer: An Oxfam Report on Western Connections with World Hunger* (Oxford: Oxfam, 1986).
33 Black, *A Cause for Our Times*, 269.
34 Also see Michael D. Wilkinson, "Lobbying for Fair Trade: Northern NGDOs, the European Community and the GATT Uruguay Round," *Third World Quarterly* 17, no. 2 (1996): 251–67.
35 Kevin Watkins, former Head of Research, Oxford International, interview with the author, Oxford, 13 June 2011.
36 For an extended critique unusual for the time, see Kevin Watkins, *Fixing the Rules: North-South Issues in International Trade and the GATT Uruguay Round* (London: Catholic Institute for International Relations, 1992); also see Belinda Coote, *The Trade Trap: Poverty and the Global Commodity Markets* (Oxford: Oxfam, 1992).
37 Watkins, interview with the author.
38 Kevin Watkins, *The Oxfam Poverty Report* (Oxford: Oxfam International, 1995).
39 Watkins, *The Oxfam Poverty Report.*
40 Belinda Coote, *NAFTA: Poverty and Free Trade in Mexico* (Oxford: Oxfam, 1995).
41 Caroline LeQuesne, *Reforming World Trade: The Social and Environmental Priorities* (Oxford: Oxfam International, 1996).
42 On the context, see Narlikar and Tussie, "The G20 at the Cancun Ministerial: Developing Countries and their Evolving Coalitions in the WTO."
43 Eagleton-Pierce, *Symbolic Power in the World Trade Organization*; also see Adam Sneyd, *Governing Cotton: Globalization and Poverty in Africa* (Basingstoke: Palgrave Macmillan, 2011); and Donna Lee, "The Cotton Club: The Africa Group in the Doha Development Agenda," in *The WTO After Hong Kong: Progress in, and Prospects for, the Doha Development Agenda*, ed. Donna Lee and Rorden Wilkinson (London: Routledge, 2007).
44 Kevin Watkins, *Cultivating Poverty: The Impact of US Cotton Subsidies on Africa*, Oxfam Briefing Paper, 5 September 2002 (Oxford: Oxfam International, 2002).
45 Romain Benicchio, Advocacy Officer, Oxfam International, interview with the author, Geneva, 26 September 2006.
46 El Hadji A. Diouf, Programme Coordinator, Africa Trade Programme, International Centre for Trade and Sustainable Development, Geneva, interview with the author, Geneva, 29 September 2006.
47 World Trade Organization, "Doha Work Programme: Decision Adopted by the General Council on 1 August 2004" (WT/L/579), 2 August 2004, Annex A: 4.
48 Céline Charveriat and Romaine Benicchio, *Dumping: The Beginning of the End? Implications of the Ruling in the Brazil/US Cotton Dispute*, Oxfam Briefing Paper, 5 August 2004 (Oxford: Oxfam International, 2004); and Kimberly Pfeifer, Gawain Kripke and Emily Alpert, "Finding the Moral Fiber: Why Reform is Urgently Needed for a Fair Cotton Trade," Oxford Briefing Paper (Oxford: Oxfam International, 18 October 2004).

49 For instance, see Marion Fourcade, *Economists and Societies: Discipline and Profession in the United States, Britain, and France, 1890s to 1990s* (Princeton University Press, 2010); Marion Fourcade, "The Construction of a Global Profession: The Transnationalization of Economics," *American Journal of Sociology*, 112, no. 1 (2006): 145–94; Yves Dezalay and Bryant G. Garth, *Dealing in Virtue: International Commercial Arbitration and the Construction of a Transnational Legal Order* (Chicago, Ill.:University of Chicago Press, 1996); and Yves Dezalay and Bryant G. Garth, *The Internationalization of Palace Wars: Lawyers, Economists, and the Contest to Transform Latin American States* (Chicago, Ill.:University of Chicago Press, 2002).

50 Emily Jones, former policy advisor, Oxfam International, interview with the author, Oxford, 26 October 2011; and Duncan Green, former head of research, Oxfam International, interview with the author, London, 27 May 2011.

51 Bourdieu, "The Force of Law," 13.

52 Watkins, *Cultivating Poverty.*

53 Boltanski and Chiapello, *The New Spirit of Capitalism.*

54 Elaine Swan, "Commodity Diversity: Smiling Faces as a Strategy of Containment," *Organization* 17, no. 1 (2010): 77–100.

55 Boltanski and Chiapello, *The New Spirit of Capitalism.*

8 Ratcheting up accountability?

Embedded NGOs in the multilateral trade system[1]

Erin Hannah

- **Conceptualizing embedded NGOs**
- **Embedded NGOs and their quest for accountable and inclusive trade policymaking**
- **Conclusion**

For nearly 50 years, the agenda of international trade negotiations has reflected the priorities of developed countries and the rules have evolved to mirror and reinforce the developmental imperatives of the world's richest countries. Promises to redress these asymmetries and to prioritize sustainable development remain unfulfilled.[2] There is particular concern that the commercial opportunities being negotiated during the Doha Development Round of multilateral trade negotiations (2001–current) will shrink the developmental policy space available to developing countries.[3] Meanwhile, frustrated by the failure to conclude the Doha Development Round, an increasing number of states, led by the United States and the European Union (EU), are negotiating bilateral or regional free trade agreements (FTAs) and plurilateral trade agreements which threaten to accelerate liberalization, ratchet-up international trade rules and bind developing countries to more stringent disciplines and obligations than are required by the World Trade Organization (WTO) agreements in a context where relatively greater power asymmetries prevail.[4] The "bicycle theory" narrative—the notion that ever greater market opening is needed to prevent economic crisis—continues to drive further trade liberalization and many fear that this will erode special and differential treatment provisions negotiated multilaterally, make developing countries more vulnerable to import surges and marginalize them further in multilateral trade negotiations.[5]

The extension of trade rules into new areas, such as intellectual property rights, services, and investment, has rendered trade negotiations infinitely more complex, and effective participation requires sophisticated, technical expertise. There is a growing chorus of concern that developing countries lack the requisite capacity, knowledge, and resources to participate effectively in international trade negotiations, and to shape the rules that will ultimately determine their collective destinies.[6] Developing and least developed countries are often marginalized in international trade negotiations, have minimal representation in Geneva and are unable to resist domination by developed countries. Although the international trade regime is premised on rhetorical, principled commitments such as consensus, reciprocity, and most favored nation, there are vast disparities in the ability of some members to frame the agenda and advance key strategic interests.[7] Often developing country delegations lack the technical knowledge or the resources to engage in formal negotiations or to advance scientifically or economically supported evidence for their positions. Knowledge asymmetries serve to exacerbate power asymmetries further and render the international trade regime unsustainable.[8]

A new brand of actor has emerged in response to these developments. International nongovernmental organizations (NGOs) that claim to be socially progressive and which seek to re-embed global markets in broader social and environmental values, both domestically and globally, are working with developing and least developed countries in what are purported to be efforts to correct imbalances and asymmetries in the international trade regime.[9] Coined 'embedded NGOs' to distinguish them from more traditional advocacy groups and to demarcate their commitment to a socially embedded, liberal international economic order, these actors engage in demand-driven advocacy and provide research and technical trade-related expertise to developing and least developed countries with the aim to increase their negotiating capacity, carve out additional policy or development space, and promote the three pillars of sustainable development—economic, social, and environment. The overarching objective is to make the WTO more accountable, inclusive, and responsive to the needs and priorities of developing and least developed members. Embedded NGOs are based in both the global North and the global South. They are predominantly status quo-maintaining actors, as opposed to status quo-altering or transformative actors such as the Focus on the Global South or the Third World Network, in that they accept the basic tenets of free trade as essential for development and poverty alleviation, and consider mainstreaming development in the WTO a priority.[10] According to some, embedded NGOs and the up-scaling of knowledge and capacity of developing countries are at least partly responsible for putting the brakes on the Doha Development Round negotiations.[11]

Embedded NGOs have increased significantly in number in the past decade. They deserve scholarly attention because understanding the global governance of trade requires us to take all "three" of the WTOs seriously: the Organization and the Secretariat; member states; and non-state actors.[12] We need to understand better that international trade politics are about much more than interactions between member states, and embedded NGOs play effective roles in this regime. Yet, so far no robust approach has been advanced to aid our understanding. To this end, this chapter develops an analytical framework to evaluate the impact of embedded NGOs on the WTO's accountability regime.

The first section of this chapter deals with definitional issues and differentiates the work of embedded NGO from other forms of NGO advocacy. I then situate the study in the extant literature on transnational NGOs and accountability and delineate four key accountability dimensions along which we can evaluate embedded NGOs: transparency, evaluation, consultation, and correction. The discussion then shifts, in the final section, to a consideration of the challenges and obstacles encountered by embedded NGOs.

On balance, improvements in the negotiating capacity of developing countries and of the WTO's accountability regime more generally are likely to result from the provision of research and technical assistance provided by embedded NGOs, especially in areas concerning supply-side capacities that are not central to the formal Doha Development Round negotiations, such as Aid for Trade (AfT). However, the institutional and geographical attributes of embedded NGOs, the uneven engagement by embedded NGOs with developing countries, the commitment of embedded NGOs to a liberal economic order, and the internal and external accountability of embedded NGOs themselves are significant challenges that must be addressed. Further research is required to better identify and explain the variations and extent of embedded NGOs' impact on the WTO's accountability regime, and to redress power and knowledge asymmetries in the international trade regime more generally.

Conceptualizing embedded NGOs

The potential for NGOs to improve the democratic accountability of the WTO has long been a focal point for research.[13] Indeed, it is widely argued that more open trade policymaking processes that include NGOs will, by virtue of the divergence of interests represented, lead to a stronger, more legitimate, and qualitatively enhanced international trade system.[14] Some scholars evaluate the impact of formal

NGO inclusion vis-à-vis the submission of *amicus curiae* briefs to the dispute settlement process and NGO participation in WTO proceedings, public symposia, and consultations with the WTO secretariat.[15] Others examine the informal agenda-setting capacity of NGOs at the WTO in a range of issue areas such as trade and health, genetically modified organisms, environment, investment, labor standards, and development.[16] The common denominator in these studies is the view that NGO interaction with the WTO makes international trade negotiations more transparent, gives rise to public debate and contestation, and provides a voice for broader societal concerns about the impact of international trade rules.[17]

Yet, while much has been learned about the role of NGOs and other non-state actors in the WTO policymaking process, the tendency to focus on the public campaigns waged by NGOs at the WTO does not fully capture the strategies NGOs employ to influence international trade negotiations and is at odds with the evolving relationship between NGOs and various members of the international trade regime. Increasingly, highly specialized NGOs are interacting directly with WTO members in an effort to affect international trade negotiations, and this development has received inadequate attention in the literature.[18] Moreover, these NGOs are leveraging their legal and technical trade-related expertise in an effort to redress power and knowledge asymmetries in the international trade regime. There is a small but burgeoning body of literature that studies the role of NGO research in shaping global governance,[19] but the role of NGO expertise in international trade negotiations has received little attention.[20] This chapter seeks to help fill these vacancies in the literature by conceptualizing a particular brand of non-state actor, embedded NGOs, and their potential impact on the accountability of the WTO.

Embedded NGOs are best understood as one class of knowledge producer and disseminator in the international trade regime that leverages their trade-related technical and legal capacity and expertise to affect international trade politics. They are part of an epistemic community of experts defined by Haas as "network[s] of professionals with recognized expertise and competence in a particular domain and an authoritative claim to policy-relevant knowledge within that domain or issue-area."[21] They are involved in the construction, contestation, and reification of epistemes, the shared, intersubjective or taken-for-granted causal and evaluative assumptions about how the world works and ought to work.[22] Epistemes are "the attribute of science-based agents [...] who seek to socially construct policy in their image of the truth and principled beliefs," in order to promote international cooperation.[23]

According to Ruggie, experts and the knowledge they generate defines the legitimate social purpose of the international trade regime.[24] In other words, embedded NGOs are part of the community of experts that generates "the widely held accepted norms, consensual scientific knowledge, ideological beliefs deeply accepted by the collective, and so on."[25] Embedded NGOs possess an authoritative claim on knowledge and are involved in the legitimation of certain forms of trade knowledge; they possess the ability to shape the terms of debate and construct narratives that define what is both conceivable and inconceivable in trade negotiations.

States rely on experts to help them make sense of the world. Networks of experts, including embedded NGOs, assist states in defining the problems they face, and in formulating, distilling, and channeling new ideas for policy formulation. Increasing reliance on expert knowledge goes hand in hand with increasing technical complexity and uncertainty in global governance.[26] Nowhere is this more in evidence than in the international trade regime where embedded NGOs have emerged as key nodes in this network.

It is possible to discern six key characteristics common to embedded NGOs. In tandem, these characteristics distinguish embedded NGOs from other forms of NGO advocacy.

First, embedded NGOs accept the basic tenets upon which the international trade regime rests, but aim to re-embed global markets. They work to infuse global markets with mechanisms that enable social protection for the world's most vulnerable people. Embedded NGOs are part of a wider movement that aims to reinvent and reinvigorate the embedded liberal compromise in contemporary global economic governance.[27] They aim to provide both developed and developing countries with the tools, resources, ideas, and knowledge necessary to re-embed socially the international trade regime and carve out additional policy or development space for developing countries in new and novel ways. In this respect, they are reshaping the discourse and assumptions about "who is in need of protection, who bears the responsibility of protection, and what kinds of risks are worthy of protection."[28] However, they are best classified as status quo-maintaining actors, not transformative or status quo-altering actors like many advocacy NGOs, because they accept, and indeed cement, the normative underpinnings of the international trade regime. Their policy prescriptions tweak at the margins rather than propose radical, innovative change, and may even crowd out alternative voices and shrink space for resistance.

Second, embedded NGOs are highly specialized, think tank-like organizations. They are widely recognized as experts in the field of international trade and they serve as knowledge nodes and disseminators of information to activists and practitioners alike all around the world. They often work together with intergovernmental organizations such as the Food and Agriculture Organization (FAO) and the United Nations Conference on Trade and Development (UNCTAD).

Third, the work of embedded NGOs is distinct from conventional advocacy or protest work of NGOs in that they engage in demand-driven advocacy, responding to requests by both developed and developing countries for research and trade-related technical assistance in international trade negotiations. They seek to affect trade rules by building capacity and equipping countries with the knowledge, resources, and tools necessary to participate fully in trade negotiations. Fourth, embedded NGOs maintain unusually close relations with trade negotiators and often form part of developed and developing country members' official trade delegations, and they are considered by negotiators to be vital interlocutors in the development of trade policy.

Fifth, while they may engage with both developed and developing countries, embedded NGOs leverage their legal and technical trade-related expertise in areas of key strategic interest to developing countries—e.g. agriculture, health, fisheries, aid—in an effort to redress knowledge and power asymmetries in the international trade regime. Their explicit aim is to empower developing countries to articulate and defend *autonomous* policy choices in trade negotiations. The demand-driven nature of their work means that embedded NGOs are responsive to requests for assistance by countries. However, it is not always clear what constitutes developing country interests, given the variation and contestation across and within the global South. For example, there are tensions within Brazil over whether liberalization and the expansion of agribusiness or support and protection for subsistence farming should be priorities in international trade negotiations. Embedded NGOs intervene in domestic political conflicts and play a major role in helping developing countries identify their strategic interests. The co-constituted nature of developing country interests raises important questions about what motivates embedded NGOs to operate in this way and points to the sixth key characteristic.

Embedded NGOs are second-order global development actors which operate as agents of principal actors—development donors. In large measure, embedded NGOs came into existence with the outgrowth of innovation and privatization of development financing following the 2002 Monterrey Consensus on Financing for Development.[29] As the major reference points for international development cooperation, the Monterrey Consensus and the 2008 Doha Declaration[30] articulated commitments to ensuring the increased availability of aid for developing countries and to promote the internationally agreed Millennium Development Goals (MDGs) for poverty reduction and sustainable development.[31] Developed countries agreed to increase their official development assistance, and to develop and support innovative sources of financing for development.[32] The backbone of the Consensus is a commitment to encouraging private international capital flows to developing countries and using trade and financial liberalization to combat global poverty.[33] Since 2002, there has been an increased flow of development aid through NGOs that support the goals and priorities articulated by the MDGs and the Consensus. The UK's Department for International Development (DFID) provides perhaps the best illustration of this trend.

As the Organisation for Economic Co-operation and Development's (OECD) third largest bilateral aid agency, DFID distributes funds to combat global poverty through multilateral organizations such as the EU and the World Bank, bilaterally to countries through country assistance plans, and through partnerships with NGOs. International and domestic NGOs compete for short-term grants and long-term Programme Partnership Agreements.[34] For example, DFID has provided over 30 percent of total funding for the International Centre for Trade and Sustainable Development (ICTSD) since 2007.[35] As articulated in its 2013–15 business plan, the ICTSD works to align with DFID's Operational Plan which includes a commitment to "build support for open markets and wealth creation," and to "work with the European Commission, WTO and others towards securing progress on trade liberalization that promises global growth and advances the interests of poor countries."[36] These illustrations highlight the motivations of embedded NGOs, which are owing to a triple coincidence—their normative commitments to sustainable development and socially embedded global markets, their need to secure funding to secure their existence, and their need to align priorities and policy prescriptions with donors.

Embedded NGOs are based in both the global North and the global South. Prominent examples include the ICTSD (Geneva, Switzerland), International Lawyers and Economists Against Poverty (ILEAP) (Toronto, Canada and Nairobi, Kenya), European Centre for Development and Policy Management (ECDPM) (Brussels, Belgium), Trade Policy Research and Training Program (TPRTP) (Ibadan, Nigeria), the Centre for Policy Dialogue (CPD) (Dhaka, Bangladesh), and Environment and Development of the Third World—African Centre for Commerce, Integration and Development (ENDA-CACID) (Dakar, Senegal).

With the exception of one exploratory working paper that identified some of these actors working in the African context,[37] the role and impact of embedded NGOs on the international trade regime remains virtually unexplored in the literature.[38]

Embedded NGOs and their quest for accountable and inclusive trade policymaking

The need for greater accountability in global economic governance is widely recognized.[39] At a minimum, accountability requires information and transparency about the exercise of power, mechanisms to monitor and evaluate performance and institutional effectiveness, opportunities for decision makers to justify their actions, and procedures through which poor performance or abuses of power can be corrected. Moreover, most scholars agree that international organizations (IOs) should be accountable to affected persons. Indeed, as Scholte puts it,[40] an IO "would be accountable to the extent that it is transparent to those affected, consults those affected, reports to those affected and provides redress to those who are adversely affected." However, there is a wide-ranging debate over who counts as "affected," who is entitled to hold decision makers in IOs accountable, and what constitutes an abuse of power.[41]

Some scholars argue that participatory and democratic models of accountability are essential for effective and legitimate global governance.[42] Others emphasize the need for "good governance" and argue that horizontal or delegation models of accountability place sufficient limits on the exercise and abuse of power in global governance.[43] Grant and Keohane specify that multilateral IOs like the WTO, World Bank and International Monetary Fund are consistently subject to a combination of these two models of accountability and failure to distinguish between them has generated considerable confusion in contemporary discourses of accountability.[44] We can also conceive of accountability regimes based on substantive purposes, i.e. IOs are accountable to the extent that they work to fulfill their mandates. Meanwhile, the debate is rendered more complex by what Wolfe coins an "accountability trilemma"[45]—IOs with multiple accountability regimes like the WTO must trade off demands for efficacy, responsiveness and coherence.

The promise of NGOs for improving the quality of governance at the WTO clearly rests with participatory and democratic models of accountability. Although many call into question the internal legitimacy and accountability of NGOs,[46] most observers see potential for

NGOs to improve the public and democratic accountability of the WTO.[47] NGO advocacy can make international trade negotiations and WTO proceedings more transparent. They have enjoyed significant success in pressuring the WTO Secretariat to improve public access to WTO documentation and the dispute settlement process. These improvements in transparency have enhanced outside monitoring and scrutiny of WTO activities, particularly by NGOs. NGO advocacy campaigns generate greater public awareness, debate and contestation on key trade-related issues. NGOs have been instrumental in signaling the deleterious impact of trade liberalization in a range of issue areas—investment, health, genetically modified organisms, environment and labor. NGOs may also give a voice to grievances and concerns that are otherwise marginalized in international trade negotiations. In these respects, NGOs promote the development of the global public sphere, spaces where informed citizens may contest flawed choices and demand that WTO decision makers justify their actions and policies.

Given the different tactics and objectives embraced by embedded NGOs, this overview of the potential impact of NGOs on the accountability of the WTO is incomplete. While their work may enhance the global public sphere, embedded NGOs provide research and technical trade-related expertise for the expressed purpose of empowering developing countries, ensuring the WTO fulfills the Doha Development Agenda (DDA) mandate and advances the goal of sustainable development, and improving the quality of transparency, inclusivity, evaluation, and correction for WTO member states. This means that we need a more precise set of accountability criteria than those outlined above against which to evaluate the impact of their work.

According to Wolfe, there is a series of six questions that must be asked of any accountability regime: who, to whom, about what, through what process, by what standards, and with what affects?[48] Table 8.1 illustrates how these questions can be applied to the impact of embedded NGOs on the WTO's accountability regime.

Does the provision of research and technical trade-related expertise by embedded NGOs render the multilateral trade regime more accountable to WTO members, especially developing and least developed countries, and the citizens they represent? Does it increase the likelihood of fulfilling the development priorities of the Doha Round and introducing policies that serve the three pillars of sustainable development—economic, social, and environment? Does it increase the capacity of developing and least developed countries to participate in international trade negotiations? Does it result in the introduction of new rules and policies or the evaluation and adjustment of existing

Table 8.1 Accountability criteria

Who	*To whom*	*About what*	*Through what process*	*Criteria/ standard of assessment*	*With what effect on agents*
International trade system/ WTO	WTO members and the citizens they represent	Doha Development Agenda mandate; sustainable development	Inclusive participation, consultation	Introduction, evaluation and adjustment of substantive rules and policies	Sustainable economic growth, policy or development space, increased trade policy capacity

rules and policies that enable developing and least developed countries to realize sustainable economic growth, increased trade capacity, and availability of policy space to pursue development goals? In order to answer these questions, we can examine the impact of embedded NGOs on the WTO's accountability regime along four dimensions: transparency, evaluation, consultation, and correction.

Transparency

The first and least controversial dimension is transparency. In addition to making WTO documentation more widely available and increasing public visibility and awareness of the WTO, embedded NGOs aim to make information about its activities more accessible and streamlined, to the public as well as to academics, national trade negotiators, government departments, and the trade policy community. For example, the ICTSD publishes 13 weekly and monthly periodicals free of charge such as the *Bridges Weekly Trade News Digest*, *BIORes*, and the *Bridges Review*. It co-publishes, with other NGOs, a series of regional periodicals such *Passerelles* with ENDA Tiers Monde and *Eclairage sur les Négociations* with ECDPM. It maintains a pronounced presence on all major social networking cites such as Twitter and Facebook, providing up-to-the-minute information and analysis on ongoing trade-related issues. The ICTSD collaborates with other organizations and research institutes to generate approximately 100 research papers and policy briefs annually.[49] It also conducts an annual survey to take the pulse of its audience, to gather information about how best to improve the provision of research and analysis, and to identify the various uses of its outputs. We find similar initiatives in other organizations, but on a much smaller scale. For example, the TPRTP publishes the *African Journal of Economic Policy* twice annually, and ILEAP issues a series of background briefs with the goal to inform/educate researchers, trade negotiators, and policymakers.

The provision of information by such organizations is touted by embedded NGOs as politically neutral. They view themselves as conduits of non-partisan research and analysis aimed at encouraging knowledge-empowered participation in international trade policy-making. There is no doubt that the information disseminated by embedded NGOs has extraordinary reach,[50] and has educated unprecedented numbers of people about the activities of the WTO and international trade negotiations more generally. However, it must also be recognized that the information and knowledge generated by these organizations is inherently value laden with a commitment to a more liberal trade regime. By improving the transparency of the WTO, embedded NGOs are also working to construct conventional wisdom about the possibilities and desirability of global trade to work for sustainable development.

Evaluation

Second, accountability can be assessed in terms of evaluation. According to Scholte, "[a]ccountability entails an obligation to determine how affected circles have been affected."[51] Embedded NGOs monitor, scrutinize, and assess the development and implementation of trade policy. They aim to provide credible, evidence-based, and policy-oriented assessments of new and existing rules. By conducting independent impact assessments, they provide developing countries with additional information and interpretations of official reports and assessments offered by the WTO Secretariat and other IOs.

The ICTSD has developed a series of impact assessment methodologies and implemented them in a range of issue areas. For example, in an effort to assist developing countries to develop and articulate their respective positions on the special safeguard mechanism (SSM) for agriculture, the ICTSD collaborated with personnel from the South Centre and FAO to develop a methodology for identifying sensitive products (SP).[52] The aim was to help individual countries operationalize the SP and SSM concepts in order to protect food security, livelihood security, and rural development.[53] The ICTSD initially conducted in-country field testing of the methodology in six G33 coalition[54] countries—Barbados, Honduras, Kenya, Pakistan, Peru, and Sri Lanka.[55] Additional studies took place in 2006 and 2007.[56] These country studies form the basis for the G33 coalition's SP lists in WTO negotiations.[57]

The ICTSD also developed a simulation exercise designed to evaluate the impact of various SSM proposals on individual G33 members.[58] The simulation was applied to six countries[59] to determine how the use of different triggers and remedies would affect different countries' access to the SSM and the effectiveness of the SSM in bridging gaps between import and domestic prices.[60] The findings of this report were reflected in the G33 positions on trigger mechanisms and remedies between 2008 and 2010.[61]

Aid for Trade is another area where embedded NGOs have sought to develop mechanisms for monitoring and evaluating new and proposed rules. ILEAP has been a leader in producing assessments designed to help developing countries mainstream trade into national development strategies and to capitalize on the provision of official development assistance—concessional loans and grants—for trade-related programs and projects.[62] The ICTSD also recently developed a methodology to evaluate the effectiveness and impact of AfT at the country level in WTO member states.[63]

In addition, embedded NGOs also evaluate and utilize the impact assessment reports conducted by other IOs. For example, ENDA-CACID led a platform of West African organizations in commissioning and producing reports in response to EU Sustainability Impact Assessment reports in Economic Community of West African States (ECOWAS)-EU Economic Partnership Agreement (EPA) negotiations. They cited concerns raised by the EU's Sustainability Impact Assessment to argue that the level of liberalization on the negotiating table would have deleterious effects on employment and manufacturing in West Africa.[64] They also leveraged their legal capacity to challenge the conventional wisdom that WTO law obliges parties to FTAs to liberalize 90 percent of their trade flows. West African NGOs conducted their own legal assessments, researched EPA alternatives, and funneled information to West African negotiators that was hitherto unavailable and even denied by the EU. According to Trommer, the West African tariff liberalization offer of 60 percent resulted from the research and assessments conducted by NGOs.[65] Though formally outside the purview of the WTO's accountability regime, by evaluating the empirical and legal basis of the EU's trade and development vision in EPA negotiations, NGOs raised broader questions about the desirability of liberalization and integration in West Africa and the linkages between free trade and sustainable development for least developed countries.

Overall, embedded NGOs show potential for improving the evaluation dimension of the WTO's accountability regime and of the international trade regime more generally. However, this brief illustration of their activities raises questions about impact and uptake. Future research should explore the conditions under which the production of knowledge and information, impact assessments and metrics impact negotiations and translate into policy change and agenda setting.[66] We also require a better understanding of the implications if the research and assessments by embedded NGOs are faulty or based on inaccurate information. Finally, we must explore questions related to power and autonomy and be aware that embedded NGOs may be constructing and reinforcing patterns of dependence or over-reliance for developing and least developed countries.

Consultation

The third dimension of accountability is consultation. Those affected by the rules should have meaningful opportunities to shape outcomes and be included in negotiations leading to the construction and implementation of new rules.[67] The primary aims of embedded NGOs are to improve the quality of participation and empower developing countries to articulate and defend policy choices in international trade negotiations. Indeed, the stated purpose of the ICTSD is to:

> [empower] stakeholders in trade policy through information, networking, dialogue, well-targeted research, and capacity building. ICTSD identifies knowledge gaps in international trade rule- and policymaking from a sustainable development perspective; it mobilizes the best expertise around the world through dialogue and research to address those gaps in a solution-oriented way; it processes the knowledge generated through these processes so that it is applied and relevant for international policymaking processes; and it delivers this knowledge to sustainable development constituencies in a timely manner.[68]

Embedded NGOs also prioritize autonomous capacity building. According to ILEAP,

> in order for developing countries to compete effectively and equally in international trade negotiations, they need more than

> access to the advice of dedicated professionals. They must also develop their own capacity to act for themselves, including the ability to negotiate effectively, to define and assess options, to identify the appropriate experts, and to evaluate their performances.[69]

Embedded NGOs aim to equip developing countries to participate effectively in international trade negotiations and shape the rules that will ultimately determine their collective destinies through a four-pronged strategy. First, they aim to increase the supply of experts in developing countries by offering mentorships and conducting in-country training sessions. For example, in March 2011, ILEAP partnered with the Commission of ECOWAS and the West African Economic and Monetary Union to host a regional training workshop for the West African Technical Working Group on Trade in Services. The objective was to help regional experts better understand the "elements that are required to design, manage and implement a more comprehensive approach to services sector development," and to develop their capacity to advance these positions in international trade negotiations. They were trained in the application of a methodology designed to conduct regulatory audits and competitiveness assessments in different services-related sectors with the objective to establish "knowledge anchors" in the region that could provide advice and support to their respective governments.[70] ILEAP also offers a Fellow Program in Geneva through which students or recent graduates of advanced degrees in law, economics, or related programs from developing countries work to monitor and report on international trade negotiations. They receive negotiation skills training, signal to ILEAP areas that may require its services, and act as conduits of information between capital-based and Geneva-based researchers and negotiators.[71]

The second prong of the capacity-building strategy is the staging of in-country or regional workshops for broad-based multi-stakeholder dialogue, collaboration and networking on substantive and technical aspects of international trade negotiations. Since 2005, the ICTSD has hosted a series of such workshops on the SSM and SP within G33 member states. As part of the in-country field testing of the SP methodology, local researchers, trade officials and academics were brought together to consult with farmers and civil society organizations at the local and sub-national levels to discuss import sensitivities and the potential impacts of further liberalization. In November 2011, ILEAP and the ICTSD partnered to host a sub-Saharan Africa-wide workshop in Nairobi, Kenya, on trade in services negotiations and services sector development. The event brought together a range of actors including national and regional officials responsible for trade in services negotiations, non-state actors from the sub-Saharan African private sector and civil society, academic researchers, think tanks, and non-African experts from IOs, NGOs, and donors.[72] There are numerous additional examples of such initiatives by developing country-based embedded NGOs that are designed to increase the range of input, research, expertise, and evidentiary basis of developing country positions in trade negotiations, such as the CPD's Young Scholars Seminar Program and the Capacity Building Training Workshop on Trade Facilitation.[73]

A parallel initiative, and the third prong of the capacity-building strategy, is the staging of workshops and meetings in Geneva. These meetings often take place in parallel to ministerial meetings at the WTO and are designed to facilitate networking, coalition building and innovative thinking and analysis among a range of stakeholders including academics, policy researchers, intergovernmental organizations, NGOs, parliamentarians, businesses, and national trade officials. The objective is to generate inputs and ideas on sustainable development and trade policy for future and ongoing negotiations. The Trade and Development Symposiums, for example, hosted by the ICTSD, serve this purpose.[74]

The final and least documented dimension of capacity building is the inclusion of embedded NGO representatives in the official trade delegations of WTO member states at Ministerial Conferences. Although it is acknowledged that these actors have a "significant" presence in official trade delegations,[75] to date little is known about the extent, formal role or impact of the inclusion of these actors,[76] or how this compares to the inclusion of other private actors such as business associations.[77]

Correction

The most important test of accountability and the final dimension along which we can evaluate the impact of embedded NGOs on the WTO's accountability regime is correction. Is the WTO doing what it said it would do and learning from its mistakes by correcting the harmful consequences of its policies or introducing policy changes to address its shortcomings?[78] A commitment to redress persistent inequalities and unfair terms of trade between developed and developing countries constitutes the foundation for the Doha Development Round. Indeed, the primary objective, as articulated in the Ministerial Declaration in Qatar in 2001, is to reform the international trade regime such that it promotes economic growth and sustainable development in the poorest regions of the world.[79] Paragraph 1 of the Ministerial Declaration establishes that progressive elimination of barriers to trade is the coveted path to achieving these goals:

> The multilateral trading system embodied in the World Trade Organization has contributed significantly to economic growth, development and employment throughout the past fifty years. We are determined, particularly in the light of the global economic slowdown, to maintain the process of reform and liberalization of trade policies, thus ensuring that the system plays its full part in promoting recovery, growth and development. We therefore strongly reaffirm the principles and objectives set out in the Marrakech Agreement Establishing the World Trade Organization, and pledge to reject the use of protectionism.

Paragraph 2 also explicitly recognizes "the need for all our peoples to benefit from the increased opportunities and welfare gains that the multilateral trade regime generates." WTO members affirmed their commitment to sustainable development, the idea that "acting for the protection of the environment and the promotion of sustainable development can and must be mutually supportive." Furthermore, the needs and interests of developing countries were to be placed at the heart of the work program adopted by the Doha Ministerial Declaration provided they are consistent with the principles outlined in Paragraph 1.

In terms of more tangible commitments, trade-related technical assistance was promised in the interest of filling the capacity deficit in international trade negotiations. WTO members acknowledged the need to improve the volume and quality of developing and least developed country participation in trade negotiations, and to help them make effective use of the flexibilities contained in existing Agreements. In this vein, WTO members also promised to address implementation-related issues raised by the Like-Minded Group (LMG) of developing countries concerning imbalances in the WTO Agreements.[80] Essentially, the LMG raised almost 100 items of concern. In addition to outlining the difficulties experienced by least developed and developing countries in implementing their own commitments, the LMG addressed the failure of developed countries to implement a range of commitments including "policy space" provisions.[81]

The notion of "policy space" gained currency during the Uruguay Round of multilateral trade negotiations. At its core, this concept is founded on the premise that the burden of adapting to new trade rules and disciplines falls most heavily on countries with the least capacity to do so. It also recognizes that international trade rules place downward pressure on developing countries' ability to regulate domestically and to promote industrial policy, thereby constraining their ability to pursue sustainable development priorities and industrial development. The idea is to carve out space from WTO disciplines to allow developing countries sufficient policy space or flexibility and time to adjust to new trade rules. Such space is most commonly manifested in the form of special and differential treatment (SDT) for developing countries.[82] SDT provisions include:

- longer time periods for implementing agreements and commitments;
- measures to increase trading opportunities for these countries;
- provisions requiring all WTO members to safeguard the trade interests of developing countries;
- support to help developing countries build the infrastructure for WTO work, handle disputes and implement technical standards; and
- provisions related to least-developed country members.[83]

Moreover, Paragraph 44 of the Doha Declaration includes special provisions for the review and, where appropriate, re-articulation of SDT provisions with the objective of "making them more precise, effective and operational." In sum, the new rules being negotiated at the WTO should enable developing and least developed countries to realize sustainable economic growth, increased trade capacity, and availability of policy space to pursue development goals.

Embedded NGOs seek to empower developing countries to demand that the WTO fulfill this agenda and further the goal of sustainable development. Their tactics, outlined above, are designed to provide assistance to developing countries to mainstream trade into national development strategies and ensure they are consistent with their broader economic, social and environmental agendas. On the other hand, they are designed to provide the networks, tools, resources, ideas, and knowledge necessary to enable developing countries to articulate these priorities in international trade negotiations. Embedded NGOs seek to assist developing countries to socially embed the international trade regime and carve out additional policy or development space in new and novel ways. In order to evaluate the impact of embedded NGOs on the WTO's accountability regime along this dimension, we must assess the extent to which the provision of research and technical trade-related assistance helps developing countries realize the introduction of new rules and policies or the evaluation and adjustment of existing rules and policies that serve these ends.

Conclusion

Embedded NGOs are highly specialized NGOs that engage in demand-driven advocacy and leverage their legal and technical trade-related expertise across a range of issue areas—such as fisheries, agriculture, services, or aid—in order to promote sustainable development priorities, carve out policy or development space from international trade rules, and increase the trade policy and negotiating capacity of developing and least developed countries. This chapter has developed an analytical framework for evaluating the impact of embedded NGOs on the WTO's accountability regime by delineating four dimensions for analysis—transparency, evaluation, consultation, and correction. There are a number of factors we nevertheless need to bear in mind when considering embedded NGOs.

First, there are issues with the institutional and geographic attributes of embedded NGOs. They are overwhelmingly based in the global North and are directed by Western-educated, middle-class people. They also have far more resources and access to the WTO than NGOs located in the global South. These factors raise the question of whether Northern-based embedded NGOs are the appropriate actors to provide a voice or act as a mediating agent for developing and least developed countries in international trade negotiations.[84] We must also inquire into whether there is a Western bias in the research and technical assistance provided by embedded NGOs[85] that may serve to reproduce social hierarchies or inequalities.[86]

Second, although embedded NGOs may empower and give a voice to otherwise marginalized actors in the international trade regime, there is uneven engagement across issue areas and developing and least developed countries. This issue was raised, for example, in a 2007 independent, third-party evaluation of ILEAP[87] and may also serve to exacerbate inequalities in the international trade regime.[88]

Third, there are concerns about accountability, and these issues are not particular to embedded NGOs. Indeed, critics question whether most NGOs have sufficient transparency, representativeness, and participation mechanisms to ensure their own internal accountability.[89] Also at issue is the external accountability of NGOs and the question of to whom they are accountable and by what mechanisms.[90]

Finally, and most significantly, embedded NGOs are knowledge producers in global trade. They are central to the construction of conventional wisdom about the limits and possibilities of trade to work for development, and they impact the strategies, resources, and patterns of empowerment in the global South. The creation and dissemination of knowledge in global trade is inherently political. Given that they are predominantly status quo-maintaining, second-order development actors, embedded NGOs endorse a liberal international economic order. Future research should further investigate the conditions under which one becomes a knowledge producer and how non-state actors acquire and legitimate knowledge.[91] We also need to explore how the construction and dissemination of knowledge by embedded NGOs reinforces dominant trade narratives and power asymmetries in global trade.

In order to understand better how these dynamics are at play in global trade and to evaluate the impact of embedded NGOs on the WTO's accountability regime, future research should trace the provision of research and technical trade-related assistance by embedded NGOs to developing and least developed countries in the context of ongoing WTO negotiations. Possible issue areas of focus include fisheries subsidies negotiations, agriculture negotiations, services negotiations, and AfT negotiations. These are areas of key strategic concern to developing countries and constitute both major stumbling blocks and windows of opportunity in the ongoing Doha Round of multilateral trade negotiations. Embedded NGOs are actively engaged in the provision of research and technical trade-related assistance to both developed and developing countries in these areas. Analyses of these areas would provide insight into the differing nature of relationships between NGOs and a variety of WTO members. Moreover, the areas vary in terms of the types of policies (positive, regulative policies versus negative policy space) advocated by embedded NGOs. Therefore, comparative case studies of embedded NGO advocacy in these areas would shed light on the varied role and impact of embedded NGO expertise, and help to elucidate some of the opportunities and constraints on embedded NGO agency in international trade negotiations.

Another fruitful avenue for research is the role of embedded NGOs in the negotiation of North-South FTAs, such as the EU's Economic Partnership Agreements. In light of the failure of WTO members to conclude the current round of multilateral trade negotiations, a growing number of countries are circumventing the multilateral trade regime in favor of regional FTAs. It would be worthwhile to compare whether embedded NGOs show more or less promise in affecting regional or multilateral trade negotiations and to explore how the challenges outlined above play out in the different negotiating contexts, especially given the widespread concern that FTAs serve to ratchet-up trade disciplines and exacerbate power and knowledge asymmetries in the international trade regime.

Notes

1 This chapter is a revised version of an article first published as "The Quest for Accountable Governance: Embedded NGOs and Demand Driven Advocacy in the International Trade Regime," *Journal of World Trade* 48, no. 3: 457–479. I kindly thank the publisher, Kluwer Law, for allowing me to reproduce the material here.

2 Rorden Wilkinson, *What's Wrong with the WTO and How to Fix it* (Cambridge: Polity Press, 2014).

3 James Scott and Rorden Wilkinson, "The Poverty of the Doha Round and the Least Developed Countries," *Third World Quarterly* 32, no. 4 (2011): 611–627.

4 Tony Heron, *Pathways from Preferential Trade: The Politics of Trade Adjustment in Africa, the Caribbean and Pacific* (New York: Palgrave Macmillan, 2013); Sanoussi Bilal, Phillipe de Lombaerde and Diana Tussie, *Asymmetric Trade Negotiations* (Farnham: Ashgate Publishing, 2011); Ben Richardson, "Restructuring the EU-ACP Sugar Regime: Out of the Strong there Came Forth Sweetness,"*Review of International Political Economy* 16, no. 4 (2009): 673–697; and Tony Heron and Gabriel Siles-Brügge, "Competitive Liberalization and the 'Global Europe' Services and Investment Agenda: Locating the Commercial Drivers of the EU-ACP Economic Partnership Agreements," *Journal of Common Market Studies* 50, no. 2 (2012): 250–266.

5 Rorden Wilkinson, "Of Butchery and Bicycles: The WTO and the 'Death' of the Doha Development Agenda," *The Political Quarterly* 83, no. 2 (2012): 395–401; and Alisa DiCaprio and Silke Trommer, "Bilateral Graduation: The Impact of EPAs on LDC Trade Space," *Journal of Development Studies* 46, no. 9 (2010): 607–627.

6 Amrita Narlikar, "Fairness in International Trade Negotiations: Developing Countries in the GATT and WTO," *The World Economy* 29, no. 8 (2006): 1005–1028.

7 Fatoumata Jawara and Aileen Kwa, *Behind the Scenes at the WTO: The Real World of International Trade Negotiations*, 2nd edition (Toronto: Zed Books, 2004).

8 Diana Tussie, *The Politics of Trade: The Role of Research in Trade Policy and Negotiation* (Ottawa: International Development Research Centre, 2009).

9 John Gerard Ruggie, "International Regimes, Transactions and Change: Embedded Liberalism and the Post-war Economic Order," *International Organization* 36, no. 2 (1982): 379–415.

10 Faizel Ismail, "Mainstreaming Development in the World Trade Organization," *Journal of World Trade* 39, no. 1 (2005): 11–21.

11 Donna Lee, "Global Trade Governance and the Challenges of African Activism in the Doha Development Agenda Negotiations," *Global Society* 26, no. 1 (2012): 83–101.

12 The notion of a third sector of global governance is drawn from Thomas G. Weiss, Tatiana Carayannis and Richard Jolly, "The 'Third' United Nations," *Global Governance* 15, no. 1 (2009): 123–142.

13 Daniel C. Esty, "Non-governmental Organizations at the World Trade Organization: Cooperation, Competition and Exclusion,"*Journal of International Economic Law* 1, no. 1 (1998): 123–147; Rorden Wilkinson, "Managing Global Civil Society: The WTO's Engagement with NGOs," in *The Idea of Global Civil Society: Politics and Ethics in a Globalising Era*, ed. Randall Germain and Michael Kenny (Abingdon and New York: Routledge, 2005), 156–174; Hannah Murphy, "Rethinking the Roles of Non-governmental Organizations at the World Trade Organization," *Australian Journal of International Affairs* 66, no. 4 (2012): 468–485; and Jens Steffek, "Awkward Partners: NGOs and Social Movements at the WTO," in *The Oxford Handbook on the World Trade Organization*, ed. Amrita Narlikar, Martin Daunton and Robert Sterns (Oxford: Oxford University Press, 2012), 301–319.

14 Sylvia Ostry, "Dissent.com: How NGOs are Re-making the WTO," *Policy Options* 22 (2001): 6–15; Steve Charnovitz, "The WTO and Cosmopolitics," *Journal of International Economic Law* 7, no. 3 (2004): 675–682; and Marc Williams, "Civil Society and the WTO: Contesting Accountability," in *Building Global Democracy? Civil Society and Accountable Global Governance*, ed. Jan Aart Scholte (Cambridge: Cambridge University Press, 2011), 105–128.

15 Peter Van den Bossche, "NGO Involvement in the WTO: A Comparative Perspective," *Journal of International Economic Law* 11, no. 4 (2008): 717–749; and Martina Piewitt, "Participatory Governance in the WTO: How Inclusive is Global Civil Society?" *Journal of World Trade* 44, no. 2 (2010): 467–488.

16 Susan K. Sell and Assem Prakash, "Using Ideas Strategically: The Contest Between Business and NGO Networks in Intellectual Property Rights," *International Studies Quarterly* 48, no. 1 (2004): 143–175; Duncan Matthews, "The Role of International NGOs in the Intellectual Property Policy: Making and Norm-setting Activities of Multilateral Institutions," *Chicago-Kent Law Review* 82, no. 3 (2006): 1369–1387; Baogang He and Hannah Murphy, "Global Social Justice at the WTO? The Role of NGOs in Constructing Global Social Contracts," *International Affairs* 83, no. 4 (2007): 707–727; Tracey Epps, "Reconciling Public Opinion and WTO Rules Under the SPS Agreement,"*World Trade Review* 7, no. 2 (2008): 359–392; Daniel C. Esty, "Environmental Governance at the WTO: Outreach to Civil Society," in *Trade, Environment and the Millennium*, ed. Gary P. Sampson and Bradnee Chambers (Tokyo, New York and Paris: United Nations University Press, 1999), 119–144; Elizabeth Smythe, "Just Say No! The Negotiation of Investment Rules at the WTO," *Journal of Political Economy* 33, no. 4 (2003): 60–83; Robert O'Brien, Anne Marie Goetz, Jan Aart Scholte and Marc Williams, *Contesting Global Governance: Multilateral Economic Institutions and Global Social Movements* (Cambridge: Cambridge University Press, 2000); and Marc Williams, "Civil Society and the World Trading System," in *The Politics of International Trade: Actors, Issues and Regional Dynamics*, ed. Dominic Kelly and Wyn Grant (New York: Palgrave Macmillan, 2005), 30–46.

17 Jan Aart Scholte, *Building Global Democracy? Civil Society and Accountability in Global Governance* (Cambridge: Cambridge University Press, 2011).

18 Notable exceptions include Mark Halle and Robert Wolfe, *Process Matters: Sustainable Development and Domestic Trade Transparency* (Winnipeg: International Institute for Sustainable Development, 2007); Andreas Dür and Dirk de Bièvre, "Inclusion without Influence? NGOs in European Trade Policy," *Journal of Public Policy* 27, no. 1 (2007): 79–101; and Silke Trommer, *Transformations in Trade Politics: Participatory Trade Politics in West Africa* (London and New York: Routledge 2013).

19 O'Brien et al., *Contesting Global Governance*; Robert W. Cox, "An Alternative Approach to Multilateralism in the Twenty-first Century," *Global Governance* 3, no. 1 (1997): 103; Fred Carden, *Knowledge to Policy: Making the Most of Development Research* (Ottawa: International Development Research Centre, 2009); Diana Stone and Simon Maxwell, *Global Knowledge Networks and International Development* (Oxford: Routledge, 2004); and Scholte, *Building Global Democracy?*

20 Tussie, in *The Politics of Trade*, has orchestrated one of the most extensive appraisals of the role of independent and commissioned research within the trade policymaking processes of individual countries and in the formation of coalitions in multilateral trade negotiations. However, the focus is not the provision of research by international NGOs.

21 Peter Haas, "Introduction: Epistemic Communities and International Policy Coordination," *International Organization* 46, no. 1 (1992): 1, 3.

22 Haas, "Introduction," 1, 3; Martha Finnemore, "International Organizations as Teachers of Norms: The United Nations Educational, Scientific, and Cultural Organization and Science Policy," *International Organization* 47, no. 4 (1993): 565–597; Martha Finnemore, *National Interests in International Society* (New York: Cornell University Press, 1996); John Gerard Ruggie, "Territoriality and Beyond: Problematizing Modernity in International Relations," *International Organization* 47, no. 1 (1993): 139–174; Emanuel Adler, "The Emergence of Cooperation: National Epistemic Communities and the International Evolution of the Idea of Nuclear Arms Control," *International Organization* 46, no. 1 (1992): 101–145; Emanuel Adler, "Seeds of Peaceful Change: The OSCE's Security Community-Building Model, in Security Communities," in *Security Communities*, ed. Emanuel Adler and Michael Barnett (Cambridge: Cambridge University Press, 1998), 119–160; Jeffery W. Legro, "Whence American Internationalism," *International Organization* 54, no. 2 (2000): 253–289; and Erin Hannah, "NGOs and the European Union: Examining the Power of Epistemes in the EC's TRIPS and Access to Medicines Negotiations," *Journal of Civil Society* 7, no. 2 (2011): 179–206.

23 Emanuel Adler and Steven Bernstein, "Knowledge in Power: The Epistemic Construction of Global Governance," in *Power in Global Governance*, ed. Michael Barnett and Raymond Duvall (Cambridge: Cambridge University Press, 2005), 295.

24 Ruggie, "International Regimes, Transactions and Change," 382–383.

25 Adler and Bernstein, "Knowledge in Power," 303.

26 Emanuel Adler and Peter Haas, "Conclusion: Epistemic Communities, World Order and the Creation of a Reflective Research Program," *International Organization* 46, no. 1 (1992): 367–390.

27 Ruggie, "International Regimes, Transactions and Change"; and Steven Bernstein and Louis W. Pauly, ed., *Global Liberalism and Political Order: Toward a New Grand Compromise?* (Albany, NY: State University of New York Press, 2007).
28 Andrew Lang, "Reconstructing Embedded Liberalism: John Gerard Ruggie and Constructivist Approaches to the Study of the International Trade Regime," *Journal of International Economic Law* 9, no. 1 (2006): 81–116.
29 United Nations Department of Economic and Social Affairs (UNDESA), "Monetary Consensus on Financing for Development," the final text of agreements and commitments adopted at the *International Conference on Financing for Development Monterrey, Mexico*, 18–22 March 2002, www.un.org/esa/ffd/monterrey/MonterreyConsensus.pdf.
30 United Nations, "Follow-up International Conference on Financing for Development to Review the Implementation of the Monterrey Consensus," A/CONF.212/L.1/Rev.1, 9 December 2008, http://ec.europa.eu/development/icenter/repository/Doha_declaration_2008_en.pdf.
31 Louis W. Pauly, "The United Nations in a Changing Global Economy," in *Global Liberalism and Political Order: Toward a New Grand Compromise?* ed. Steven Bernstein and Louis W. Pauly (Albany, NY: State University of New York Press, 2007).
32 For example, EU members have introduced a broad range of innovations including air tax levies, tax write-offs, lottery proceeds, debt for development swaps, and establishing an International Financing Facility. See the EU Accountability Report on Financing for Development, http://ec.europa.eu/europeaid/what/development-policies/financing_for_development/accountability_report_2012_en.htm.
33 Susanne Soederberg, "Recasting Neoliberal Dominance in the Global South? A Critique of the Monterrey Consensus," *Alternatives: Global, Local, Political* 30, no. 3 (2005): 325–364.
34 Mark Tran, "UK Aid Money: The Key Datasets You Need to Know," *The Guardian*, 26 September 2012, www.theguardian.com/global-development/datablog/2012/sep/26/uk-aid-money-key-datasets.
35 DFID also provides major funds to other embedded NGOs such as ILEAP and ECDPM. For further information on DFID projects see http://devtracker.dfid.gov.uk.
36 DFID Business Case and Summary, *Support to the International Centre for Trade and Sustainable Development (ICTSD) 2013–15* (London: Department for International Development, 2012), http://projects.dfid.gov.uk/IATI/document/3730456.
37 Sylvia Ostry and Thomas K. Tieku, "Trade Advocacy Groups and Multilateral Trade Policymaking of African States," MCIS Briefings (Toronto: Munk Center for International Studies, 2007).
38 Steffek, "Awkward Partners."
39 Robert O. Keohane, "Accountability in World Politics," *Scandinavian Political Studies* 29, no. 2 (2006): 75–87; David Held and Mathias Koenig-Archibugi, ed., *Global Governance and Public Accountability* (Malden: Wiley-Blackwell, 2005); and Alnoor Ebraim and Edward Weisband, *Global Accountabilities: Participation, Pluralism, and Public Ethics* (Cambridge: Cambridge University Press, 2007).
40 Scholte, *Building Global Democracy?* 18.

41 Ruth W. Grant and Robert O. Keohane, "Accountability and Abuses of Power in World Politics," *American Political Science Review* 99, no. 1 (2005): 29–43.

42 David Held, *Democracy and the Global Order: From the Modern State to Cosmopolitan Governance* (Stanford, Calif.: Stanford University Press, 1995); Yannis Papadopoulos, "Accountability and Multi-level Governance: More Accountability, Less Democracy?" *Western European Politics* 33, no. 5 (2010): 1030–1049; and Jens Steffek, "Public Accountability and the Public Sphere of International Governance," *Ethics & International Affairs* 24, no. 1 (2010): 45–68.

43 Giandomenico Majone, *Dilemmas of European Integration: The Ambiguities and Pitfalls of Integration by Stealth* (Oxford: Oxford University Press, 2005); and Carol Harlow and Richard Rawlings, "Promoting Accountability in Multi-level Governance: A Network Approach,"*European Law Journal* 13, no. 4 (2007): 542–562.

44 Grant and Keohane, "Accountability and Abuses of Power in World Politics."

45 Robert Wolfe, "Who is Accountable at the World Trade Organization?" Paper presented at the *52nd International Studies Association Annual Convention*, Montreal Quebec, March 2011.

46 Martina Piewitt, Meike Rodekamp and Jens Steffek, "Civil Society in World Politics: How Accountable are Transnational CSOs?" *Journal of Civil Society* 6, no. 3 (2010): 237–258; and Sungjoo Cho, "A Quest for WTO's Legitimacy," *World Trade Review* 4, no. 3 (2005): 391–399.

47 Williams, "Civil Society and the World Trading System"; and Steffek, "Awkward Partners."

48 Wolfe, "Who is Accountable at the World Trade Organization?" 5.

49 See International Centre for Trade and Sustainable Development, http://ictsd.org.

50 For example, the ICTSD estimates that its publications are read by 20,000 policymakers in 80 countries each year.

51 Scholte, *Building Global Democracy?*

52 Luisa Bernal, *Methodology for Identification of Special Products (SP) and Products for Eligibility Under the Special Safeguard Mechanism (SSM) by Developing Countries* (Geneva: ICTSD, 2005).

53 ICTSD, "Special Products and the Special Safeguard Mechanism: Strategic Options for Developing Countries," Issue Paper 6 (Geneva: ICTSD, 2005).

54 The G33 Coalition comprises large and small import-sensitive developing countries.

55 A summary of the key findings is provided by the ICTSD, "Special Products and the Special Safeguard Mechanism."

56 A second round of field testing took place in 2006 in Ecuador, Fiji Islands, Papua New Guinea, Vietnam and the Philippines. Notably, the Philippines was the only G33 country in this round. In 2007, the methodology was applied in China, Indonesia, Mali, Tanzania, Uganda, Nigeria and the Eastern Caribbean states. See Paul Mably, "Centralized Production: The Group of 33," in *The Politics of Trade: The Role of Research in Trade Policy and Negotiations*, ed. Diana Tussie (Ottawa: International Development Research Centre, 2009), 239–270.

57 Mably, "Centralized Production."

58 Raul Montemayor, "Implications of the Proposed Modalities for the Special Safeguard Mechanism: A Simulation Exercise—Agriculture and Sustainable Development Series," Issue Paper 10 (Geneva: ICTSD, 2007).
59 China, Ecuador, Fiji, Indonesia, the Philippines and Senegal.
60 ICTSD, *The Special Safeguard Mechanism: Findings from a Simulation Exercise, Information Note: Number 2* (Geneva: ICTSD, 2007).
61 WTO, *G33 Submission on the SSM*, Communication by the G33 to the Committee on Agriculture: Special Session, 3 June, JOB(08)47, 2008; WTO, *Refocusing Discussions on the Special Safeguard Mechanism (SSM): Outstanding Issues and Concerns on its Design and Structure*, Submission by the G33 to the Committee on Agriculture: Special Session, TN/AG/GEN/30, 28 January 2010; WTO, *Price and Volume Cross-check Conditionalities*, Submission by the G33 to the Committee on Agriculture: Special Session, JOB/AG/3/, 5 February 2010; WTO, *G33 Submission on the SSM: Seasonality*, Communication by the G33 to the Committee on Agriculture: Special Session, JOB/AG/4/, 5 February 2010; and WTO, *Issues and Concerns on the Price-based Special Safeguard Mechanism: Some Analysis and Technical Contributions for the Design and Structure*, Communication by the G33 to the Committee on Agriculture: Special Session, 11 February 2010.
62 See for an example, Amanda Sunassee-Lam, Axel de la Maisonneuve, Dominique Njinkeu and Hugh Cameron, "Aid for Trade for Tanzania: Case Study," a study drafted for the workshop, *Trade Negotiations and Development for the EAC: EPAs and the WTO* (Arusha, Tanzania: ILEAP in collaboration with the East African Community Secretariat, 2005), www.ileap-jeicp.org/downloads/Aid%20For%20Trade%20For%20Tanzania%20-%20Case%20Study_ExecSumm.pdf.
63 See for example, Ratnaker Adhikari, *Evaluating Aid for Trade Effectiveness on the Ground: A Methodological Framework*, ICTSD Programme on Competitiveness and Sustainable Development Issue Paper no. 20 (Geneva: ICTSD, 2011).
64 Trommer, *Transformations in Trade Politics.*
65 Silke Trommer, "Activists Beyond Brussels: Transnational NGO Strategies on EU-West African Trade Negotiations,"*Globalizations* 8 (2011): 113–126.
66 Clive George, *The Truth About Trade: The Real Impact of Liberalization* (Toronto: Zed Books, 2010).
67 Scholte, *Building Global Democracy?*
68 International Centre for Trade and Sustainable Development, "About ICTSD," http://ictsd.org/about/.
69 International Lawyers and Economists Against Poverty (ILEAP), www.ileap-jeicp.org/programmes/index.html.
70 ILEAP, *Supporting Service Sector Development and Negations: Aide Memoire*, www.ileap-jeicp.org/downloads/accra_march_11/services-training_west-africa_draft_aide-memoire_agenda_rev_1.pdf.
71 ILEAP, "Fellowships for Enhancing Expertise," www.ileap-jeicp.org/capacity_building/fellowships.html.
72 ILEAP, "High Level Meeting to Discuss Services Reforms and Negotiations for Development in Sub-Sahara Africa: For Immediate Release," 13 November 2011, www.ileap-jeicp.org/programmes/meetings_workshops/nairobi_nov_2011.html.

73 Centre for Policy Dialogue (CDP), "CDP-ARTNeT Capacity Building Training Workshop on Trade Facilitation," 21 October 2010, http://cpd.org.bd/index.php/cpd-artnet-capacity-building-training-workshop-on-trade-facilitation/.
74 ICTSD, "Bali Trade and Development Symposium," www.ictsdsymposium.org.
75 Rorden Wilkinson, "The WTO in Hong Kong: What it Really Means for the Doha Development Agenda," *New Political Economy* 11, no. 2 (2006): 291–304; and Sylvia Ostry, "The World Trading System: In the Fog of Uncertainty," *Review of International Organization* 1, no. 2 (2006): 139–152.
76 Steffek, "Awkward Partners."
77 Consumer Unity & Trust Society (CUTS), *Towards More Inclusive Trade Policy Making: Process and Role of Stakeholders in Select African Countries* (Geneva: CUTS Geneva Resource Centre, 2009).
78 Scholte, *Building Global Democracy?*
79 WTO, *Refocusing Discussions on the Special Safeguard Mechanism (SSM)*.
80 For an overview of the activities of the LMG in the run-up to Doha as they relate to implementation-related issues, see Amrita Narlikar and John Odell, "The Strict Distributive Strategy for a Bargaining Coalition: The Like-Minded Group and the World Trade Organization," in *Negotiating Trade: Developing Countries in the WTO and NAFTA*, ed. John Odell (Cambridge: Cambridge University Press, 2006), 115–144.
81 According to the WTO, *Price and Volume Cross-check Conditionalities*, 40 of the 100 issues raised were addressed at the Doha Ministerial Conference in the Decision on Implementation-related Issues and Concerns. The remaining items are the subject of current negotiations.
82 For further discussion of policy space as it pertains to developing countries see Kevin Gallagher, *Putting Development First: The Importance of Policy Space in the WTO and International Financial Institutions* (Toronto: Zed Books, 2005). The notion of special and differential treatment is not new—it was coined by the first secretary-general of UNCTAD in 1964. It was introduced to the international trade regime through the 1970 so-called "Enabling Clause" and was reaffirmed by developed countries during the Tokyo Meeting of the General Agreement on Tariffs and Trade (GATT) in 1973. Although its popularity waned in the late 1970s and early 1980s as neoliberal ideas took hold, special and differential treatment is a perennial feature of multilateral trade rules.
83 WTO, *Special and Differential Treatment Provisions* (Geneva: WTO Trade and Development Committee, n.d.), www.wto.org/english/tratop_e/devel_e/dev_special_differential_provisions_e.htm.
84 Jens Steffek and Patrizia Nanz, "Emergent Patterns of Civil Society Participation in Global and European Governance," in *Civil Society Participation in European and Global Governance: A Cure for the Democratic Deficit?* ed. Jens Steffek, Claudia Kissling and Patrizia Nanz (New York: Palgrave MacMillan, 2008).
85 Tanja Brühl, "Representing the People? NGOs in International Negotiations," in *Evaluating Transnational NGOs: Legitimacy, Accountability, Representation*, ed. Jens Steffek and Kristina Hahn (New York: Palgrave Macmillan, 2010).

86 Bernard Beauzamy, "Transnational Social Movements and Democratic Legitimacy," in*Legitimacy beyond the State?: Re-examining the Democratic Credentials of Transnational Actors*, ed. Eva Erman and Anders Uhlin (New York: Palgrave Macmillan, 2010).

87 Tom Pengelly, Bernard Wood, Sisule Musungu and Tamara Asamoah, *Evaluation of International Lawyers and Economists Against Poverty (ILEAP): Final Report 2007* (London: SANNA Consulting, 2007), http://idl-bnc.idrc.ca/dspace/bitstream/10625/43676/1/130239.pdf.

88 Darren Halpin and Peter McLaverty, "Legitimating INGO Advocacy: The Case of Internal Democracies," in *Evaluating Transnational NGOs: Legitimacy, Accountability, Representation*, ed. Jens Steffek and Krisina Hahn (New York: Palgrave Macmillan, 2010).

89 Piewitt et al., "Civil Society in World Politics?"

90 Jonas Tallberg and Anders Uhlin, "Civil Society and Global Democracy: An Assessment," in *Global Democracy: Normative and Empirical Assessments*, ed. Daniele Archibugi, Mathias Koenig-Archibugi and Raffaele Marchetti (Cambridge: Cambridge University Press, 2011).

91 Matthew Eagleton-Pierce, *Symbolic Power in the World Trade Organization* (Oxford: Oxford University Press, 2013).

9 Southern trade intellectuals in expert knowledge creation[1]

James Scott

- **The role of intellectuals in international politics**
- **The privileges of power**
- **Identifying Southern trade intellectuals and their relationship with the rising powers**
- **Framing the Doha Round impasse**
- **The emancipatory potential of Southern trade intellectuals?**
- **Conclusion**

The emergence, or re-emergence, of the so-called "rising powers" of the global South is frequently seen as a serious challenge to the stability of the prevailing, Western-dominated order. However, while the rise of Brazil, India, and China has undoubtedly altered the dynamics of World Trade Organization (WTO) negotiations, the broader implications remain obscure due to continuing areas of uncertainty. The extent to which the rising powers truly challenge the existing system remains questionable,[2] as does the level of influence that they have attained.[3]

This chapter looks beyond the dynamics of the conspicuous small group negotiations in the WTO to try to understand the changes taking place beyond the high-profile, direct negotiations. It argues that more subtle shifts in the dynamics of trade governance can be perceived, one of which is the increasing involvement of the rising powers in providing expert knowledge and intellectual leadership to the developing world. Specifically, it is the contention of this chapter that there is emerging a new set of trade specialists from the global South, primarily originating from the rising powers, who operate as a loose epistemic community providing an alternative source of expert knowledge around trade negotiations. They have frequently acquired their knowledge from direct experience as trade negotiators, and they cohere around a shared commitment to a broadly "new developmentalist"[4] understanding of global trade.

This group, and the intellectual leadership that it is able to exercise, has weakened the dominance previously enjoyed by the Western powers over trade analysis and broadened the range of voices providing expert opinion on trade matters. This development forms an important area of leadership provided by the rising powers to less developed countries, which continue to suffer severe trade analysis constraints. That said, concerns remain over whether this epistemic community, being largely tied to the rising powers, can be wholly trusted by other developing countries. Overreliance on the intellectual leadership of this group must be guarded against.

In making this argument, the chapter draws on, and seeks to extend, the insights generated by analyses of epistemic communities and how they influence international politics. It applies this framework to investigate the way in which the identified group of Southern trade intellectuals have articulated an interpretation of the pattern and progress of the Doha Development Agenda (DDA) negotiations, particularly in providing an alternative framing of the impasse in the Doha Round that challenges the narrative put forward by the United States and European Union (EU). This intellectual leadership has enabled other developing countries to resist the rich countries' pressure to conclude the round more strongly than would otherwise have been possible, despite the lack of real development content that the DDA offers. The case provides an example of an epistemic community operating in an area in which there is no objective interpretation of events; this is in contrast to much of the existing literature on epistemic communities, which draws heavily on the role of scientific knowledge in influencing political outcomes.

The chapter unfolds as follows. The next section examines the role given to intellectuals within the various strands of international political economy theory, with a particular focus on epistemic communities. Following that, the chapter sets out the privileged position that the traditional Western powers have enjoyed in trade analysis and in interpreting events, as it is against this set of narratives that the set of Southern intellectuals cohere. In section four the chapter turns to identifying some of the people who fall into the category of Southern trade intellectuals, though only an indicative rather than a prescriptive list is given. Section five explores the role of this group of intellectuals in articulating an interpretation of the current impasse in the DDA that deflects and nullifies the narrative of the United States and EU and the blame that they direct towards the rising powers. The penultimate section examines some of the benefits this has brought for other developing countries and highlights potential concerns, before the final section draws some conclusions.

The role of intellectuals in international politics

The issue of intellectual leadership within international politics has grown over time. Goldstein and Keohane argue that ideas are important variables in explaining foreign policy under a variety of circumstances, though more basic political interests also remain at work.[5] Somewhat similarly, within the "new institutionalism" ideas have been turned to as a means of overcoming various theoretical shortcomings, bolstering existing analytical tools.[6] Peter Hall, for instance, uses ideas as a means of understanding significant institutional change, which has been a consistent challenge in historical institutionalism.[7]

The works of Antonio Gramsci and those that have been derived therefrom, such as that of Robert Cox and Stephen Gill, have also given a central role to ideas and the intellectuals who propagate them in understanding the international system. Gramsci's conceptualization of intellectuals brings to the fore the function that they have in defining, promoting and sustaining what Cox terms collective images of social order—that is, "differing views as to both the nature and the legitimacy of prevailing power relations, the meaning of justice and public good, and so forth."[8] In this way, knowledge production is inherently bound up with identity and interests.[9]

Gramscian frameworks offer important insights, but the grounding of intellectuals in particular social forces is somewhat problematic in the context of the subject examined in this chapter. The economies and associated class structures found within the rising powers are at present too dissimilar to form a coherent analytical basis from which to draw a set of like-minded intellectuals. For this reason, this chapter adopts a theoretical approach based in social constructivism, which has provided some of the greatest advances in analyzing the role of ideas and intellectuals in shaping politics.

John Ruggie's pioneering work in social constructivism examined the role that ideas such as liberal trade theory play within the global arena, and how ideas are a crucial element in understanding how a dominant state creates a particular international order. In this conception, "[p]olitical authority represents a fusion of power with legitimate social purpose," which in the post-World War II context, Ruggie famously characterized as "embedded liberalism"—the wedding of a liberal trade and monetary regime with the right to intervene in the domestic economy to protect core interests (such as employment) and provide economic stability.[10] Ruggie traces the emergence across the industrial world of a set of social objectives around such intervention, highlighting the importance of key intellectuals such as John Maynard

Keynes. Thus for Ruggie, intellectuals and the ideas they promote play a central role in defining the "legitimate social purpose" that provides the content of an international regime.

The concept of epistemic communities set out by Peter Haas draws from social constructivism and sets out how groups of intellectuals operate to construct and disseminate particular worldviews.[11] Haas argues that how states "identify their interests and recognize the latitude of actions deemed appropriate in specific issue-areas of policymaking are functions of the manner in which the problems are understood by the policymakers or are represented by those to whom they turn for advice under conditions of uncertainty."[12] Networks of experts serve a crucial function in this process, helping states to identify their interests and framing issues for collective debate. Under certain conditions such networks may form epistemic communities, defined as "network[s] of professionals with recognized expertise and competence in a particular domain and an authoritative claim to policy-relevant knowledge within that domain or issue-area."[13] Epistemic communities provide interpretations of social and physical phenomena and can become important actors at both national and transnational levels.

Much of the subsequent work on epistemic communities focused only on scientific groups, but this was explicitly not the original conception Haas put forward.[14] Notably, for present purposes high-level diplomats are identified as potential members of epistemic communities, holding a privileged position in translating expert knowledge into political action.[15]

Those using the epistemic communities concept have made numerous insights and refinements to the theory. Johannes Lindvall finds that expert ideas have "real but limited effects on policy."[16] Expert ideas are used instrumentally, he argues, to pursue prior held aims, rather than at a more fundamental level of formulating policy objectives.[17] Schot and Schipper question whether epistemic communities need to cohere around a shared set of causal and normative beliefs as Haas assumes.[18] They find in the case of European transport policy that an epistemic community can be effective even without these features if engaged in a common policy initiative. Ponte and Cheyns highlight the possibilities that epistemic communities hold for benefiting weaker groups if used well.[19] Meanwhile, by contrast, Rethel finds that marginalized groups can find their political exclusion exacerbated by the operation of epistemic communities.[20]

Collectively, the epistemic communities literature provides powerful insights into how intellectuals gain traction in political processes through operating in collective, loosely formed groups of experts. By forming networks of recognized experts, epistemic communities are able to provide ready analysis and frames of understanding to important communities, including politicians, who may lack the expertise (or in some cases simply the time) to comprehend fully the issues in question. These networks are important non-state actors that are able to influence the direction of international negotiations.

While the rising powers remain secondary to the established powers, their influence will be heavily conditional upon the degree to which they can provide wider diplomatic leadership to other developing countries. Intellectual leadership in trade policy is one area in which that is taking place. The following section examines the privileged position enjoyed by the most powerful Western states in setting the terms of trade debates and the structures of ideational power with which the epistemic community, identified below, must contend.

The privileges of power

As Erin Hannah demonstrates,[21] drawing from Adler and Bernstein,[22] at the core of the global trade system is a legal/liberal episteme which is highly resistant to change and defines the bounds of what policy options are possible. Epistemes are identified as "the deepest level of the ideational world," which endow privileged actors "with the authority to determine valid knowledge or to reproduce the knowledge on which an episteme is based."[23] The legal/liberal episteme in the trade system not only constrains what potential policies are available, but is the lens through which members are judged to be acting in compliance with the regime. States, particularly the weakest,[24] feel strong social pressure to remain within the bounds of compliant behavior as dictated by the prevailing episteme, or more specifically, by those in a position to be the interpreters and arbiters of that episteme.[25] This forms a potent constraining force pressuring others to conform to the policy preferences of prevailing powers. In the present context, opposition to the agenda put in place by the most powerful actors relies on legitimation through rigorous, well-articulated intellectual advocacy.

The perspective of the dominant Western states is further aided by their influence over other key organizations of global governance. Reflecting on her experience as a Nicaraguan WTO delegate, Gloria María Carrión Fonseca argues that:

> WTO negotiations are frequently influenced by studies and analyses presented by institutions who share a fervent belief in the

> tenets of free trade. The World Bank, the IMF [International Monetary Fund], regional banks like the Inter-American Development Bank and the WTO itself thus acquire structural power during negotiations, because their vision of the economy and development prevails and their arguments, statistics and rationales are never questioned. The negotiators generally accept their analyses as absolute truths.[26]

Developing countries are particularly susceptible in this regard. With limited staff and relatively high staff turnover, there is comparatively little build-up of knowledge among many developing countries.[27] This lack of rooted knowledge accumulation places them in a particularly weak position to withstand the pressure of the dominant episteme and the interpretation of events put forward by the most powerful actors, assisting their incorporation into the hegemonic trade agenda.

WTO members that oppose that agenda are treated as pariahs, standing in the way of progress—a "won't-do" country in former US Trade Representative Robert Zoellick's dismissive phrase.[28] When developing countries seek to oppose the most powerful countries too stridently they are slapped down. The G20, for instance, was dismissed by one US delegate as a "third-world chest thumping festival led by Brazil and India," following its rejection of the offer on agriculture the rich countries put forward at the Cancún Ministerial Meeting of 2003.[29] Characterizing developing countries as "won't-do" countries that stand in the way of progress is thus used as a means of disciplining behavior and ensuring that the direction of trade governance continues to favor the most powerful states, consonant with the (qualified) liberalizing agenda they favor.

This highlights why it is crucial that alternative, well-articulated narratives are put forward that challenge those of the rich Western countries. That said, the assertion of a "developing country perspective,"[30] as it were, is not new, but in present times the emergence of the rising powers has instilled a confidence and security to dissenting voices. There have always been developing country ambassadors and diplomats who have sought to argue their case and refused to accept meekly the dominant discourse, but in the past they have often been silenced by pressure from the United States and EU, which have been known to push ministers to remove representatives in Geneva considered to be too forthright.[31]

The reliance on Western aid and the weak understanding within many capitals of what happens in Geneva facilitates this process. While this is still a problem today, it is diminishing as new donors emerge, lessening the leverage the traditional donors have. Thus the structural changes in the global economy are diminishing the ability of the most powerful states to dominate proceedings by silencing dissenters within Geneva, facilitating the emergence of powerfully placed alternative voices.

The picture that emerges is that the most powerful states have always enjoyed a privileged position with respect to dictating the interpretation of events and whether others are acting in conformity with the spirit of the system. Furthermore, the United States and EU are known, at times, to use more coercive means to silence dissent from developing countries. Yet, these two leading WTO members are increasingly challenged over their interpretation of events by a group of intellectuals from the global South operating as an epistemic community. The next section begins to identify who falls into this group.

Identifying Southern trade intellectuals and their relationship with the rising powers

The intellectuals of interest here form a loose epistemic community, the members of which frequently, though not always, draw their expertise from direct experience of trade negotiations as former or current representatives of developing countries in the General Agreement on Tariffs and Trade (GATT)/WTO. Many are from rising powers (broadly defined), while others have a link to the rising powers through the organizations they head being funded primarily by the BRICS (Brazil, Russia, India, China, and South Africa) countries.

A prescriptive list of the members of this group is not possible since membership of the group is not rigidly defined. The list given below is, for this reason, indicative only and by no means meant to be a complete delineation of who falls into the group of relevant Southern trade intellectuals. Attempts to form any such list would be impossible and counterproductive since epistemic communities are seldom rigidly demarcated but have blurred boundaries. An overly expansive list of individuals would inevitably risk including marginal players, clouding the analysis. As such, those identified here are those individuals who are particularly prominent—those at the core of the epistemic community. Focusing on them forms a means of beginning the analysis, through examining the contribution of what might be seen as archetypal examples.

These core members include:

- Debapriya Bhattacharya, former ambassador and permanent representative of Bangladesh to the WTO and the United Nations

(UN), former special advisor on least developed countries (LDCs) to the UN Conference on Trade and Development's (UNCTAD) secretary-general;
- Ujal Singh Bhatia, former ambassador of India to the WTO and current Appellate Body member;
- Faizel Ismail, South Africa's former ambassador and permanent representative at the WTO;
- Martin Khor, executive director of the South Centre;
- Pradeep Singh Mehta, secretary-general of the Consumer Unity and Trust Society (CUTS) International, India;
- Ricardo Meléndez-Ortiz, former permanent representative of Colombia to Geneva, including acting as a negotiator in the Uruguay Round and director of the International Centre for Trade and Sustainable Development (ICTSD); and
- Sun Zhenyu, former ambassador of China to the WTO.

The individuals identified above each have personal claims to expertise. However, personal position and claims to knowledge are not necessarily sufficient to wield influence but must, at times, be enhanced through the position of the intellectuals within key institutions. A number of these prominent Southern trade intellectuals achieve greater impact through being leaders of trade-focused nongovernmental organizations (NGOs), enabling them to direct research outputs towards core concerns of the developing world and helping to increase the dissemination of their ideas. This is true of Ricardo Meléndez-Ortiz—founder and executive director of ICTSD; Debapriya Bhattacharya—executive director of the Centre for Policy Dialogue in Dhaka, Bangladesh; Sun Zhenyu—chair of the China Society for World Trade Organization Studies, Beijing; and as already noted, Martin Khor—head of the South Centre; and Pradeep Singh Mehta—founder and director of CUTS International. Importantly, the outlets for publishing commentary and analysis provided by these organizations are frequently used to publish the work of other members of the epistemic community, cementing it as a group.

Through past or present direct involvement in trade negotiations combined with being in prominent positions within trade-based research organizations, the intellectuals identified above have (to recap Peter Haas) "recognised expertise and competence [...] and an authoritative claim to policy-relevant knowledge within that domain or issue-area."[32] Though this is a diverse group, which should by no means be considered to present a fully consistent set of opinions across all individuals, a core set of beliefs is nonetheless discernible. The intellectual tradition around which this group coheres pushes, to varying degrees, against free-trade orthodoxy and seeks to open up greater space for government intervention in pursuit of development goals. Though cognizant of the benefits of trade and of trade liberalization, the group highlights the inequalities and inequities of the current trade system and seeks to carve out opportunities for developing countries to pursue an active trade policy as part of national development strategies.[33] This set of policies forms part of what has been termed the "new developmentalism,"[34] which in turn draws from ideas relating to the "developmental state,"[35] in which the government plays a key role in directing resources (both state and private) into sectors delivering high productivity.

Many of those identified above are from BRICS countries, but the importance of the rising powers to this epistemic community stretches further. Finding themselves with much greater fiscal resources, the emerging powers are expanding their support for Geneva-based organizations performing trade analysis for developing countries. For example, the South Centre—which articulates an analysis across a range of international issues from a stance strongly rooted in the interests of the global South—increasingly being financed by the rising powers. In 2008, the latest available data, 37 percent of the South Centre's donations came from South Africa, India and China. In this way, the ability of the South Centre and its Executive Director Martin Khor to provide intellectual leadership is partly enabled by the rise of the global South.

In addition, the emergence of the rising powers also precipitates important cultural changes. Specifically, it has changed the dynamics of what is considered to be valid knowledge. As Robert Zoellick, in his incarnation as president of the World Bank, has put it:

> The new multipolar economy requires multipolar knowledge. With the end of the outdated concept of the Third World, the First World must open itself to competition in ideas and experience. The flow of knowledge is no longer North to South, West to East, rich to poor. Rising economies bring new approaches and solutions.[36]

The emergence of the rising powers has altered the landscape of what knowledge is considered valid and which experiences are considered relevant to policy formulation. The epistemic community identified here has been bound up with these changes. The following section examines the role that they have played in the struggle to frame the collapse of the Doha Round in 2008 and in countering the narrative put forward by the United States and EU.

Framing the Doha Round impasse

The collapse of the Doha Round of negotiations generated a great deal of debate and analysis over what caused the failure of the talks. Immediately following the failure of the 2008 Mini-Ministerial that finally put the round on ice, the United States and EU began to try to frame the failure of the talks in a way that depicted their own actions in the most positive light and placed blame for the collapse elsewhere, portraying the round's failure as a consequence of the rising powers being overly belligerent and failing to make sufficient concessions. The United States placed the blame squarely on India and China. US officials claimed to have "swallowed hard and accepted" a compromise proposal, while China and India were, they claimed, "obstacles to the round" that had put the DDA into the "gravest danger."[37] This stance was picked up and repeated uncritically by elements of the media,[38] illustrating the privileged position afforded the rich countries in framing debates around trade. Subsequent scholarly analyses of the details of the collapse painted a different picture, finding that "the Americans were the ones who could most accurately be described as abandoning it."[39] China, meanwhile, had played a bridging role between India and the United States.[40] Nonetheless, the "blame game" over the collapse of the DDA continued over subsequent years, with a string of US trade representatives, sometimes supported by the EU, arguing that the failure of the talks was down to the failure of the emerging powers to make offers that reflect their newfound importance to the global economy.[41]

Though the Doha Round remains deadlocked, nearly all WTO members remain rhetorically at least committed to closing a deal at some point, and the success of the Bali Ministerial Conference in December 2013 reignited hopes in this regard.[42] How the failure of the talks is understood by wider constituents, including most importantly the wider membership of the WTO—the roughly 120 countries not involved in the July 2008 Mini-Ministerial—is crucial to determining where greatest pressure for further concessions will be felt. Naturally, if the rich countries are able to dominate the debate in this regard, the pressure for concession from the developing world will rise concomitantly.

The epistemic community identified above has been at the forefront of resisting the US/EU narrative and countering it with an alternative. They have sought to frame the failure of the DDA as having little to do with the rising powers but being, instead, a consequence of the rich countries' poor offers (particularly on reducing agricultural subsidies), excessive demands (particularly in non-agricultural market access—NAMA), and refusal to respect the negotiating mandates. This has formed a shared, coherent intellectual interpretation of the DDA negotiations and the impasse therein that the group has propagated within academic circles, in the media and through presentations at a variety of trade-related events.

Prominent among the latter is the WTO's annual Public Forum, which brings together a range of stakeholders (including business groups, academics and NGOs) with delegates and representatives of other international organizations. This is not only an important forum for shaping public perceptions of the WTO negotiations, but also a significant channel for delegates from low-income countries to hear and learn from a range of opinions, particularly for those who are not usually resident in Geneva. The Southern trade intellectuals identified above are among the most prolific participants in the Public Forum. Ricardo Meléndez-Ortiz, for instance, participated in 11 panels between 2009 and 2012, while Pradeep Mehta has five and Ujal Singh Bhatia four. Very few others contribute as frequently.

The combined output of this epistemic community in scholarly journals, trade journals, newspapers, online media, and at public events forms a very comprehensive set of contributions, of which only a general outline can be drawn here. While differences may be found in the details and emphasis among the various members of the group, there is a sufficient core agreement that can be said to form a coherent shared interpretation.

Ujal Singh Bhatia has published commentaries in a variety of outlets which flatly reject the accusations leveled by the United States and EU at the rising powers. He has argued that the rich countries had made demands for additional flexibilities in agriculture that would "drain the agricultural negotiations of whatever ambition was achieved through the formula cuts."[43] Furthermore, he placed the blame for the collapse squarely at the feet of the United States, arguing that "[t]he reasons for the present impasse are not systemic. They have less to do with faulty institutional design than with the concerns of one large member, specifically the domestic political compulsions of the US […] The US has defensive red lines across the range of negotiating areas."[44] In this sense, Bhatia turns the narrative being propounded by the United States and EU on its head and situates the inadequacies of rich-country agricultural concessions at the root of the impasse.

Martin Khor at the South Centre has also provided a stream of analyses that push back at the US-EU narrative in a similar vein. He has highlighted the "imbalance" in the current texts between the cuts in industrial tariffs required of developing countries with those of the developed countries' agricultural policies.[45] Echoing Bhatia, Khor places blame for the impasse in the talks with the United States, with the rest of the world waiting "for the US to give up its unreasonable demands."[46] Khor has repeatedly drawn attention to what he (and many developing countries) feel to be the central problem with the Doha Round as it currently stands, namely that:

> there is little development content left in the proposals on the table [...] Further, in the core negotiating issues of agriculture and industrial tariffs [...] the special treatment for developing countries has been whittled away. In fact it is the developed countries that are getting special treatment.[47]

Much of Khor's output is published through the South Centre (of which he is executive director) in its *South Bulletin*, which is widely read by delegates from developing countries. His analysis of the Doha Round thereby has a direct route to influence the broader group of developing countries and shape their perceptions of the Doha Round impasse.

For Faizel Ismail, the primary concerns are the unwillingness of the rich countries to stick to the mandates on which the round was launched and, like Khor, the steady erosion of the development content of the round.[48] Again, it is the United States and its domestic political constraints that he argues are the greatest impediment to a deal, with the United States "unwilling to work on the basis of [the] multilateral texts," and seeking to placate business lobbies demanding more market access into the major emerging markets.[49] Elsewhere, however, Ismail also highlights the role that the EU has played in pushing a similar, albeit less extreme, agenda to that of the United States.[50] Faizel Ismail has consistently brought the discussion back to the mandates agreed at the launching of the round at the 2001 Doha Ministerial, and subsequently reaffirmed at the Hong Kong Ministerial of 2005, and the attempts by the rich countries to ignore them.[51]

Others have focused on the comparison between the texts on agriculture and NAMA. The offers made by the rich countries in agriculture will not lead to any reduction of the current level of agricultural subsidies, representing a continued failure to deal with an "endemic problem with international trade."[52] By contrast, the Southern trade intellectuals have argued that the current package in agriculture and NAMA will result in greater market opening among the developing countries (particularly China) than among developed ones.[53]

Debapriya Bhattacharya has sought to maintain attention on the failure to deliver on the promised benefits to LDCs. Most notably, at the Hong Kong Ministerial Meeting of 2005, LDCs were promised movement toward the provision of duty-free, quota-free market access. Bhattacharya has consistently highlighted the failure of the major players (which includes the BRICS but is mainly aimed at the rich countries) to make good these promises, engaging instead in negotiations on issues most of interest to themselves.[54] Like others within the epistemic community, Bhattacharya brings attention to the failure of the major powers to negotiate on the basis of the mandates agreed at the launching of the Doha Round.

The point made here is not to establish, or even comment upon, which of these competing narratives is true. To do so would misunderstand the manner in which multilateral trade negotiations take place. There is no objective way to assess the commitments made in trade negotiations, and the GATT/WTO has always relied on a looser, more fluid means of assessing the reciprocity expected in deals.[55] It is only the *perceptions* among members concerning whether or not the offers made by other participants are sufficient that matter. This is a central component of the principle of "diffuse reciprocity" that Keohane identifies in operation in the GATT/WTO, in which "the definition of equivalence is less precise, one's partners may be viewed as a group rather than as particular actors, and the sequence of events is less narrowly bounded."[56] Clearly defined, objective measures of the contributions of each member participating in the DDA are not warranted, and are probably not even possible.

Rather, the point here is to highlight the role being played by this core group of intellectuals from the global South in articulating a counter-narrative to that presented by the rich countries. Furthermore, this battle over how the impasse is framed has important wider ramifications. It is precisely because there are no objective measures of which members have made greater concessions than others that subjective perceptions matter so much, and hence the way in which the collapse is framed—how it is contextualized and understood by a broader audience—becomes critical.

For present purposes, the other developing countries are a key part of that audience. Frequently lacking sufficient institutional capacity and with a fairly high rate of turnover of their small Geneva-based staff, low-income countries rely more than others on the leadership and analysis provided by institutions and individuals that they consider reliable. The epistemic community examined here has been crucial in providing leadership to these other, weaker states. Such states can be seen to have echoed the narrative put forward by the Southern trade intellectuals concerning the collapse of the DDA, though they also add their own interpretation of events. This is seen, for example, in the statements made following the collapse by the Africa Group, African, Caribbean and Pacific (ACP) Group and LDC Group (collectively known as the G90). The G90 statement on the 2008 Mini-Ministerial notes the crucial importance of the "development content of the Doha Development Round," before going on to "call on the major trading developed partners to show leadership and explore all possible efforts to reach the necessary convergence among all the Members on the major issues underpinning the negotiations."[57] By placing the onus on the developed countries to find a solution, the G90 countries are clearly adopting a position much closer to that of the epistemic community explored here.

This is also clearly seen in the statement of the ministers of the Africa Group, which is forthright about who is blocking progress, stating: "developed countries are [...] the ones who demanded it [i.e. the launching of the DDA] and they are the ones blocking the movement forward."[58] They also echo the stance of demanding a "real and effective substantial reduction of trade distorting domestic support in rich industrialized countries," attention to the problem of import surges in agriculture and sufficient flexibilities in NAMA "to nurture and safeguard our industrial base," and to protect policy space.[59]

In this way, the articulation of a more development-oriented framing of the impasse in opposition to that of the United States and EU has helped to prevent the rich countries from setting the terms of the debate over why the impasse was reached, helped to prevent those other more marginalized countries from acquiescing to a Doha Round agenda that is not in their interests, and thereby helped to ensure that the Doha Round did not follow the pattern of previous, asymmetric trade rounds.[60] While this is positive, the next section examines some potential problems associated with the rise of intellectual leadership by the rising powers.

The emancipatory potential of Southern trade intellectuals?

Understanding the impacts of prospective trade deals has been a perennial problem for developing countries. It is widely accepted that many developing countries simply did not know what the Uruguay Round entailed and it was only when they began to implement it that they realized the imbalance it held between the elements included for developing countries vis-à-vis those included for benefit of the developed countries.[61] This experience highlighted the critical importance played by technical capacity and trade policy analysis in facilitating successful engagement in negotiations. As Debapriya Bhattacharya puts it:

> Information and skilled analysis of that information are the key determinants of a party's ability to negotiate a successful outcome. The highly technical nature of trade negotiations means that success will depend on each party's ability to develop solid arguments based on reliable information and exhaustive analysis.[62]

The growth of NGOs working on trade has provided one route to addressing this problem, though debate remains over whether these institutions hold the potential to make global governance more accountable to weaker constituents.[63] Arguably, NGOs cannot be relied upon to fulfill this function since many are disengaging from the WTO due to its ongoing "impasse."[64]

To understand the resilience of networks that provide a more developmentally oriented trade analysis, it is important to look in more detail at the individuals involved. As noted above, the epistemic community identified here gains their expertise, and thereby their influence, primarily from having been former trade negotiators and having worked, and continuing to work, directly in trade governance. For this reason, we can expect them to be a more stable source of trade expertise to developing countries than many alternatives. The foci of NGO campaigns come and go, along with the provision of accompanying reports and analysis. Epistemic communities built on individuals who have been engaged with the trade system sometimes for decades are likely to be more durable.

Yet, dangers remain for weaker states. The rising powers, given their clear export competitiveness, have an interest in pursuing a process of encouraging market opening among the developed countries while maintaining as much policy space for themselves as possible to aid their ongoing development strategies, and it is no surprise that this is what the Southern trade intellectuals identified in this paper generally advocate, given their links to the BRICS. However, LDCs and other low-income countries often face a different set of challenges that are not necessarily shared with the rising powers. For example, many rightly fear that significant market opening by the major developed countries will lead to a damaging erosion of preferences that will harm the export interests of Africa and other marginalized areas. In this regard, there is a clear potential conflict between the interests of the rising powers and those of the LDCs.

In addition, it is important that any intellectual leadership given by the rising powers does not translate into a creeping acceptance of the exclusion of low-income countries from this inner negotiating circle. As the quote from Bhattacharya highlights above, being able to understand and articulate your trade interests is of great importance if you are to gain a successful outcome, but simply being present at the negotiating table will always remain paramount.

As such, caution must be exercised to ensure that the LDCs and other low-income countries do not come to rely too heavily on the trade analysis and the intellectual leadership of the epistemic community identified in this paper. Ultimately, it is essential that these marginalized countries are able to improve their own domestic capabilities and state capacities to formulate trade policy since reliance on any other sources will always be problematic.

Conclusion

The impact of the epistemic community examined here illustrates the importance within global governance of the role played by experts in framing international issues in areas of uncertainty and differing interests. Much of the existing epistemic communities literature, as noted above, has focused on the role of epistemic communities of scientists advocating established scientific knowledge to politicians who lack the expertise to understand the issue fully. This chapter examines a different case, in which there is no objective truth to the matter at hand (i.e. the factors at play in the impasse in the Doha Round). Rather, there are only contending perspectives being advocated by the various groups involved. Yet epistemic communities here still play a key role in influencing the agenda and in articulating the perspective of the relatively weak, ensuring that their voice is not drowned by the more powerful. Echoing the analysis of Ponte and Cheyns,[65] the present case reinforces the finding that for small or weak states promoting one expert group over another is a crucial element in defending their interests within international politics. Epistemic communities emerging from the global South thereby form an important means of resistance by developing countries to adverse political pressures over how key international events are framed. It is through these means that marginalized states can seek to challenge the core episteme governing trade and the privileges that it gives the architects of the system.

Within trade governance, the emergence of this group of intellectuals and the effect that they have had on the DDA, and on trade policy formulation more widely, form one area in which we can see the shift in trade politics that the rising powers have brought about. Until the Doha Round is concluded (if it is concluded), it is not possible to assess fully the extent to which the traditional dominance of the United States and EU on trade negotiations has been loosened. Nor is it possible to ascertain the extent to which the rest of the (non-rising) developing world has been able to secure greater concessions. In this context, the identification of this epistemic community of Southern trade intellectuals offers one means of identifying how the shifting forces of global production have altered the dynamics of international trade negotiations.

The provision to the developing world of alternative sources of trade analysis is welcome, and has weakened the previous dominance that the rich world, and the institutions that they control, had in supplying trade advice to poor countries.[66] The result is that the traditional powers have been less able than before to push the rest of the members into a multilateral deal regardless of the distribution of benefits.

We see then that the contours of WTO negotiations are being altered by the rising powers, but in subtle ways. Too much focus has been placed on the altered "geometry" of the negotiations (i.e. which members are included in which negotiations) and on the battles within small group meetings held between the United States, EU, Brazil, China and India. While these high-profile changes are important, their impact can be overstated. To understand the changes being brought to the WTO by the rising powers demands attention to the more subtle shifts in the dynamics of negotiations. This is less about the direct substance of negotiation—which remains largely a debate over how far and how fast to liberalize which sectors. Rather, the changes are found in the nuances surrounding that process—the framing of key events and the battle over who is empowered to interpret the negotiating process.

Notes

1 A version of this chapter appeared as "The Role of Southern Intellectuals in Contemporary Trade Governance," *New Political Economy*, online first, DOI: 10.1080/13563467.2014.951615. The author would like to thank *New Political Economy* for permitting it to be reprinted.

2 Gregory Chin and Ramesh Thakur, "Will China Change the Rules of Global Order?" *The Washington Quarterly* 33, no. 4 (2010): 119–38; and Kristen Hopewell, "New Protagonists in Global Economic Governance: Brazilian Agribusiness at the WTO," *New Political Economy* 18, no. 4 (2013): 603–23.

3 Robert H. Wade, "Protecting Power: Western States in Global Organizations," in *Global Governance at Risk*, ed. David Held and Charles Rogers (Malden, Mass. and Cambridge: Polity Press, 2013), 77–110.

4 Luiz Carlos Bresser Pereira, *Globalization and Competition: Why Some Emergent Countries Succeed while Others Fall Behind* (Cambridge: Cambridge University Press, 2010).

5 Judith Goldstein and Robert O. Keohane, ed., *Ideas and Foreign Policy: Beliefs, Institutions, and Political Change* (Ithaca, NY and London: Cornell University Press, 1993).

6 See Mark M. Blyth, "Any More Bright Ideas? The Ideational Turn in Comparative Politics," *Comparative Politics* 29, no. 2 (1997): 229–50.
7 Peter A. Hall, *The Power of Economic Ideas* (Princeton, N.J.: Princeton University Press, 1989).
8 Robert W. Cox, *Approaches to World Order* (Cambridge: Cambridge University Press, 1996), 99; and Antonio Gramsci, *Selections from the Prison Notebooks* (London: Lawrence and Wishart, 1971), 5–7.
9 Stephen Gill, "Epistemology, Ontology and the 'Italian School,'" in *Gramsci, Historical Materialism and International Relations*, ed. Stephen Gill (Cambridge: Cambridge University Press, 1993), 24.
10 John G. Ruggie, "International Regimes, Transactions, and Change: Embedded Liberalism in the Postwar Economic Order," *International Organization* 36, no. 2 (1982): 382–83.
11 Peter Haas, "Introduction: Epistemic Communities and International Policy Coordination," *International Organization* 46, no. 1 (1992): 1–35.
12 Haas, "Introduction," 2.
13 Haas, "Introduction," 3.
14 See Mai'a K. Davis Cross, "Rethinking Epistemic Communities Twenty Years Later," *Review of International Studies* 39, no. 1 (2012): 137–60.
15 Davis Cross, "Rethinking Epistemic Communities Twenty Years Later," 157; Patrik Marier, "Empowering Epistemic Communities: Specialised Politicians, Policy Experts and Policy Reform," *West European Politics* 31, no. 3 (2008): 513–33.
16 Johannes Lindvall, "The Real but Limited Influence of Expert Ideas," *World Politics* 61, no. 4 (2009): 703.
17 See also Gabriel Siles-Brügge, *Constructing European Union Trade Policy: A Global Idea of Europe* (Basingstoke: Palgrave Macmillan, 2014).
18 Johan Schot and Frank Schipper, "Experts and European Transport Integration, 1945–1958," *Journal of European Public Policy* 18, no. 2 (2011): 274–93.
19 Stefano Ponte and Emmanuelle Cheyns, "Voluntary Standards, Expert Knowledge and the Governance of Sustainability Networks," *Global Networks* 13, no. 4 (2013): 459–77.
20 Lena Rethel, "The New Financial Development Paradigm and Asian Bond Markets," *New Political Economy* 15, no. 4 (2010): 493–517.
21 Erin Hannah, "NGOs and the European Union: Examining the Power of Epistemes in the EC's TRIPS and Access to Medicines Negotiations," *Journal of Civil Society* 7, no. 2 (2011): 179–206.
22 Emanuel Adler and Steven Bernstein, "Knowledge in Power: The Epistemic Construction of Global Governance," in *Power in Global Governance*, ed. Michael Barnett and Raymond Duvall (Cambridge: Cambridge University Press, 2005), 294–318.
23 Hannah, "NGOs and the European Union," 181.
24 Ian Johnstone, "The Power of Interpretive Communities," in *Power in Global Governance*, ed. Michael Barnett and Raymond Duvall (Cambridge: Cambridge University Press, 2005), 188.
25 Abram Chayes and Antonia Handler Chayes, *The New Sovereignty* (Cambridge, Mass.: Harvard University Press, 1995), 27.
26 Gloria María Carrión Fonseca, "A Nicaraguan in the World Trade Organization," *Envio*, no. 349, www.envio.org.ni/articulo/4227.

27 Rorden Wilkinson, *What's Wrong with the WTO and How to Fix It* (Cambridge: Polity Press, 2014), 56–61.
28 Robert Zoellick, "America will Not Wait for the Won't-do Countries," *Financial Times*, 22 September 2003.
29 Quoted in Sylvia Ostry, "Cancun: Can Can't? Can Do?" 2003, www.ceim.uqam.ca/pdf/construire_ostry.pdf.
30 This phrase is, of course, highly problematic. Developing countries as a group, if that group makes any analytical sense at all (see Anthony Payne, *The Global Politics of Unequal Development* (Basingstoke: Palgrave Macmillan, 2005), 213–233), are highly heterogeneous and do not all share one perspective. Even within narrower definitions, such as least developed countries, there is a plurality of perspectives and interests.
31 Fatoumata Jawara and Aileen Kwa, *Behind the Scenes at the WTO: The Real World of International Trade Negotiations* (London and New York: Zed Books, 2003), 151–2.
32 Haas, "Introduction," 3.
33 See, as one example, Ricardo Meléndez-Ortiz, "Comments in the Discussion on 'Policy Space and Trade Negotiations,'" ICTSD, 2007, http://ictsd.org/connect/bridges-tv/.
34 Bresser Pereira, *Globalization and Competition.*
35 Chalmers Johnson, *Japan, Who Governs? The Rise of the Developmental State* (New York: W.W. Norton, 1995).
36 Robert Zoellick, "Democratizing Development Economics," Speech made at Georgetown University, 29 September 2010, http://go.worldbank.org/N58SCW9BW0.
37 US trade official David Shark, quoted in Associated Press, "US: China, India Threaten Doha Round of WTO Talks," 28 July 2008.
38 For example *The Guardian*, "WTO: China Throws Up Barrier to Doha Agreement," 28 July 2008.
39 Paul Blustein, *The Nine-Day Misadventure of the Most Favored Nations: How the WTO's Doha Round Negotiations went Awry in July 2008* (Washington, DC: Brookings Institute Paper, 2008), www.brookings.edu/research/articles/2008/12/05-trade-blustein.
40 James Scott and Rorden Wilkinson, "China Threat? Evidence from the WTO," *Journal of World Trade* 47, no. 4 (2013): 761–82.
41 See for examples WTO, "Remarks by U.S. Trade Representative Ron Kirk at the Opening Plenary Session at the World Trade Organization Ministerial Conference" (2011), www.wto.org/english/thewto_e/minist_e/min11_e/min11_statements_e.htm; and Susan C. Schwab, "After Doha: Why the Negotiations are Doomed and What We Should Do About it," *Foreign Affairs* 90, no. 3 (2011): 104–17.
42 Rorden Wilkinson, Erin Hannah and James Scott, "The WTO in Bali: What MC9 Means for the Doha Development Agenda and Why it Matters," *Third World Quarterly* 35, no. 6 (2014): 1032–50.
43 Ujal Singh Bhatia, "A Few Developing Countries Cannot Be the Bankers of the Round," *South Bulletin* 46, no. 3 (2010): 7.
44 Ujal Singh Bhatia, "Sources of the WTO's Impasse," *VOX* (2011), www.voxeu.org/article/sources-wto-s-impasse.
45 Martin Khor, "Long Stalemate Ahead for WTO Talks," *South Bulletin* 46, no. 3 (2010): 2.

46 Khor, "Long Stalemate Ahead for WTO Talks," 3; Martin Khor, "Crunch Time at the WTO," *Gulf Daily News*, 4 May 2011.
47 Martin Khor, "Behind the Impasse in WTO's Doha Talks," *South Bulletin* 54 (2011): 2. See also Martin Khor, "The Twists and Turns of the Doha Talks and the WTO," *South Bulletin* 68 (2012); and Martin Khor, "WTO: Stingy with the Poor, Generous with the Rich," *Inter Press Service*, 1 October 2013.
48 Faizel Ismail, *Reforming the World Trade Organization: Developing Countries in the Doha Round* (Jaipur: CUTS International and Friedrich Ebert Stiftung, 2009), 88–93.
49 Faizel Ismail, "How to Break the Impasse of Doha Round," *South Bulletin* 46, no. 3 (2010): 6.
50 Faizel Ismail, "Is the Doha Round Dead? What is the Way Forward?" *World Economics* 13, no. 3 (2012): 149–50.
51 Faizel Ismail, "Narratives and Myths in the WTO Doha Round," *Economic and Political Weekly* 47, no. 31 (2012): 55–60.
52 Pradeep Singh Mehta, "Comments to the Warwick Commission," Video (2007), www.youtube.com/WarwickCommission; and Pradeep Singh Mehta, Bhipul Chatterjee and Joseph George, "The Doha Development Agenda: Prospective Outcomes and African Perspectives," in *Trade, Poverty, Development: Getting Beyond the WTO's Doha Deadlock*, ed. Rorden Wilkinson and James Scott (Abingdon: Routledge, 2013), 187–202.
53 See, for example, Sun Zhenyu, "The Doha Round and the Future of the WTO," in *Trade, Poverty, Development: Getting Beyond the WTO's Doha Deadlock*, ed. Rorden Wilkinson and James Scott (Abingdon: Routledge, 2013), 141–154; and Ricardo Meléndez-Ortiz, "The Trade Round of Unbelievers," *Development and Cooperation (D+C)*, no. 8–9 (2006), www.giz.de/E+Z/content/archive-eng/index.html.
54 Debapriya Bhattacharya, *Ongoing WTO Doha Round Negotiations Concerns and Interests of Bangladesh and other LDCs* (Dhaka, Bangladesh: CPD, 2009), www.cpd.org.bd/pub_attach/DR99.pdf.
55 See Rorden Wilkinson, *Multilateralism and the World Trade Organization: The Architecture and Extension of International Trade Regulation* (Abingdon: Routledge, 2006).
56 Robert O. Keohane, "Reciprocity in International Relations," *International Organization* 40, no. 1 (1986): 4.
57 WTO, "Statement of African, ACP and LDC Groups on the WTO Mini-Ministerial Meeting Geneva, 25 July 2008," TN/C/12, 28 July 2008.
58 Africa Group, *Press Statement by Hon. Uhuru Kenyatta, Deputy Prime Minister and Minister for Trade (Kenya), On Behalf of the African Group at the WTO Mini-Ministerial Meeting, Geneva: 25th July 2008* (Geneva: Africa Group, 2008), www.trade.go.ke/downloads/Press%20Releases/.
59 Africa Group, *Press Statement by Hon. Uhuru Kenyatta*.
60 The battle over how to frame issues is seen throughout the WTO. For a very useful exploration of this and more broadly of the role played by discourse in exacerbating and ameliorating power asymmetries, see Matthew Eagleton-Pierce, *Symbolic Power in the World Trade Organization* (Oxford: Oxford University Press, 2013).
61 See Sylvia Ostry, "The Uruguay Round North-South Grand Bargain: Implications for Future Negotiations," in *The Political Economy of*

International Trade Law: Essays in Honour of Robert E. Hudec, ed. Daniel L.M. Kennedy and James D. Southwick (Cambridge: Cambridge University Press, 2002), 285–300; and J. Michael Finger and Julio J. Nogués, "The Unbalanced Uruguay Round Outcome: The New Areas in Future WTO Negotiations," *The World Economy* 25, no. 3 (2002): 321–40.

62 Debapriya Bhattacharya, "Least Developed Countries in Trade Negotiations: Planning Process and Information Needs," *Asia-Pacific Trade and Investment Review* 1, no. 1 (2005): 83.

63 See Silke Trommer, *Transformations in Trade Politics: Participatory Trade Politics in West Africa* (Abingdon: Routledge, 2014); Clark A. Miller, "Democratization, International Knowledge Institutions, and Global Governance," *Governance* 20, no. 2 (2007): 325–57; and for contrast Bill Paterson, "*Transformismo* at the WTO," in *Gramsci and Global Politics: Hegemony and Resistance*, ed. Mark McNally and John Schwarzmatel (Abingdon: Routledge, 2009), 42–57; and Erin N. Hannah, "The Quest for Accountable Governance: Embedded NGOs and Demand Driven Advocacy in the International Trade Regime," *Journal of World Trade* 48, no. 3 (2014): 457–79.

64 Wilkinson et al., "The WTO in Bali."

65 Ponte and Cheyns, "Voluntary Standards, Expert Knowledge and the Governance of Sustainability Networks."

66 See James Scott, "The Use and Misuse of Trade Negotiation Simulations," *Journal of World Trade* 42, no. 1 (2008): 87–103.

Index

Routledge Global Institutions Series

109 Expert Knowledge in Global Trade (2016)
edited by Erin Hannah (University of Western Ontario), James Scott (King's College London), and Silke Trommer (University of Helsinki)

108 World Trade Organization (2nd edition, 2016)
Law, economics, and politics
by Bernard M. Hoekman (European University Institute) and Petros C. Mavroidis (European University Institute)

107 Women and Girls Rising (2015)
Progress and resistance around the world
by Ellen Chesler (Roosevelt Institute) and Theresa McGovern (Columbia University)

106 The North Atlantic Treaty Organization (2nd edition, 2015)
by Julian Lindley-French (National Defense University)

105 The African Union (2nd edition, 2015)
by Samuel M. Makinda (Murdoch University), F. Wafula Okumu (The Borders Institute), David Mickler (University of Western Australia)

104 Governing Climate Change (2nd edition, 2015)
by Harriet Bulkeley (Durham University) and Peter Newell (University of Sussex)

103 The Organization of Islamic Cooperation (2015)
Politics, problems, and potential
by Turan Kayaoglu (University of Washington, Tacoma)

102 Contemporary Human Rights Ideas (2nd edition, 2015)
by Bertrand G. Ramcharan

101 The Politics of International Organizations (2015)
Views from insiders
edited by Patrick Weller (Griffith University) and Xu Yi-chong (Griffith University)

100 Global Poverty (2nd edition, 2015)
Global governance and poor people in the post-2015 era
by David Hulme (University of Manchester)

99 Global Corporations in Global Governance (2015)
by Christopher May (Lancaster University)

98 The United Nations Centre on Transnational Corporations (2015)
Corporate conduct and the public interest
by Khalil Hamdani and Lorraine Ruffing

97 The Challenges of Constructing Legitimacy in Peacebuilding (2015)
Afghanistan, Iraq, Sierra Leone, and East Timor
by Daisaku Higashi (University of Tokyo)

96 The European Union and Environmental Governance (2015)
by Henrik Selin (Boston University) and Stacy D. VanDeveer (University of New Hampshire)

95 Rising Powers, Global Governance, and Global Ethics (2015)
edited by Jamie Gaskarth (Plymouth University)

94 Wartime Origins and the Future United Nations (2015)
edited by Dan Plesch (SOAS, University of London) and Thomas G. Weiss (CUNY Graduate Center)

93 International Judicial Institutions (2nd edition, 2015)
The architecture of international justice at home and abroad
by Richard J. Goldstone (Retired Justice of the Constitutional Court of South Africa) and Adam M. Smith (International Lawyer, Washington, DC)

92 The NGO Challenge for International Relations Theory (2014)
edited by William E. DeMars (Wofford College) and Dennis Dijkzeul (Ruhr University Bochum)

91 21st Century Democracy Promotion in the Americas (2014)
Standing up for the Polity
by Jorge Heine (Wilfrid Laurier University) and Brigitte Weiffen (University of Konstanz)

90 BRICS and Coexistence (2014)
An alternative vision of world order
edited by Cedric de Coning (Norwegian Institute of International Affairs), Thomas Mandrup (Royal Danish Defence College), and Liselotte Odgaard (Royal Danish Defence College)

89 IBSA (2014)
The rise of the Global South?
by Oliver Stuenkel (Getulio Vargas Foundation)

88 Making Global Institutions Work (2014)
edited by Kate Brennan

87 Post-2015 UN Development (2014))
Making change happen
edited by Stephen Browne (FUNDS Project) and Thomas G. Weiss (CUNY Graduate Center)

86 Who Participates in Global Governance? (2014)
States, bureaucracies, and NGOs in the United Nations
by Molly Ruhlman (Towson University)

85 The Security Council as Global Legislator (2014)
edited by Vesselin Popovski (United Nations University) and Trudy Fraser (United Nations University)

84 UNICEF (2014)
Global governance that works
by Richard Jolly (University of Sussex)

83 The Society for Worldwide Interbank Financial Telecommunication (SWIFT) (2014)
Cooperative governance for network innovation, standards, and community
by Susan V. Scott (London School of Economics and Political Science) and Markos Zachariadis (University of Cambridge)

82 The International Politics of Human Rights (2014)
Rallying to the R2P cause?
edited by Monica Serrano (Colegio de Mexico) and Thomas G. Weiss (The CUNY Graduate Center)

81 Private Foundations and Development Partnerships (2014)
American philanthropy and global development agendas
by Michael Moran (Swinburne University of Technology)

80 Nongovernmental Development Organizations and the Poverty Reduction Agenda (2014)
The moral crusaders
by Jonathan J. Makuwira (Royal Melbourne Institute of Technology University)

79 Corporate Social Responsibility (2014)
The role of business in sustainable development
by Oliver F. Williams (University of Notre Dame)

78 Reducing Armed Violence with NGO Governance (2014)
edited by Rodney Bruce Hall (Oxford University)

77 Transformations in Trade Politics (2014)
Participatory trade politics in West Africa
by Silke Trommer (Murdoch University)

76 Committing to the Court (2013)
Rules, politics, and the International Criminal Court
by Yvonne M. Dutton (Indiana University)

75 Global Institutions of Religion (2013)
Ancient movers, modern shakers
by Katherine Marshall (Georgetown University)

74 Crisis of Global Sustainability (2013)
by Tapio Kanninen

73 The Group of Twenty (G20) (2013)
by Andrew F. Cooper (University of Waterloo) and Ramesh Thakur (Australian National University)

72 Peacebuilding (2013)
From concept to commission
by Rob Jenkins (Hunter College, CUNY)

71 Human Rights and Humanitarian Norms, Strategic Framing, and Intervention (2013)
Lessons for the Responsibility to Protect
by Melissa Labonte (Fordham University)

70 Feminist Strategies in International Governance (2013)
edited by Gülay Caglar (Humboldt University, Berlin), Elisabeth Prügl (the Graduate Institute of International and Development Studies, Geneva), and Susanne Zwingel (the State University of New York, Potsdam)

69 The Migration Industry and the Commercialization of International Migration (2013)
edited by Thomas Gammeltoft-Hansen (Danish Institute for International Studies) and Ninna Nyberg Sørensen (Danish Institute for International Studies)

68 Integrating Africa (2013)
Decolonization's legacies, sovereignty, and the African Union
by Martin Welz (University of Konstanz)

67 Trade, Poverty, Development (2013)
Getting beyond the WTO's Doha deadlock
edited by Rorden Wilkinson (University of Manchester) and James Scott (University of Manchester)

66 The United Nations Industrial Development Organization (UNIDO) (2012)
Industrial solutions for a sustainable future
by Stephen Browne (FUNDS Project)

65 The Millennium Development Goals and Beyond (2012)
Global development after 2015
edited by Rorden Wilkinson (University of Manchester) and David Hulme (University of Manchester)

64 International Organizations as Self-Directed Actors (2012)
A framework for analysis
edited by Joel E. Oestreich (Drexel University)

63 Maritime Piracy (2012)
by Robert Haywood (One Earth Future Foundation) and Roberta Spivak (One Earth Future Foundation)

62 United Nations High Commissioner for Refugees (UNHCR) (2nd edition, 2012)
by Gil Loescher (University of Oxford), Alexander Betts (University of Oxford), and James Milner (University of Toronto)

61 International Law, International Relations, and Global Governance (2012)
by Charlotte Ku (University of Illinois)

60 Global Health Governance (2012)
by Sophie Harman (City University, London)

59 The Council of Europe (2012)
by Martyn Bond (University of London)

58 The Security Governance of Regional Organizations (2011)
edited by Emil J. Kirchner (University of Essex) and Roberto Domínguez (Suffolk University)

57 The United Nations Development Programme and System (2011)
by Stephen Browne (FUNDS Project)

56 The South Asian Association for Regional Cooperation (2011)
An emerging collaboration architecture
by Lawrence Sáez (University of London)

55 The UN Human Rights Council (2011)
by Bertrand G. Ramcharan (Geneva Graduate Institute of International and Development Studies)

54 Responsibility to Protect (2011)
Cultural perspectives in the Global South
edited by Rama Mani (University of Oxford) and Thomas G. Weiss (The CUNY Graduate Center)

53 The International Trade Centre (2011)
Promoting exports for development
by Stephen Browne (FUNDS Project) and Sam Laird (University of Nottingham)

52 The Idea of World Government (2011)
From ancient times to the twenty-first century
by James A. Yunker (Western Illinois University)

51 Humanitarianism Contested (2011)
Where angels fear to tread
by Michael Barnett (George Washington University) and Thomas G. Weiss (The CUNY Graduate Center)

50 The Organization of American States (2011)
Global governance away from the media
by Monica Herz (Catholic University, Rio de Janeiro)

49 Non-Governmental Organizations in World Politics (2011)
The construction of global governance
by Peter Willetts (City University, London)

48 The Forum on China-Africa Cooperation (FOCAC) (2011)
by Ian Taylor (University of St. Andrews)

47 Global Think Tanks (2011)
Policy networks and governance
by James G. McGann (University of Pennsylvania) with Richard Sabatini

46 United Nations Educational, Scientific and Cultural Organization (UNESCO) (2011)
Creating norms for a complex world
by J.P. Singh (Georgetown University)

45 The International Labour Organization (2011)
Coming in from the cold
by Steve Hughes (Newcastle University) and Nigel Haworth (University of Auckland)

44 Global Poverty (2010)
How global governance is failing the poor
by David Hulme (University of Manchester)

43 Global Governance, Poverty, and Inequality (2010)
edited by Jennifer Clapp (University of Waterloo) and Rorden Wilkinson (University of Manchester)

42 Multilateral Counter-Terrorism (2010)
The global politics of cooperation and contestation
by Peter Romaniuk (John Jay College of Criminal Justice, CUNY)

41 Governing Climate Change (2010)
by Peter Newell (University of East Anglia) and Harriet A. Bulkeley (Durham University)

40 The UN Secretary-General and Secretariat (2nd edition, 2010)
by Leon Gordenker (Princeton University)

39 Preventive Human Rights Strategies (2010)
by Bertrand G. Ramcharan (Geneva Graduate Institute of International and Development Studies)

38 African Economic Institutions (2010)
by Kwame Akonor (Seton Hall University)

37 Global Institutions and the HIV/AIDS Epidemic (2010)
Responding to an international crisis
by Franklyn Lisk (University of Warwick)

36 Regional Security (2010)
The capacity of international organizations
by Rodrigo Tavares (United Nations University)

35 The Organisation for Economic Co-operation and Development (2009)
by Richard Woodward (University of Hull)

34 Transnational Organized Crime (2009)
by Frank Madsen (University of Cambridge)

33 The United Nations and Human Rights (2nd edition, 2009)
A guide for a new era
by Julie A. Mertus (American University)

32 The International Organization for Standardization (2009)
Global governance through voluntary consensus
by Craig N. Murphy (Wellesley College) and JoAnne Yates (Massachusetts Institute of Technology)

31 Shaping the Humanitarian World (2009)
by Peter Walker (Tufts University) and Daniel G. Maxwell (Tufts University)

30 Global Food and Agricultural Institutions (2009)
by John Shaw

29 Institutions of the Global South (2009)
by Jacqueline Anne Braveboy-Wagner (City College of New York, CUNY)

28 International Judicial Institutions (2009)
The architecture of international justice at home and abroad
by Richard J. Goldstone (Retired Justice of the Constitutional Court of South Africa) and Adam M. Smith (Harvard University)

27 The International Olympic Committee (2009)
The governance of the Olympic system
by Jean-Loup Chappelet (IDHEAP Swiss Graduate School of Public Administration) and Brenda Kübler-Mabbott

26 The World Health Organization (2009)
by Kelley Lee (London School of Hygiene and Tropical Medicine)

25 Internet Governance (2009)
The new frontier of global institutions
by John Mathiason (Syracuse University)

24 Institutions of the Asia-Pacific (2009)
ASEAN, APEC, and beyond
by Mark Beeson (University of Birmingham)

23 United Nations High Commissioner for Refugees (UNHCR) (2008)
The politics and practice of refugee protection into the twenty-first century
by Gil Loescher (University of Oxford), Alexander Betts (University of Oxford), and James Milner (University of Toronto)

22 Contemporary Human Rights Ideas (2008)
by Bertrand G. Ramcharan (Geneva Graduate Institute of International and Development Studies)

21 The World Bank (2008)
From reconstruction to development to equity
by Katherine Marshall (Georgetown University)

20 The European Union (2008)
by Clive Archer (Manchester Metropolitan University)

19 The African Union (2008)
Challenges of globalization, security, and governance
by Samuel M. Makinda (Murdoch University) and F. Wafula Okumu (McMaster University)

18 Commonwealth (2008)
Inter- and non-state contributions to global governance
by Timothy M. Shaw (Royal Roads University)

17 The World Trade Organization (2007)
Law, economics, and politics
by Bernard M. Hoekman (World Bank) and Petros C. Mavroidis (Columbia University)

16 A Crisis of Global Institutions? (2007)
Multilateralism and international security
by Edward Newman (University of Birmingham)

15 UN Conference on Trade and Development (2007)
by Ian Taylor (University of St. Andrews) and Karen Smith (University of Stellenbosch)

14 The Organization for Security and Co-operation in Europe (2007)
by David J. Galbreath (University of Aberdeen)

13 The International Committee of the Red Cross (2007)
A neutral humanitarian actor
by David P. Forsythe (University of Nebraska) and Barbara Ann Rieffer-Flanagan (Central Washington University)

12 The World Economic Forum (2007)
A multi-stakeholder approach to global governance
by Geoffrey Allen Pigman (Bennington College)

11 The Group of 7/8 (2007)
by Hugo Dobson (University of Sheffield)

10 The International Monetary Fund (2007)
Politics of conditional lending
by James Raymond Vreeland (Georgetown University)

9 The North Atlantic Treaty Organization (2007)
The enduring alliance
by Julian Lindley-French (Center for Applied Policy, University of Munich)

8 The World Intellectual Property Organization (2006)
Resurgence and the development agenda
by Chris May (University of the West of England)

7 The UN Security Council (2006)
Practice and promise
by Edward C. Luck (Columbia University)

6 Global Environmental Institutions (2006)
by Elizabeth R. DeSombre (Wellesley College)

5 Internal Displacement (2006)
Conceptualization and its consequences
by Thomas G. Weiss (The CUNY Graduate Center) and David A. Korn

4 The UN General Assembly (2005)
by M. J. Peterson (University of Massachusetts, Amherst)

3 United Nations Global Conferences (2005)
by Michael G. Schechter (Michigan State University)

2 The UN Secretary-General and Secretariat (2005)
by Leon Gordenker (Princeton University)

1 The United Nations and Human Rights (2005)
A guide for a new era
by Julie A. Mertus (American University)

Books currently under contract include:

The Regional Development Banks
Lending with a regional flavor
by Jonathan R. Strand (University of Nevada)

Millennium Development Goals (MDGs)
For a people-centered development agenda?
by Sakiko Fukada-Parr (The New School)

The Bank for International Settlements
The politics of global financial supervision in the age of high finance
by Kevin Ozgercin (SUNY College at Old Westbury)

International Migration
by Khalid Koser (Geneva Centre for Security Policy)

Human Development
by Richard Ponzio

The International Monetary Fund (2nd edition)
Politics of conditional lending
by James Raymond Vreeland (Georgetown University)

The UN Global Compact
by Catia Gregoratti (Lund University)

Institutions for Women's Rights
by Charlotte Patton (York College, CUNY) and
Carolyn Stephenson (University of Hawaii)

International Aid
by Paul Mosley (University of Sheffield)

Global Consumer Policy
by Karsten Ronit (University of Copenhagen)

The Changing Political Map of Global Governance
by Anthony Payne (University of Sheffield) and
Stephen Robert Buzdugan (Manchester Metropolitan University)

Coping with Nuclear Weapons
by W. Pal Sidhu

Global Governance and China
The dragon's learning curve
edited by Scott Kennedy (Indiana University)

The Politics of Global Economic Surveillance
by Martin S. Edwards (Seton Hall University)

Mercy and Mercenaries
Humanitarian agencies and private security companies
by Peter Hoffman

Regional Organizations in the Middle East
by James Worrall (University of Leeds)

Reforming the UN Development System
The Politics of Incrementalism
by Silke Weinlich (Duisburg-Essen University)

The United Nations as a Knowledge Organization
by Nanette Svenson (Tulane University)

The International Criminal Court
The Politics and practice of prosecuting atrocity crimes
by Martin Mennecke (University of Copenhagen)

BRICS
by João Pontes Nogueira (Catholic University, Rio de Janeiro) and Monica Herz (Catholic University, Rio de Janeiro)

The European Union (2nd edition)
by Clive Archer (Manchester Metropolitan University)

Governing Climate Change (2nd edition)
by Peter Newell (University of East Anglia) and Harriet A. Bulkeley (Durham University)

Protecting the Internally Displaced
Rhetoric and reality
by Phil Orchard (University of Queensland)

The Arctic Council
Within the far north
by Douglas C. Nord (Umea University)

For further information regarding the series, please contact:

Nicola Parkin, Editor, Politics & International Studies
Taylor & Francis
2 Park Square, Milton Park, Abingdon
Oxford OX14 4RN, UK
Nicola.parkin@tandf.co.uk
www.routledge.com

For Product Safety Concerns and Information please contact our EU representative GPSR@taylorandfrancis.com
Taylor & Francis Verlag GmbH, Kaufingerstraße 24, 80331 München, Germany

www.ingramcontent.com/pod-product-compliance
Ingram Content Group UK Ltd.
Pitfield, Milton Keynes, MK11 3LW, UK
UKHW022110190926
475702UK00013B/1367
* 9 7 8 0 8 1 5 3 7 7 2 3 8 *